PASTERNAK

PASTERNAK

A critical study
by
HENRY GIFFORD

THE BRISTOL PRESS

A CIP catalogue record for this book is available from the British Library

ISBN 1 85399 174 0

©Cambridge University Press 1977, 1991

First published in 1977 by
Cambridge University Press.

This edition published in 1991 by:
Bristol Classical Press
226 North Street
Bedminster
Bristol BS3 1JD

The Bristol Press is an imprint of Bristol Classical Press

Printed in Great Britain by
Booksprint, Bristol

To Rosamond

Contents

Author's Note, 1990

Much valuable work has been done on Pasternak since 1977 when this book was first published. The reader today may wish to consult some of the following biographies and studies:

BARNES, Christopher, *Boris Pasternak: A Literary Biography Volume I 1890-1928,* Cambridge, 1989

CORNWALL, Neil *Pasternak's Novel: Perspectives on 'Doctor Zhivago',* Keele, 1986

FLEISHMAN, Lazar, *Boris Pasternak: The Poet and His Politics,* Cambridge, Mass., 1990

FLEISHMAN, Lazar ed., *Boris Pasternak and His Times* Berkley, 1989

LIVINGSTONE, Angela ed., *Pasternak on Art and Creativity,* Cambridge, 1985

O'CONNOR, KatherineTiernan, *Boris Pasternak's 'My Sister–Life',* Ann Arbour, 1988

PASTERNAK, Evgeny, *Boris Pasternak: The Tragic Years 1930-60,* London, 1990

This is an opportunity to remove two misapprehensions. I quote on p.122 Pasernak's own statement that he read his paper on 'Symbolism and Immortality' immeadiately before accompanying his father to Tolstoy's deathbed in 1910. Professor Barnees points out that the paper was actually written in 1913.

The title of Pasternak's first autobiography, as Professor Fleishman has found, does not derive from a 'safe conduct'. The term *okhrannaya gramota* in the first Soviet years signified a document 'confirming the inviolability of valuable private cultural collections'. As yet, no exact counterpart has been suggested in English, 'preservation order' being the nearest.

Foreword

In the pages that follow an attempt has been made to describe and appraise the achievement of Boris Pasternak as poet, writer of prose fiction, and translator. This required that he should be seen in relation to the profound crisis which made the life of a poet so difficult in Pasternak's country almost from the beginning of his career. So my celebration of him – and such, with no more than occasional hesitancy, it has turned out to be – has inevitably gained a wider reference. Pasternak was not the only important Russian poet of the time; his integrity and courage are less isolated than some people, unacquainted with the work of certain among his contemporaries, might assume. In writing this book I have been conscious that the case of Pasternak – and of Osip Mandelstam and Anna Akhmatova, to name no others – could become exemplary for the whole world. Poetry will have to save itself by its own exertions.

It is a pleasure for me to acknowledge help from various quarters. First of all, I must thank the Leverhulme Trustees for a grant in the year 1972–3 and the University of Bristol for its willingness to concede a year's leave of absence and the financial means to enjoy it. I am indebted to the following friends and colleagues: George Reavey, who sent me much that was interesting and not easily available, including his own 'First Essay Towards Pasternak' which came out in *Experiment* (Cambridge, 1930); Stephen Dodgson for advice on Scriabin; Stephan Körner for coaching me on Cohen, and for his constant interest in this project; Richard Peace and Christopher Ricks who read chapters to my profit; and Angela Livingstone who allowed me to see her translation of *Safe Conduct* and a paper on Pasternak and Rilke afterwards delivered at the Cerisy-la-Salle Colloquium in September 1975. I express my gratitude to Margaret Milsom for typing the manuscript, and to Marjorie Taylor and Janet Redcliffe for much miscellaneous help.

I must also thank Michael Black for suggesting various improve-

xi

ments, Jane Hodgart for her care in going over the typescript, and Tony Edwards for timely assistance with the proofs.

For the last thirty years I have spent more hours on the study of Russian literature than may seem legitimate for a full-time member of an English Department. In this I was encouraged by C. L. Wrenn, once my tutor in Old and Middle English, whose Ilchester lecture at Oxford in 1951 is among the earlier appreciations of Pasternak in this country. I should also like to acknowledge the benevolent complicity of L. C. Knights, for twelve years head of my department.

The text from which quotations are taken is that of the Michigan edition in three volumes by G. P. Struve and B. A. Filippov. This has been supplemented where necessary by use of the Moscow edition of 1965, which carries the admirable essay by Sinyavsky. All translations are my own. In rendering both poetry and prose I have kept as near the original as could be without excessive clumsiness. These are glosses and no more: the translation of poetry should be left to poets.

H. G.

Bristol,
September 1975

Abbreviations

The following abbreviations have been used in the notes and
bibliography

OSP	*Oxford Slavonic Papers*
PSS	*Polnoe sobranie sochineniy*
RLT	*Russian Literature Tri-Quarterly*
SEER	*Slavonic and East European Review*
Sobr. soch.	*Sobranie sochineniy*
Soch.	*Sochineniya*
SP	*Stikhotvoreniya i poemy*

Transcription

I have endeavoured in transcribing Russian words to follow the
system practised by *The Slavonic and East European Review* though
I have not used *y* before the soft vowel *e* initially or when it follows
another vowel. However, certain proper names are excepted, e.g.
Burliuk, Scriabin, Tchaikovsky, Wladimir Weidlé.

I

A Portrait of the Artist

I

Boris Leonidovich Pasternak gave an account of himself twice in autobiographies. The first of these he wrote on the threshold of middle age, the second only a few years before his death. From the other works a little more may be deduced of the life he led. There are glimpses of it at various moments. One section of his poem *Nineteen Five* is entitled 'Childhood' and here he may be seen as a fourteen-year-old schoolboy caught by the romance of that first revolution: the seniors already in the party 'have the look of eagles', the boys play at parliament in class, or make up fantasies about 'the illegal district of Gruziny' in Moscow.[1] At the opening of another narrative poem, *Spektorsky*, he mentions poverty at the time his son had been born, and the work he was then engaged upon at the end of 1924 – hunting out references to Lenin in the foreign press.[2] Again, his prose story *The Last Summer* draws upon certain episodes of his own life just before and during the First World War;[3] elsewhere he refers to his presence at the Ninth Congress of Soviets in 1921 when he heard Lenin speak;[4] and something is to be learned about his friendships from poems dedicated to such people as Larisa Reisner or the Meyerholds, husband and wife. But it is clear beyond dispute that Pasternak had no interest in the publicity that so many artists have sought in our time. Without going so far as T. S. Eliot in the dissociation of his personal life from his poetry, he wished to be known to the world entirely through the writing he had done. Almost every line of this bears the stamp of a highly individual genius. But unlike some of his most gifted contemporaries, unlike Blok or Esenin or Mayakovsky or Akhmatova, Pasternak while being omnipresent in his poetry and prose fiction does not make it a direct transcript of his life or an apparent self-portrait. Here I shall attempt to give no more than a few notes on the man himself and the world he lived in, before proceeding to his choice of vocation and to the manifold works he has left.

1

II

In 1924 he was called upon to write a brief autobiographical statement, which after giving the place of his birth, Moscow, and the year, 1890, continues: 'I owe much if not everything to my father, Academician Leonid Osipovich Pasternak, and to my mother, an outstanding pianist.'[5] Two years later he wrote to his parents: 'Sometimes it seems to me that. . .if ever I have achieved something, then somewhere in the depths of my being I had been doing it for you.'[6] From Leonid Pasternak and his wife Rosa Kaufman their elder son inherited the gifts and the dedication of an artist. They came from Odessa, she a child prodigy who at the age of twenty was teaching in its conservatoire, he the leading Russian impressionist, a fine portrait painter, and, through his drawings for Tolstoy's *Resurrection* and the large part he took in producing a famous illustrated edition of Lermontov, the founder of Russian illustrative art.[7] It was in 1893 that Pasternak first came to know Tolstoy, who had been attracted by his work at an exhibition of the group known as the Wanderers [*Peredvizhniki*].[8] They were personal friends when Tolstoy in 1898 invited him to illustrate *Resurrection*. Leonid was already teaching at the Moscow School of Painting, Sculpture and Architecture, in which he was active for the best part of thirty years until his resignation not long before leaving Russia for good in 1921.

Leonid Pasternak was Jewish; but though anti-semitism lay not far below the surface in Russia and from time to time broke out alarmingly, his son grew up a Muscovite of Muscovites, with the accent, idiom and manners of the place as his birthright.[9] Years later the widow of Leonid Andreev visiting the elder Pasternaks in Berlin reported that theirs remained very much a Moscow home.[10] Pasternak's most eminent contemporary among Russian poets, Osip Mandelstam, was also the child of Jewish parents. Judaism, he noted in his memoirs, is like a grain of musk that will permeate a whole house.[11] But nowhere in Boris Pasternak's writings can that odour be detected. There are two passages in *Doctor Zhivago* deploring segregation on the part of the Jews since they are destined above all peoples to transcend their racial identity and to be 'dissolved without trace among the others whose religious foundations they have themselves laid'.[12] The contrast with Mandelstam is a telling one. He had grown up in St Petersburg, fascinated by its military splendours

2

but unable to banish from his exultation in them a sense that for him they were alien. Such glories belonged by right to the son of a corps commander, and Mandelstam's father was a Jewish dealer in skins who spoke what his son has recorded as a very imperfect form of Russian.[13] Pasternak felt at home in Moscow, without any such misgivings. Mandelstam's widow, allowing herself a touch of malice, has described him as 'a domesticated creature of a familiar Moscow sort, very much attached to the comforts of home and his dacha in the country'.[14]

The comforts of home are evident in the innumerable sketches and paintings Leonid Pasternak made of domestic scenes: his daughters beside their mother at the piano or with their German governess; the old nurse at her mending; the two little boys in sailor suits bent over a book. This is like the warm encircling family life of the Sventitskys in *Doctor Zhivago*. It meant more to Rosa Pasternak than her musical career, which she abandoned as a public performer for the sake of husband and children. Its leisure and tranquillity are beautifully preserved by Leonid in a watercolour of 1892 which depicts his young wife playing the piano by candlelight. The room deep in shadow appears to be empty, shared only with the artist who observes her. Rosa is concentrated on the music which her eyes transmit from the score to her fingers. In the privacy of that scene, as one artist represents the performance of another, can be found what for Boris Pasternak was a supreme value. Zhivago tries to recover it at Varykino, when Lara's child has been put to bed, the candle is lit, and the poet takes his place at the large writing table.[15]

Josephine Pasternak in prefacing the letters written by Marina Tsvetaeva to Leonid comments on the resemblance between Marina's Moscow upbringing and Boris's. It would have interested her to explore the parallels: 'Of their mothers who illustrated music and purity of heart, of their fathers so Russian and at the same time so closely connected with European culture, of the atmosphere of love for all that is best in the German people, of their tolerance, of their real, not ostentatious, religious feeling.'[16] There was nothing narrow in this Muscovite culture of the two families, hospitable as it was to German poetry, art, music and philosophy, thus preparing Pasternak to make the most of his sojourn in Marburg when his mother had saved the money for him to go abroad. The Moscow of Pasternak's youth was stirring with new ideas of every description in the arts. It was changing into a modern city some dozen years before the First World War, though much remained of its past – the 'forty times forty' belltowers, the general aspect at once thronged and perceptibly rural, as the town outgrew the vast, straggling village it had been. To Moscow, even Soviet Moscow after the purges of 1937, Leonid Pasternak still hoped to return until the outbreak of the Second World War made this impossible. For his son, as for the friends of Zhivago looking out over its roofs at the end of the novel, this was a 'holy city'.[17] Boris Pasternak spent nearly all his life in Moscow, or after 1936 at the writers' settlement not far away at Peredelkino.

Leonid Osipovich gave his son an example of modesty, freedom and uncompromising determination in art. He was fortunate in being able to live for his family and his work, on terms of easy friendship with remarkable men, among them Tolstoy, Rilke and the painters Repin, Polenov and Serov; fortunate to have developed his talent without hindrance or frustration; and throughout a long life to have preserved such equanimity and openness. Leonid as an impressionist liked to work rapidly; he caught his subjects in motion, he filled his paintings with light and air, and came increasingly to take pleasure in colour. Like his son, he had the ability to penetrate to the essence of things, particularly in his portraits. It might be said that Boris Pasternak's poetry combines the impressionism of his father's painting with the virtuosity of his mother's keyboard technique. But, more important still, they initiated him into a way of life that called for dedication, generous feeling, and a love of the unassuming and the domestic.

III

Thus Pasternak had many advantages at the beginning. Another was the date of his birth. It may seem a strange irony to assert that any Russian was lucky to have been born in the year 1890. As Pasternak wrote in his first autobiography, *Safe Conduct* [*Okhrannaya gramota*, 1931]:

The boys roughly of my age were thirteen in 1905 and in their twenty-second year before the war. Both these critical moments coincided with two red-letter dates of our history. Their puberty [*detskaya vozmuzhalost'*] and their coming of age for military service were at once like the clamps that held a transitional epoch. Our time the whole way through [*vo vsey tolshche*] is stitched with their nerves.[18]

The good fortune of Pasternak was not that exceptional trials lay ahead of him – even though John Berryman held the artist to be 'extremely lucky who is presented with the worst possible ordeal which will not actually kill him'.[19] This may sound plausible to those who have not known general terror. It is true indeed that Blok – in 1913 before the real test had come – once compared the artist's nerves to the strings of a piano and said that 'a few blows from the heel merely *strengthen* the strings' of that 'internal piano'.[20] But terror such as Pasternak's contemporaries knew will tighten the strings to breaking-point. Wladimir Weidlé remarks on the poetry written by Mandelstam shortly before his final arrest: 'The most terrible thing in the Voronezh poems – and in some pre-Voronezh ones – is that there may be sensed in them a spiritual torment which passes the limits of what can find utterance in art; that torment which shatters art.'[21] Pasternak was to feel something of that anguish near the end of his life, when the storm broke over *Doctor Zhivago*. And he shared in the common anxieties of his time – one so laden with disaster that to have been present was only to be reckoned good fortune by the connoisseurs of chaos.

Yet it was an undoubted advantage to find himself the contemporary of so many good poets in Russia. Aleksandr Blok was ten years older than Pasternak, and that interval means that he belonged to another generation. Of the poets who made their debut in the years just preceding the First World War and who thus properly form Pasternak's own generation the eldest, Velemir Khlebnikov, was his senior by five years; the youngest, Sergey Esenin, by five years his junior. Anna Akhmatova was born in 1889, Osip Mandelstam in 1891, Marina Tsvetaeva in 1892, Vladimir Mayakovsky in 1893. Together they made a constellation such as had not been known since the Pushkin *Pléiade*. There could be no second Pushkin, but several of the later group are more notable poets than those next to him in the *Pléiade*, Baratynsky and Yazykov. The particular generation at the centre of which Pasternak stands chronologically was given an opportunity unparalleled since the age of the great novelists.

If we take the year 1910 as the high-water mark of the modern movement in the arts, then the opportunity becomes plain. At that time, although the revolution of 1905 had failed, Russia could not be sealed off from the west as in earlier periods of repression. It was closely involved in the cultural life of Europe, then seized by an extraordinary ferment. Camilla Gray points out 'exactly how close the Russian *avant-garde* [in painting] stood to the progressive groups in other European centres. Many of the Munich "Blaue Reiter" group were, in fact, Russians.'[22] She says further:

After 1910 the influence of the various schools had become so wide-spread and intermingled with each other that one can no longer point to Russia as being a directly imitative home of various movements. It has become a centre in its own right of which the 'Knave of Diamonds' exhibition was a testimony.[23]

As for the poets, from the Symbolist group onwards they had been alive to developments in the west, and Bryusov, Balmont and Annensky all did much translation. There was every reason for Russian authors at this time to feel confident. They could look to the examples of Tolstoy, Dostoevsky and Chekhov – universally recognised as taking a high place among the moderns. The earlier part of the twentieth century came under Russian influence in many ways, but especially in fiction and in the ballet (now gaining attention as a serious form). For Pasternak to attain manhood just at this time could not fail to quicken his awareness: the possibilities were clear, the moment decisive for change.

IV

Innovation in the arts went with a growing unrest in society. Blok, always highly sensitive to atmosphere, has described the tension in those years just preceding the First World War. Looking back from 1919, when he wrote the foreword to his poem *Retribution* [*Vozmezdie*], he recalled: 'The winter of 1911 was filled with. . . trepidation. I remember the discussions at night from which there first grew an awareness that art, life and politics can neither be separated nor run together.' It was an awareness, too, of 'irreconcilable contradictions that called out for reconciling'.[24]

In the first chapter of this poem he had described the nineteenth century as 'an iron and truly harsh age' [*zheleznyy,/Voistinu zhestokiy vek*] and then observed that in the twentieth 'the darkness of life' had become 'still more homeless, still more terrible':

> Двадцатый век . . . Еще бездомней,
> Еще страшнее жизни мгла. . .[25]

He completed that chapter in 1916,[26] when the darkness was already thickening; but the image of a home exposed to the elements had been with him much earlier. A poem of 1910 speaks of his 'ancient house' as having been penetrated by the blizzard:

> Старый дом мой пронизан метелью. . .[27]

This image was to acquire its full meaning for Pasternak with *Doctor Zhivago*, but long before he wrote that another prophetic line of Blok's had been realised in a way that the poet may scarcely have foreseen (it had been written by the February of the year in which the war broke out):

Холод и мрак грядущих дней. . .[28]

[The cold and gloom of future days.]

There is a passage in the Epilogue to *Doctor Zhivago* recording how Zhivago's friends Gordon and Dudorov, who have just heard the dreadful story of Tanya, now in the year 1943 want to appropriate another celebrated line of Blok's, 'We are the children of Russia's terrible years' [*My deti strashnykh let Rossii*] for her generation which had undergone a real terror.[29] Pasternak and his contemporaries were not born in a time that merits this description, but they were certainly to see its coming and to bear its full impact. Blok in his foreword to *Retribution* wrote some other words whose shadow would lengthen over the decades: 'all our years. . .have been tinged so indelibly that each numeral seems written in blood; we cannot forget those numerals; they have been written upon our own faces.'[30]

The first signs that the sheltered world of Pasternak's childhood was about to break up had come with the revolution of 1905. Lara in *Doctor Zhivago* saw the events of that time as having over them 'a film of innocence';[31] Mandelstam in his memoirs compared the boys who took part in that revolution with Nikolenka Rostov in *War and Peace* at the time of joining the hussars.[32] The young people who had lived through that crisis retained their innocence and their hope. Half a dozen years after the revolution had been suppressed, so Pasternak writes in *The Last Summer*, they

never talked about the past because deep down they all knew there would again be a revolution. As the result of a delusion which even in our time [1929] may be forgiven, they imagined it would come like a play that has been temporarily taken off and is suddenly put on again with the permanent company, that is with all of them in their old parts.

Natasha in this story 'believed like them all that the finest thing in her youth had merely been postponed, and when the hour struck it would not pass her by'.[33] What none of them realised was that the play when it was revived would have an entirely new second act, and the leading parts were no longer for them to take. That would be the moment of passing into an inconceivable era, the transition, as

Akhmatova put it, from the nominal to the real twentieth century [*ne kalendarnyy,/Nastoyashchiy dvadtsatyy vek*[34]].

As everybody now recognises, the revolution of October 1917 drove iron wedges into the national life, between one class and another, between the past and the future, and between the sensibility of one generation – Pasternak's own – and that of its successor. The new world was estranged from the old. Nowhere did this show more patently than in the arts. For these the immediate and the most grave consequence was a broken culture. Within a few years very many of the writers, painters and musicians had gone abroad. There was a brief period at the beginning of the 1920s when Berlin, the first gathering place of exile, communicated freely with Moscow. Then final decisions had to be taken. Some, like Ehrenburg or Alexey Tolstoy, returned to what was now the Soviet Union; others, among them Pasternak, Akhmatova and Mandelstam, had made their choice to stay at home, however cheerless home might become. For a very large number the situation was summed up in the title of a verse collection by Tsvetaeva, who had accepted voluntary exile: *After Russia*.[35]

The separation of Russian culture into two increasingly hostile parts destroyed the conditions which for many years had given it strength and variety. In the middle stretch of the nineteenth century, a balance had been maintained between two opposing schools of thought. The positivism of Belinsky's successors, Chernyshevsky, Dobrolyubov and Pisarev, had been held in check by the imaginative and religious tendencies of the great novelists, above all Tolstoy and Dostoevsky, whose minds were energised by this challenge to their own sense of the world. The debate, continuing right up to the October revolution, sometimes shifted its ground, and the alignments were always liable to change. The benefits of it to Russian intellectual life depended on the forces in conflict being matched more or less evenly. At one time, before the emergence of the Symbolist poets, positivism seemed likely to gain the day. However in the years preceding the revolution of 1917 a strong and vitalising interplay of these tendencies had again developed. But it was not to last. Very soon the balance had been altered, and apparently beyond any reversal. The difficulties for writers then multiplied to the point where even exceptional talent and the highest artistic courage were not enough to gain them a hearing.

The problem they had to face was twofold: that of alienation from the people, an old cause of uneasiness, and, more painful still, alienation from themselves. Ever since the last decades of serfdom thinking men and women had been conscience-stricken by their inability to communicate with the people. This sense of alienation had not been absolute, and in the first months after the February revolution of 1917 many must have hoped that the long-lost unity of the nation was being restored. But once power had been assumed in the people's name, and the right of the proletariat to dictate became the foundation of the new society, then the intellectual found his position, always unsure in Russia, beginning to crumble. If he wished to stay in the country and work for the Soviet regime, it was made clear that he would have to renounce former principles and habits of mind. The artist must submit his own conscience to a higher imperative, the revolutionary will of the people. The choice before Pasternak and his generation was very plain: either the state must be paramount in literature as elsewhere, or the writer must owe responsibility to his art alone. Very few writers in history have become official spokesmen without damaging their integrity. Yet in the circumstances of a popular revolution (and the movement gathering after February 1917 was certainly this), with the civil war that followed, and the dangers of foreign intervention, it was not easy to resist the claims of the state. Mayakovsky in particular very conspicuously pledged himself to the idea of a genuinely proletarian art which the people would think important – an art accessible to all, uplifting, guiding the masses, celebrating the dignity of the worker who had been set free from capitalist exploitation. This was not so different from the truly popular and edifying art that Tolstoy had wanted. Pasternak like many others was prepared for a while to accept the 'social demand', though he interpreted it on his own lines. He did not deny the claims of a proletarian society upon his services, but he defended the right of an artist to be an artist.

However, long before the repressions of the 1930s, the writer was to find that fidelity to his own past would be very difficult. So began the alienation from himself. No doubt the sense of being excluded from what they had once known and loved was strongest in poets from St Petersburg, which lost its name, its primacy as a capital, and its memories, and became for a while derelict. But though the rupture was not so clearly symbolised for others, they too were exiles from their own youth, obliged to leave behind them so much that would be uninteresting or unintelligible to the new kind of reader. The personal life, the 'incorrect' ideas and the 'subjective' attitudes, were manifestations of weakness, and the writer who

9

wanted to depict the new Soviet reality and its heroes would have first to escape from himself. The fearful price that Mayakovsky had to pay for the reorientation of his art in annulling so much of what he had been and in his eventual suicide was brought home poignantly to Pasternak. Their friendship and later estrangement helped him probably more than anything else to define his own purposes and to abide by them.[36]

V

Pasternak once he had found his vocation contrived to follow it in a manner that, given the circumstances of Soviet life, is extraordinary. For the millions who have read *Doctor Zhivago*, Pasternak has come, like the hero of his novel, to represent the artist in quint-essential form. When he wrote his memoirs it was only the development of an artist that he described. The portrait that emerges from the impressions of his contemporaries hardly needs to be amplified from other sources. No doubt when Pasternak's letters have been collected and edited, and a full biography is written, new touches will be added to that portrait. Yet it seems unlikely that the biographical details of a life so much subordinated to his art will add a great deal to the understanding of what he wrote. Pasternak's story is in the main one that consists of absences and immunities. Because he had been lamed as a boy he took no part in the First World War. By the time of the Second he was over fifty and only saw the front in 1943 as a visitor after repeated applications. Although in the first decade of Soviet power he wrote some narrative poetry on political themes he is largely absent from Soviet literature, just as his appearances on the platform to read his verse were not frequent. (He had no desire to join the countless 'music hall heroes' who imitated Mayakovsky's very successful public readings.)[37] Most surprisingly of all he was a writer who kept his independence without a finger being laid upon him. Not until the uproar following his Nobel award did he come into the harsh light of publicity. There had, of course, been occasions on which he received the benefits of 'comradely criticism' and his deficiencies in outlook and performance were pointed out to him. But through all the perils of a time when no writer could feel secure Pasternak stayed true to himself. He had to face more than one period in which publication of his own work was difficult, or even impossible. But he never became a casualty in the general rout.

It was not that he lacked courage. Aleksandr Gladkov the playwright tells of his refusal in 1936 (an unpropitious time for such an action) to sign a letter of protest about André Gide's book *Retour de l'U.R.S.S.* Pasternak made his excuse that he had not read it. But then nor had those who signed the letter. For them it was enough that *Pravda* had condemned the book as 'all lies'.[38] In the same year at a writers' congress he affirmed that 'unexpectedness is the greatest gift that life can rejoice us with' – just when the planners had really fastened their grip on Soviet literature.[39] Nor did he ever think twice before intervening to save a fellow poet in distress, as Mandelstam was in 1934, or to visit his widow when nobody else would come near her.[40] It is recorded that when two years before he had heard Mandelstam's recent outspoken poems Pasternak said: 'I envy your freedom. For me you are a new Khlebnikov. And just as alien to me as he is. I need non-freedom.'[41] Thus he knew the political risk involved, but in due course he overcame his cautiousness. And indeed the 'non-freedom' he chose would be any other man's freedom in the circumstances, unless that man were Mandelstam or Solzhenitsyn.

Pasternak never traded his conscience for personal safety, and would have been quite incapable of doing so. That he did not have to suffer in the prisons and camps where so many others went constitutes the greatest of his immunities. Edmund Wilson among others has speculated on the reasons for this. It may be that his friendship with Stalin's second wife Alliluyeva saved him, or his excellent translations of Georgian poetry, or possibly the superstitious awe Stalin felt for him as a poet with magical powers.[42] He was fortunate here, as in other respects; but consideration of his own welfare does not seem ever to have weighed seriously with Pasternak. While not living as a saint of poetry like the unworldly Khlebnikov, he disregarded the many temptations of the era to compromise his art or to lose faith in himself.

VI

Viktor Shklovsky caught sight of Pasternak once at the Moscow Press Club, when the poet was having his first success. In the novel *Zoo* Shklovsky, a hard-bitten observer, describes the impression he gave: 'A happy man. He will never be embittered. He will surely be loved, pampered and great to the end of his life.'[43] The prophecy came true only in a very relative sense, and was made finally to sound hollow by the scandal that *Doctor Zhivago* provoked. Yet happy and without bitterness he remained to an extraordinary degree. The joyfulness of Pasternak, his gratitude for being alive and able to respond as an artist, was another gift of fortune, which made him puzzling to those more careworn and perplexed than himself. Ilya Ehrenburg, one of his earliest admirers,[44] came to the conclusion after forty years that 'Boris Pasternak did not live for himself – he was not a selfish man – but he lived in himself and through himself.' And he adds: 'A talk with him, even an intimate one, was really two monologues.'[45] The sister of Marina Tsvetaeva gives much the same impression. Pasternak met her at a Moscow railway station on her return from abroad. In a tersely evolving style very like Marina's she has recorded:

He gazes when looking at a person past him (through him, perhaps). Absorbed not in him – in something of his own (and swallowing him into that something of his own. But perhaps with this 'him' he never comes into contact all through the conversation). A state of sleepwalking.
He has recognised me! He smiles... And his eyes are (only for a moment, true, but still) so devoted.[46]

The intensity of his inner life was revealed by the trouble he had in communicating the thoughts that crowded upon him. Anna Akhmatova recalling one conversation said: 'He spoke, as always, extraordinarily. It can't be repeated or remembered, but it was all full of a palpitating life.'[47] He was indeed celebrated for his impatient, confused utterance [*kosnoyazychie*], the drawback which he acknowledges in a letter to the Georgian poet, his close friend Paolo Yashvili. There he speaks of 'an everlasting inability to express the essence alone of what is felt, without complicating details'.[48] But if in speech and in letters his tumultuous thoughts fell over themselves, as a poet he could control the onrush, and what had been a social impediment became an artistic strength. Poetry, as the playwright Afinogenov noted in 1937, was for Pasternak 'the substance of life'. In that year of disasters Afinogenov found him to be 'a splendid example of the inspired man'.[49] Like the albatross in Baudelaire's famous sonnet, Pasternak had to contend with his trailing 'wings of a giant'. The inspired man could not break out of impassioned monologues.

Anna Akhmatova, sympathetic, admiring, and sometimes irritated or amused, was alert to what she called 'Pasternakian Pasternak' – the singular being about whom you could say no more than 'Boris is just Boris.'[50] She was often vexed by his apparent insulation from the world, accusing him of self-centredness and vanity. It would be juster to say as Lydia Chukovskaya does that Pasternak was pre-occupied with his art, and eager that in difficult days it should get a hearing.[51]

In her poem of 1936 'Boris Pasternak' she set down his most striking characteristic, that of being 'endowed with a kind of eternal childhood' [*On nagrazhdyon kakim–to vechnym detstvom*].[52] Memories of Harold Skimpole in *Bleak House* are apt to make the reader uncomfortable with this claim. But Akhmatova goes on to speak of the 'generosity and keen-sightedness' [*shchedrost'yu i zorkost'yu*] that completed the endowment. Pasternak if he remained in some sense a child was this because he never lost the impression-ability of childhood and its impulsive commitment. Not that he clung to the idyllic world of a Peter Pan: the child's imagination has been important in Russian literature for its undogmatic clarity.

Pasternak was a highly civilised man, expert in various literatures, an accomplished amateur of music, and well versed in philosophy. He represented the finest culture of the age and the place he grew up in. Yet, for all the elaboration of technique in his poetry and prose which so dazzled readers in the 1920s, it is rather simplicity that gives the keynote to Pasternak's character. The account of the life Zhivago led in retreat with his family at Varykino bears a relation to the experience of Pasternak at Peredelkino.[53] The world is today familiar with an image of the poet in his garden, sleeves rolled back, resting from the work there which, he told Gladkov, always relieved his anxieties.[54] Boris Pasternak tilling the soil or walking the woods may not seem the appropriate figure for a Soviet setting. He could change places with Hardy at Dorchester, or even with Emerson or Thoreau at Concord. Quiet rural days were not a means of escape from the realities of his time. He would maintain the opposite. In the 'homeless' twentieth century it was a great thing to keep alive for himself and for all who could still appreciate them the round of domestic pursuits and family happiness.

2

Music and Marburg

I

In the first two parts of *Safe Conduct*, the autobiography Pasternak began to write at the end of the 1920s, he describes his search for a vocation. Coming from that particular family, and continually meeting artists of every kind among his father's friends, he never doubted that this vocation should be artistic. But he only turned to poetry after two false starts – one in music, and one in philosophy.

Safe Conduct records the decisive moments that led to that choice. He always singled out particular experiences which, as he told the widow of the Georgian poet Tabidze, had given him a life 'so happy...set forth with such quiet concentrated meaning like a book'.[1] Listing there what had been most important to him he begins with 'the example of what my father did, the love of music and A. N. Skryabin' [Scriabin]. Again, he had written to another Georgian poet, Yashvili, in 1932, after a first visit to his country, that henceforth Tiflis would take its place for him with other memorable images. Its significance would rank beside that of 'Chopin, Scriabin, Marburg, Venice and Rilke'.[2] The present chapter explores the meaning for Pasternak of the first three – Chopin, Scriabin and Marburg. These names appear very often in his writing, especially the first two. The Marburg episode fills the centre panel of his triptych in *Safe Conduct*, between those on Scriabin and Mayakovsky. It gave rise to the best known of his early poems (before *My Sister Life*) – a lyric named 'Marburg' first published in the collection of 1917, *Above the Barriers*. His time at Marburg was the immediate prelude to self-realisation as a poet, which led to his writing verse, in the summer of 1913, 'often and regularly, as one practises painting or composes music'[3]–like Leonid Pasternak ('the example of what my father did') or Scriabin. It was in Marburg that his second and final renunciation came about, when he gave up

14

philosophy just as three years before going there he had made the first and probably more difficult renunciation – that of music.

II

Aleksandr Pasternak, younger brother of the poet, has written in a memoir about their childhood: 'Music from the very day we were born went at our side.'[4] The incident which in Pasternak's recollection marked the ending of infancy and an arrival at self-awareness concerned music. He describes in his *Essay in Autobiography* of 1957 how he was awakened by the sound of a trio (probably by Tchaikovsky for piano, cello and violin, his mother being the pianist) when in November 1894 Tolstoy was visiting their house.[5] In the smoke-filled room he saw two old men, one of them Tolstoy, the other N. N. Gué the painter, who used to say he had only two real friends, Tolstoy and the boy Boris (at this time still under four).[6] The music had affected him with 'yearning and panic':

> Why did I weep and why is my suffering so memorable to me? I had grown accustomed to the sound of the piano at home, my mother played it professionally. The voice of the piano seemed to me an inseparable attribute of music itself. The timbre of the strings, particularly in chamber ensembles, was not familiar to me and it disturbed me as though real cries for help and news of disasters had come from outside through the air-vent in the window.[7]

In this way Tolstoy, 'whose spirit permeated our whole house', music, and a sense of the reality beyond his home were all associated in one poignant remembrance. It seems no accident that here, at the threshold of Pasternak's imaginative awareness, music and literature should have been intertwined.

'Poets who are not interested in music are, or become, bad poets.' This statement by Ezra Pound[8] ignores the many good poets who lacked the musical intelligence of Dante or of Pound himself. Sometimes the poet who insists upon the importance of music – Blok is a case in point – thinks of it as something abstract, an ideal of harmony, a condition to which poetry should aspire, without himself having much expert knowledge of music. Pasternak is unusual in the degree to which music possessed him. For six years in his boyhood, from the day when he met Scriabin, he thought, as did everyone else who knew him as a boy, that to compose music would be his vocation. When in 1909 he took some of his work for Scriabin to hear, it was good enough to earn the excited approval of the most admired Russian composer at that time. Even after Pasternak had renounced music he would stay on intimate terms with it, playing the piano, on which he had been in youth a talented improviser. His greatest love in music was for the work of Chopin.

The piano, as we have already heard, seemed to Pasternak 'an inseparable attribute of music itself'.[9] His article on Chopin of 1945 (published in a Leningrad paper)[10] makes explicit and elaborates the beliefs about this composer which, to judge from many references in his poetry, he had held for at least thirty years. Pasternak looked on Chopin as one of 'the main pillars and founders of instrumental music', the other being Bach. And what he particularly admired in them was their 'realism':

Chopin was a realist in the same sense as Lev Tolstoy. His art is thoroughly original not from its unlikeness to rivals but from its likeness to nature... It is always biographical not out of self-centredness but because, like the other great realists, Chopin regarded his own life as a means of apprehending every life in the world.[11]

A poem of 1931, *'Opyat' Shopen ne ishchet vygod'* ['Once more Chopin seeks no gain for himself'], is a poem to the evocative force of his music:

> Гремит Шопен, из окон грянув,
> А снизу, под его эффект
> Прямя подсвечники каштанов,
> На звезды смотрит прошлый век.

> [Thunder of Chopin rolls from the windows
> And below under its impact
> Straightening the chestnuts' candlesticks
> Last century looks at the stars.]

It is Chopin who 'alone lays the road of escape/From likelihood to simple truth' [*Odin npokladyvaet vykhod/Iz veroyatiya v pravotu*] – to a realism that brings 'the entire nineteenth century' at the sound of the piano's 'resonant ritual' to 'fall on to the ancient pavement'.[12]

'The significance of Chopin', he claims in the article of 1945, 'is wider than music.' In his work music rediscovered itself, and from the *Études*, where you find 'Chopin at his most Chopinesque', can be derived 'a theory of childhood' and 'an introduction to death'. What they teach is 'history, the *structure* of the universe and whatever is more remote and general than playing the piano'.[13] Such claims for Chopin's *Études* may seem pitched extravagantly high, the more so when in an article that seeks to rescue Chopin from the imputation of romanticism, Pasternak apparently uses the language itself of pure romantic impressionism. We may protest that he attributes to Chopin's music those semi-divine powers of revelation which were claimed by Scriabin. But it would be wrong to assume in the first place that Pasternak went very far with Scriabin towards those ultimate mammoth delusions of the creative will. To some extent he may indeed have come to interpret Chopin in the light of his own intense preoccupation with Scriabin throughout the years of adolescence. However, what he says about the realism of Chopin forms part of an aesthetic creed in which Tolstoy is no less important, and he attributes this concern with actualities also among musicians to Bach, and among poets to Verlaine, for example, and to Blok.[14] It becomes more a question of the value he puts upon Chopin than of the terms in which he expresses that value. After all, the greatest art should indeed provide 'a theory of childhood' (in the sense that Sir Thomas Browne can look for 'the true Theory of death') and it can also prepare the mind for death, the concern with which, as Yury Zhivago discovers when still a student, continually drives the artist to fresh creation.[15]

At the end of his life, when writing the *Essay in Autobiography*, Pasternak still upheld Chopin as an ideal for the poet. He speaks in the second chapter of attempts by Andrey Bely, Khlebnikov and others to devise a new vocabulary and to transform the means of poetic expression:

I have never understood these pursuits. In my view the most astonishing discoveries have been made when the content so overfilled the artist's mind that it allowed him no time to consider, and he hurried on to utter his new statement in the old language, without examining whether it was old or new.[16]

The example Pasternak chooses of a genuine innovation within the old is Chopin who contented himself with developing the established idiom of Mozart and Field. This is the difficult and less obvious kind of originality, discussed by T. S. Eliot in relation to Samuel Johnson's verse, when the artist can still impose his 'personal stamp' on a medium already familiar to contemporaries.[17] And Pasternak was willing to see a further illustration in Scriabin, who 'with *very nearly* the resources of his predecessors renovated the feeling of music to its foundations at the very beginning of his career'.[18]

The Pasternak family met Scriabin in 1903 when they were neighbours on holiday. He was then working on his Third or 'Divine' Symphony, and as the fragments of this took shape on his piano they floated across a wooded valley to the ears of Boris

Pasternak and his brother who were out botanising.[19] Aleksandr Pasternak describes what they heard as more like a music lesson, with the player now inching forward, now falling back to the notes already achieved. Boris evokes in his recollection the thunder of the finished symphony, 'like a town under artillery fire'. Those who could judge and compare Scriabin's performance at the keyboard with that of other acknowledged masters are agreed that he was a remarkably fine executant. According to Arthur Lourié, 'Scriabin's playing was probably the most distinguished after Chopin's.'[20] In the words of a review written at the beginning of the composer's career, 'Scriabin plays as it were intimately – just as if he were improvising, or confessing to himself his most secret inspirations.'[21] Lourié explains the difficulty of appreciating Scriabin's own work as due to the fact that 'apparently his music grew out of improvisation rather than composition'. Chopin of course was a celebrated improviser, a fact recalled by Pasternak in the final part of his essay;[22] and it is improvisation that in Pasternak's poem 'Music' ['*Muzyka*', 1956] brings alive (as Chopin did in the other poem quoted above)

> The boulevard in a downpour, rumbling wheels,
> The life of the streets, the lot of the lonely

[*Bul'var pod livnem, stuk kolyos/Zhizn' ulits, uchast' odinochek*].[23]

Before Pasternak himself made poetry his business, but after he had abandoned music as a career, there was a time when, much in the manner of Chopin portraying in musical caricature 'a noted English traveller, a Parisienne in rapture, a poor Jewish old man',[24] he would improvise sketches on the piano of people who came in to the literary circle he had joined.[25] While never making public verse improvisations – as Mickiewicz once had in the salons of St Petersburg – Pasternak seems to have regarded this process of headlong commitment to the medium as natural to the inspired artist. This was how he composed his poems of 1917 and 1918.[26] This too would appear to have been the method of Yury Zhivago when he gave himself up to the writing of poetry for a few nights at Varykino;[27] and there is the same impetuous procedure when Seryozha of *The Last Summer* begins to draft the scenario for his verse play: 'In places he produced words that do not exist in the language. He left them temporarily on the paper, so that afterwards they could bring him to more immediate channels. . .leading to the colloquial speech that is formed from the union of rapture with everyday things [*s obikhodom*].'[28]

In the *Essay in Autobiography* he insists that 'the Scriabin by whom I lived and was nourished as by my daily bread remained the Scriabin of the middle period, approximately from his Third to his Fifth Sonata'.[29] On Scriabin's return from Switzerland, Pasternak, with his mother and brother, attended rehearsals of the *Poème de l'extase*, and although later he thought its title pretentious, he still regarded the music as being 'above and more serious than its name'.[30] The *Poème de l'extase* marked the full emergence of Scriabin the arch-romantic. When in 1906 the Marxist theoretician Plekhanov and his wife met Scriabin they were told by him that this work was permeated by the spirit of the revolution 'and by the ideals for which the Russian people was then struggling'.[31] Scriabin's apocalyptic frenzy belonged to the hour, and perhaps Lunacharsky was justified when he claimed him in 1925 as having been 'adopted by the epoch of revolution'.[32] Lunacharsky's essay that sought to give Scriabin a secure place in the new pantheon spoke of 'the extraordinary passion' with which he had converted 'the little light of Chopin into a raging elemental fire'. Now that the intensities of Scriabin's heyday, the abandonment to cosmic hope which came so easily then, and all the accompanying rhetoric no longer seem credible, it is hard not to dismiss them as what Eliot once called unkindly so much 'romantic detritus'.[33] True, upon the arrival of Scriabin's centenary he has lately been treated with more respect; the originality of his extreme chromaticism, quite distinct from that of Schoenberg and the Viennese atonalists, is now recognised; his messianic delusions, the bad librettos he composed for his heaven-storming cantatas, the portentous lighting effects – none of these prevented him from writing impressive keyboard work to the last. Even so, Mandelstam's verdict (which does not deny his power) has to be reckoned with. He called Scriabin 'a tempter who combined the Dionysian principle with the dementia of those Russian sectarians who burned themselves to death in coffins'.[34]

Pasternak is not blind to the excesses of Scriabin or, more plainly, to his 'reverse side', the insatiable self-love which leads to a moral nihilism (so that the intended Prometheus becomes Satan). Listening to the disputes between him and Leonid Pasternak, Boris found that they agreed on nothing but 'the nature and function of art'.[35] Scriabin's attacks on Tolstoy, his Nietzschean advocacy of the superman and refusal to acknowledge a moral law were not at all pleasing to Pasternak's father; and it is upon this example of Scriabin, who did not disguise his contempt for the uncreative, that

Pasternak blames his own arrogance in boyhood.[36] (It may be that a poem by Yury Zhivago, 'The Miracle' (No. 20), about the cursing of the fig tree for its barrenness, bears faintly the imprint of Scriabin, though it deals with a philistinism no less obdurate and more stifling than any he encountered.) All the same, Pasternak is willing to concede that Scriabin's 'egocentricity was appropriate' – though 'justified in his case alone'.[37] He defends the ideas he held about the superman as deeply national, and expressing 'the immemorial Russian urge to extremes'. Scriabin believed that 'not only should music be supermusic for it to signify at all, but that everything in the world should surpass itself so as to be itself. A man and his work must include the element of infinity which determines a phenomenon and imparts its character.'[38]

Pasternak was prepared to rank Scriabin with Dostoevsky and Blok as artists who gave something more than art, and so constituted 'a reason for endless rejoicings, a triumph made manifest and a high holiday of Russian culture'.[39] This is the settled view he took at the end of his life, and it proves that the earlier raptures, when the boy of fourteen wanted to hide 'from the steps of my divinity',[40] had not lost their power. Hearing the melodies of Scriabin 'you weep, not because you feel sad, but because the path to your innermost self has been divined with such a sure penetration'. And Scriabin is invoked as an example of 'that naturalness which in art has the decisive word'.[41] Pasternak recalled in *Safe Conduct* that Scriabin had impressed upon him the virtue of simplicity. There was a necessary paradox in this, for he also maintained that mediocre art is at the other extreme from simplicity. *Kitsch* has to be fussily elaborate, in order to hide its emptiness. The less character, the more complication.[42] A similar thought appears in a poem of the same period as *Safe Conduct*, *The Waves* [*Volny*] (1931). Here he gives the idea a classic formulation: simplicity

is what men most require,
But complication is better understood.

[*Ona* [*prostota*] *vsego nuzhnee lyudyam,/No slozhnoe ponyatney im.*][43]

The importance of Scriabin in his own day cannot be doubted. When he died in 1915 even the sceptical Mandelstam thought the event worthy to be discussed in an essay as a counterpart to the death of Pushkin.[44] It would seem clear that for Pasternak the ideal of artistic freedom and irrepressible creative power was embodied in Scriabin. Nor is it difficult to see a connection between his music

and some of Pasternak's own earlier writings. The suggestion has
been made that the First Symphony lies somewhere behind that most
characteristic and impressive volume of Pasternak's early verse,
My Sister Life, the Third behind the best of his prose works in the
1920s, *The Childhood of Luvers*.[45] When towards the end of his life
Pasternak complained about the mannerism that for him defaced his
earlier writings, the impulse to renounce them did not extend to
Scriabin's work which had meant so much to him at that period.
It continued to claim his admiration, and the fault of his own productions in Pasternak's judgment was that they did not live up to
the strict notion of simplicity placed before him by Scriabin. The
likelihood is that if they had come closer to Scriabin of the middle
period Pasternak might have looked on them more favourably.

His own poetry had at the beginning some affinities with keyboard
music. In the first place, despite their visual accuracy, the lyrics of
Above the Barriers or *My Sister Life* impress most of all by the
intricate organisation of sound effects. Dale Plank seems fully
justified in referring to 'chords' which harmonise the separate
instances of a particular set of vowels and consonants in a passage.
He can point also to the enactment of meaning through sound
devices – a feature common enough in all good poetry, but extremely prominent in the earlier lyrics of Pasternak.[46] The musical
analogy makes better sense in relation to Pasternak's poems than it
does, for example, in relation to Eliot's *Four Quartets*, because the
resemblance in Eliot's work is largely one of conception – as it is
also (incidentally) with Pasternak. Both can show the development
of themes,[47] and their verse has been shaped on the pattern of a
musical structure. But Eliot was never a practising musician. For
him the analogy is suggestive rather than inevitable, whereas for
Pasternak the exploration of music, and particularly of keyboard
music, was a step towards discovering his poetic vocation. The
writing of poetry which he began seriously in the summer of 1913
grew directly out of his association with Scriabin which had begun
ten years earlier in the summer of 1903.

Pasternak was to reject music as a vocation solely on the grounds
that he lacked perfect pitch. The story has been told dramatically in
Safe Conduct:[48] how he went to Scriabin, played his own compo-
sitions to the master's growing delight, and then hazarded his entire
musical future on a secret gamble – as on the tossing of a coin.
He would confess the deficiency of his musical ear, a shortcoming
which he knew to be shared by Scriabin himself. If Scriabin admitted

this in his own case, then a career in music would be proper for Pasternak. If on the other hand he pointed out that Wagner and Tchaikovsky lacked perfect pitch, whereas countless piano-tuners were obliged to have it, then the omen would be unfavourable. In the event he made the latter reply, and Pasternak, at the moment of supposed triumph, turned his back on music, exactly as three years later, and having received the same seal of approval from his master, he would reject philosophy.

The excuse of an imperfect ear he knew to be not wholly relevant, since the same supposed handicap had not prevented Scriabin from achieving a brilliant success in music. That it should have troubled him, that it allowed play to his superstition and instinct for self-denial,[49] shows the working in Pasternak's mind of an intuitive sense which guided him to the right vocation. And here too the example of Scriabin may have helped. What had particularly won his boyhood devotion was the ineffable lightness, the grace and spontaneity of this artist.[50] They were the signs of genius fully at one with itself. In Pasternak's addiction to music there was a hidden strain; as he says, 'in spite of the successes in composition, I was helpless when it came to the practical part'.[51] He felt deeply dissatisfied with his piano-playing. In fact, he saw what only the capacity for a real vocation could show him, that in music for all the appearances he would remain an amateur. And perhaps also with Scriabin, as later with Mayakovsky, Pasternak would have found it essential to shake off his influence. Becoming a composer he might have remained Scriabin's gifted pupil and liegeman. As a poet, he was compelled by the seriousness of his dedication to strike out for himself. Pasternak in this mature period learnt how to transcend the limitations of Scriabin. Pasternak the young poet had caught from him in particular the note of ecstasy. He was to affirm the inexhaustible energies of the creative mind, as did Scriabin. But it was impossible for any artist to live by ecstasy alone in the times that followed for Russia upon the Great War and the October Revolution.

III

Scriabin had always maintained a deep interest in philosophical problems;[52] it was on his advice that Pasternak changed from the Law Faculty of Moscow University to that of Letters, so that he might read philosophy.[53] Like the young Russians of Turgenev's generation, he took the road to Germany. Eighty years before it had been Berlin and the study of Hegel that drew students away from St Petersburg and Moscow. Pasternak in 1912 passed Berlin by on his way to Marburg, where in the 1730s Lomonosov, the principal figure of the Russian Enlightenment, had gone to study with Christian Wolff. Marburg when Pasternak went there was famous for the presence of Hermann Cohen and of Paul Natorp, his younger colleague whose own thought had been in large measure determined by Cohen. This was the great age of the Neo-Kantian school in Germany, when most university chairs were held by its adherents, and theirs had become the *Schulphilosophie* taught almost universally in German seats of learning.[54] Cohen had been a professor at Marburg since 1876, following Friedrich Albert Lange, who ten years before Cohen's arrival published the celebrated *History of Materialism*. For the fifth edition of this work, in 1896, Cohen wrote a commendatory preface which earned him a page of sharp recrimination in Lenin's *Materialism and Empirio-Criticism* (1909).[55] Cohen and the Marburg school in general were much concerned with questions of epistemology. The crisis in physics during the last decades of the nineteenth century had encouraged him to proclaim that 'theoretical idealism has begun to shake the materialism of the scientists and perhaps will soon finally overcome it', and that 'idealism permeates modern physics'. He also believed in an ethical form of socialism, which did not accept the class struggle as a necessary condition for social change. Cohen thus has a paragraph of dishonourable mention in the Soviet *Encyclopaedia* as 'an implacable enemy of scientific socialism' whom Lenin had 'fully unmasked as an idealist and reactionary'.[56]

For Pasternak he was a philosopher of genius, and the Marburg school founded by Cohen had two overwhelming advantages: it dealt with the 'primary sources', the nature and development of scientific thinking through twenty-five centuries; and it interpreted the achievements of past philosophers with an imaginative grasp that Pasternak characterises as truly Hegelian – at once magnificent in the power of its generalisation, and precise in its mastery of concrete detail.[57] Cohen bore himself in seminars with a soldierly directness; he demanded a plain answer to his favourite question about the classical philosophers they were reading: 'Was meint der Alte?' 'What is the old man getting at?'[58] Formidable, testy, merciless in his attacks on shoddy thinking and inaccuracy, Cohen is a type of philosopher that perhaps only nineteenth-century Germany could produce, with that entire dedication to the subject in hand, that unshakable confidence in human reason, in the supreme importance of philosophy, and in his own inalienable right to pursue this calling, and this alone. When Pasternak visited Marburg again in 1923, Cohen was dead,[59] and with him an age of German speculative thought had come to its end.

An unhappy love affair precipitated Pasternak's feelings about philosophy. After he had given up music, philosophy rushed in to fill the void; but he was afterwards to recognise that there had been an excessive fervour in his application to it. 'I *felt the experience* of studying this science more violently than the subject requires.'[60] This is surely not to imply that strong feeling may not enter into the pursuit of philosophy: like mathematics or even textual scholarship – like any pure intellectual activity – it can and should excite an attention in the mind comparable to that of the artist; and such a commitment is rightly to be called passionate. However, Pasternak came to see that there was something at fault in his attitude to philosophy. He explains this by describing his thought as 'vegetative' [*kakoe-to rastitel'noe myshlen'e*]. That is to say, it ramified, and secondary themes began to take on a life of their own. He accuses himself of an intellectual bad faith. The books spread about his room were opened at quotations to prop a thesis which he did not examine with due rigour. If the mark of true science is falsifiability, then Pasternak was not scientific. And yet Cohen had formed a high opinion of his potentialities as a philosopher – witness the ritual invitation to a Sunday lunch. But Pasternak insists that his pursuit of philosophical truth was not 'disinterested' [*beskorystnyy*].[61] The praise of Chopin in the lyric of 1931 quoted above had been that 'once more he seeks no gain for himself' [*ne ishchet vygod*],[62] and another lyric of the same year says about the woman he loves 'Your meaning is, like the air, disinterested' [*Tvoy smysl, kak vozdukh, beskorysten*].[63] Pasternak demands a purity of concentration in music, in poetry, in love, which seems almost like the notion of grace. He had not been able to achieve this state in his own dedication to music. Now after that unpremeditated journey to Berlin with the girl who had refused him, it became clear that the world had changed. On the summer morning that followed there was revealed to him 'the laconic freshness of life' [*svezhiy lakonizm zhizni*]. He felt a sense of 'brotherhood with the enormous summer sky... Momentarily', he tells, 'all had been forgiven me. I should have at some time in the future to work off my debt to the morning for its confidence in me.'[64] And so immediately on his return to Marburg he gathered up the books in his room, thus dismantling the unwritten thesis and ending his hope of philosophy as a vocation.

Pasternak did not replace it by poetry for another year, though the experience of something like dedication – of being obliged to make his return for an initiation into brotherhood with the elements – would suggest that, in Wordsworth's phrase, vows were made for him:

> bond unknown to me
> Was given, that I should be, else sinning greatly,
> A dedicated Spirit.[65]

As we have seen, the bond for Pasternak was not actually unknown, but he may not have recognised the precise nature of its discharge through writing poetry. Otherwise, those two early mornings of summer, Wordsworth's like Pasternak's belonging to his student days, are equally solemn, equally decisive it would seem for the young men who experienced them.

What did Cohen and Marburg do for Pasternak? The question takes that form because the city itself with memories of the thirteenth-century saint Elizabeth of Hungary, the Reformation and Giordano Bruno appealed very strongly to his imagination. Here was immemorial Germany, the landscape familiar to him from Rilke:

> In jenen kleinen Städten, wo herum
> die alten Häuser wie ein Jahrmarkt hocken[66]

> [In those little towns where all round
> the ancient houses crouch like a fair]

Pasternak was deeply responsive to German poetry, and residence in Marburg seems to have been the right preparation for his visit that followed to Italy. It was still possible in 1912 for a young Russian to share the romantic feelings about Germany that earlier generations had known in the nineteenth century. The words that he uses after describing how he left Marburg are keyed perhaps deliberately in the tone of Turgenev: 'Farewell, philosophy, farewell youth, farewell Germany!'[67] And Cohen is carefully set in that innocent and engaging picture. He bears more than slight resemblance to Lemm, the German musician in Turgenev's *A Nest of Gentlefolk*, although Lemm's genius had gone unrecognised. It could be said that the moral effect of Cohen upon Pasternak reinforced that of his own father. Here was a further example of disinterestedness – of that selfless concern for truth which Turgenev had so much admired in the idealists Granovsky and Stankevich, both of whom formed their minds in Germany. And Marburg must have seemed the appropriate setting for such a virtue. Marburg had known earlier the self-abnegation of Elizabeth of Hungary, whose legend Pasternak glances at in *Safe Conduct*.[68]

It is less simple to decide about the intellectual endowment that Pasternak may have received from Cohen. One thing is certain: just as, when giving up music as his profession, Pasternak did not ultimately part with music, but retained for it the keenest appreciation, so during his forty-odd years of writing verse he did not give up a philosophical habit of mind. This expression needs at once to be qualified. There have been poets in his time, such as Paul Valéry, Wallace Stevens or Jorge Guillén, who at least on occasions, and when writing some of their more important poems, could be described as metaphysicians in verse. (I avoid the term 'metaphysical poets' because it suggests either an English seventeenth-century connotation, or a more or less deliberate turning on the part of a modern poet towards Donne or Marvell.) And Eliot in *Four Quartets* is another such metaphysician in verse. These poets when they give scope to their philosophical interest are indeed engaged on the creation of concepts;[69] their procedure is obviously unlike that of the formal metaphysician, because they do not as a rule in their poetry conduct a sustained argument. What they offer is more a series (and it may seem a haphazard series) of meditations, closer to the style of Pascal in his *Pensées*; they do not advance by numbered paragraphs which mark the stages of an argument that consolidates each step and moves on. Poetic thinking such as theirs will take up a motif in the way that music does, by a process of variations and constant returns. Yet without a philosophical training or a philosophical interest these poets could not have written as they did – and did frequently in their capital works. Again, the prose of Eliot or Valéry is highly conscious that it bears a relation to philosophical thinking. Whether as poets or critics, they are concerned almost exclusively with order in the universe, in ethics or in art (Eliot liked to conceive the whole of Western literature as forming an ideal order).[70] Such poets directly or indirectly follow the example of Dante; and it is possible, perhaps even necessary, to regard their work as creating a structured whole.

Pasternak does not belong to this company. It is true that certain poems reflect his training and interests as a philosopher. One section of *My Sister Life* carries the title 'Occupation with Philosophy' ['*Zanyat'e filosofiey*'] and the first two poems are called 'The Definition of Poetry' ['*Opredelenie poezii*'] and 'The Definition of

26

the Soul' ['*Opredelenie dushi*'].[71] The section includes another
poem 'The Definition of Creativeness' ['*Opredelenie tvorchestva*'].[72] But the reader who expects to find something like
Andrew Marvell's 'The Definition of Love', with its clear formulations and careful argument, will be puzzled by Pasternak's
'Definitions'. The one on poetry begins with seven images, which
have been generally taken to represent the poetic process or its
effect,[73] although Dale Plank argues that 'the definition is a
negative one; the predicates refer to what poetry is not'.[74] It is only
with the third poem, in its final stanza, that a definition appears:

И сады, и пруды, и ограды,
И кипящее белыми воплями
Мирозданье – лишь страсти разряды,
Человеческим сердцем накопленной.

[And gardens, and ponds, and fences,
And seething with blank cries
The universe are only discharges of passion
Accumulated by the heart of man.]

Philosophy is an adjunct to Pasternak's lyric expression, just as it
appears to be for his prose. Thus, in an early critical essay 'The
Black Goblet' ['*Chornyy bokal*', 1916] he will venture a philosophical statement when he defines the true lyric as 'the condition *a
priori* of subjective possibility', or he will speak of a 'logically pro-
portional concept'.[75] Pasternak more than once formulated his
aesthetic position (notably in *Safe Conduct*) and there are interludes
of philosophical discussion from time to time in *Doctor Zhivago*,
especially with Sima in Chapter 13. But no major poem of his, nor
even any series of lyrics, is to be compared with *Four Quartets* or
'Notes toward a Supreme Fiction'. He has no shorter poems like
'The Idea of Order at Key West' or Valéry's 'Ébauche d'un ser-
pent'. Nor does he play in his poetry with concepts, as Mandelstam
does after his own fashion when reiterating symbols like the 'black
sun' or 'nocturnal sun' [*chornoe solntse, nochnoe solntse*], through
which, as his widow has shown, various meanings are brought into
relation with one another.[76] Pasternak's philosophical habit of mind
can be said to have determined his poetry in one sense alone. As
Sinyavsky has pointed out, he owes much to the impressionist painters, but he differs from them radically in his 'concern for essences'.
'The Black Goblet', Sinyavsky reminds us, creates the term 'impressionism of the eternal': 'The moment cherished by the impressionists
is filled in Pasternak's work with a content so significant that it now

tells not of the fleeting and unique but of the constant and general.'[77] Sinyavsky therefore is justified in using the expression 'an intensity of poetic thought' for that generalising activity behind the particulars sharply seized which runs through all Pasternak's life and art, and grows stronger with the years.[78] But the poet still does not qualify in the same way as Eliot or Wallace Stevens to be called a 'metaphysician in verse'.

These youthful passions for music and philosophy enlarged the possibility of his poetry. Music gave to him, as it did to another student of the art, Hopkins, an unusually dense patterning in his verse fabric. Here the term 'orchestration' can be properly applied (though one critic, Georgy Adamovich, has found the melody of Pasternak too dry and brittle, at least when heard immediately after Mandelstam's).[79] The preoccupation at this time with philosophy made it certain that his work, however impressionistic or fragmentary, would have a general coherence. He developed his own sufficient aesthetic;[80] and the separate poems, stories and memoirs form a manifest sequence of exploration, even though they do not compose, as Eliot's work seems in retrospect to compose, a deliberate order. Pasternak's most sustained act of creative thinking was that which produced *Doctor Zhivago*. Since it deals with the life of an artist as affected by the revolution, inevitably it became, among other things, a critique of other people's and Pasternak's own ideas about these two subjects which interact in the story. *Doctor Zhivago* is not a philosophy-drenched novel like Goethe's *Wilhelm Meister* or Thomas Mann's *Doctor Faustus*. Although he found it congenial throughout life to speculate about the nature and function of art, Pasternak's main concern was to demonstrate his understanding in this matter by practice. A philosophical training made him more conscious of what he was doing. But philosophy, like music, never came back to dominate Pasternak's interest. They were discarded alternatives through which he was able to arrive the more surely at his vocation.

3

A Commitment to Futurism

I

Russian poetry during the adolescence of Pasternak was dominated by Symbolism and in particular by Aleksandr Blok. Symbolism in Russia was part of that general tide which flooded Europe towards the end of the nineteenth century: the Russian variety in its first generation bore the name of Decadence, with Valery Bryusov at the head of the movement, and among its practitioners Konstantin Balmont, the ubiquitous translator whose own work, as Mandelstam observed, was 'that unusual thing, a typical translation without an original'.[1] More impressive, though not so greatly different in their views, were the Symbolists proper of the second generation, Vyacheslav Ivanov, the most consistent of their theoreticians, Andrey Bely, a brilliant analyser of rhythms and phonetic effects, and the one major poet in either generation, and probably the greatest to have appeared since Pushkin, Blok. For two decades, the last of the old century and the first of the new, Symbolism grew in strength and prominence; but by 1910 the movement was in a state of collapse.

All Symbolist poetry seems to take as one of its sacred scrolls the famous sonnet by Baudelaire, *Correspondances* (written probably about 1855)

> La Nature est un temple où de vivants piliers
> Laissent parfois sortir de confuses paroles:
> L'homme y passe à travers des forêts de symboles
> Qui l'observent avec des regards familiers.[2]

This sonnet was important for Vyacheslav Ivanov, and for other poets of the movement;[3] the Decadents in the first generation were profoundly aware of the French and Belgian *symbolistes*, as the Russian Symbolists of Ivanov's generation were drawn rather to Germany; but the forests in which these poets encountered their symbols were also rooted in Russia; Tyutchev, a near contemporary of Pushkin who lived and wrote until 1873, was described by another of the second generation, Georgy Chulkov, as 'one of the elect' and 'the first Russian Symbolist';[4] and Vladimir Solovyov, the religious thinker called by Blok 'a monk-knight' (*rytsar'-monakh*[5]), who died in 1900 having had his three visions of the 'Eternal Friend', the feminine principle or Sophia, stands behind 'the "theurgy" of Vyacheslav Ivanov, the poetics of Andrey Bely, the poetry of Aleksandr Blok'.[6]

Ivanov was typical of the movement in seeking an inward reality – proceeding, as his famous formula expressed it, 'from the real to the more real' [*a realibus ad realiora*] – and in his conviction that the artist had to reveal a hidden order through the imagination.[7] This latter idea corresponds to the 'music' that Blok believed poetry to be capable of hearing in the primal chaos from which a cosmos must be created.[8] Ivanov was the only one among the group to pursue this quest throughout his life until he died in 1949, an exile who had been brought to Rome and to the Catholic Church. But a sacerdotal manner and a vatic solemnity belonged to the Symbolists as a whole. Poetry for them was the privilege of an elect few, the seers, who venerated themselves. Blok however refused to suppress the mocking voice that told him this cult overstrained itself. From 1907 his poetry struck out another path: he gave an example in the way that Eliot says Yeats did of character – that resolute impersonality which enables an artist to mature and to achieve 'a kind of moral, as well as intellectual, excellence'.[9]

Symbolism broke down in Russia from a lack of momentum. This happens to all movements in the arts, as it does to religious or political movements: with Russian Symbolism it came rather swiftly. While the benefits to Russian poetry from the Symbolist experience were real enough – a recovered confidence in the imagination, an openness to fresh currents from Western European art, a high degree of technical skill – yet the deficiencies became ever more obvious. Mandelstam, with some exaggeration perhaps, complained that the Symbolist poets 'had between them not more than five hundred words – the vocabulary of a Polynesian';[10] and elsewhere he says that 'the Russian Symbolists had sealed up all words, all images, designating them exclusively for liturgical use'. The result was that 'all the utensils were in rebellion. The broom asked to knock off work, the pot on the stove no longer wanted to cook, but demanded for itself an absolute significance (as though cooking were not one).

They drove the master out of his house, and he no longer dares to go in.'[11]

Mandelstam's own solution, which he took with Nikolay Gumilyov, Anna Akhmatova and a few other St Petersburg poets who later fell away, was that of the movement called Acmeism. They wanted to be at home on earth – not in the transcendental regions of the Symbolists; and they chose as their mentors four European poets – Shakespeare, Rabelais, Villon and Gautier – all of whom they appreciated for a grasp of actualities. Mandelstam in his essay 'The Morning of Acmeism' (published in 1919, but perhaps written at the time of other manifestos by the group in 1913) said that Acmeism proclaimed the law of identity ($A=A$). These poets (who took their title from the Greek ἀκμή – the highest or culminating point, the bloom) demanded clear outlines, firmness of design, unambiguous meaning; they laid emphasis on architecture and not, like the Symbolists, music as an analogue to poetry; and they insisted, as Bryusov and Ivanov had, on sound craftmanship. St Petersburg owed its eighteenth-century palaces in the classical style to Italian architects, and Acmeist verse aimed (despite the salute to Shakespeare) at a solidity and control that were essentially Latin. Mandelstam in his essay had expressed admiration for the Middle Ages with their 'feeling for the world as a living equilibrium';[12] it was a particular sense derived from the culture of the Mediterranean that inspired the best Acmeist writing, his own and Akhmatova's.

He and Akhmatova, like Gumilyov, remained faithful to Acmeism throughout their lives, and both have a very distinguished place in Russian poetry. But Acmeism, though a salutary development when Symbolism had run into the sands, represented only one solution to the problem before poets who wanted to make a fresh start. And it belonged intimately, as I have said, to a particular place, St Petersburg, and had its strong St Petersburg allegiances – not only to Pushkin, but to his eighteenth-century predecessor Derzhavin, and to Innokenty Annensky, who had been Gumilyov's headmaster at Tsarskoe Selo, outside St Petersburg, and whose 'domestic Hellenism' deeply impressed Mandelstam.[13] Acmeism gave that 'quality of hard light' which Ezra Pound thought very welcome in the later Yeats after so many 'pseudo-glamours and glamourlets and mists and fogs since the nineties'.[14] But in its first years, before Mandelstam and Akhmatova had developed into major poets far beyond Gautier, Acmeism in the words of the critic

31

V. Zhirmunsky, seemed to have achieved 'its formal perfection, its artistic equilibrium' at the cost of some 'real concessions'; it narrowed the aims of art, 'not by the triumph of form over chaos, but by the deliberate exclusion of chaos'.[15]

The other way out of the *impasse* was that adopted by the Futurists. In Russian poetry this term embraces a host of divergencies within a general tendency – there were many varieties to what the historian of Russian Futurism has called 'the most flexible of all poetic doctrines in Russia'.[16] But common to all was the desire for a language totally unlike the now worn counters of Symbolism. 'Russian Futurism', it has been said by a critic well suited to pronounce on this matter, Renato Poggioli, 'was a highly original movement, far more seminal than its Italian counterpart in both theory and creation, particularly in the art of verse'.[17] The exact degree of its dependence at the start on Italian Futurism may still not be clear. Marinetti did make a visit both to St Petersburg and Moscow in 1910, when Russian Futurism first began to show itself; and certainly he provided the name. The Russian Futurists came to their high season in 1913, when Marinetti's second tour was a partial failure.[18] They were quite as flamboyant as Marinetti in their methods of seeking publicity. Blok's diary for 25 March 1913 notes: 'In these days, debates of the Futurists, with scandals'.[19] In the previous December David Burliuk, Vladimir Mayakovsky, Aleksey Kruchenykh, and Velemir Khlebnikov had published their manifesto *A Slap in the Face of Public Taste* [*Poshchochina obshchestvennomu vkusu*] with its declaration 'Only we are the face of our time.' Another manifesto, in February 1913, which opened the (second) book to appear under the odd name *Sadok sudey* [*Trap, or Hatchery, of Judges*] proclaimed that 'we' – the same four with four associates – 'are obsessed by new themes... We experience feelings that did not exist before us... We are new people of a new life.'[20]

These Moscow 'people of a new life' called themselves Cubo-Futurists, and the first three, Burliuk, Kruchenykh and Mayakovsky, were painters as well as poets. The close alliance between Futurist poetry and Suprematist (and later Constructivist) painting was to continue into the first decade of Soviet power. Like the painters, the poets were concerned with the destruction of the old harmonies and habits of vision. They set free the word, by breaking down all sense of decorum in their vocabulary. They proclaimed the doctrine of *zaum'* [trans-sense] which spelt the autonomy of language, its release from accepted usage and customary referents. And, along with their obsessive desire to outrage and perplex, the Futurists devoted themselves very seriously to philological questions. The linguistic circle known as *Opoyaz* [Society for the Study of Literary Language], whose most original member was Viktor Shklovsky, had close links with the Futurists. Of these the supreme experimentalist in language was Velemir Khlebnikov, whose great but eccentric talent made him, as Mandelstam put it, 'a citizen of all history, of every system of language and poetry... Khlebnikov's poetry is idiotic in the genuine Greek inoffensive meaning of that word.'[21]

Whereas Acmeism very soon met with suspicion from the Bolsheviks when they had taken power, Futurism under the leadership of Mayakovsky rapidly established itself as the authentic school of revolutionary poetry. The first Soviet Commissar of Education, Lunacharsky, was not greatly interested in their experiments, but he liked the Futurists for their enthusiasm. 'They are young', he explained, 'and youth is revolutionary.'[22] The Futurists sought to dominate Soviet culture, and now like Marinetti they celebrated the machine and the domination of man over nature. Mayakovsky's journal *Lef* speaking for the Left Front of the Arts was able to draw together Constructivist painters like Rodchenko and Lissitsky, Futurist poets (including for a while Pasternak) and the film-makers Djiga Vertov and Sergey Eisenstein. The energies of Futurism were boundless; but apart from Khlebnikov, it is only Mayakovsky and his close adherent Nikolay Aseev who survive as poets to be still read.

Futurism was largely associated with Moscow, and therefore Pasternak found himself fully exposed to it when in 1913 he wrote the poems for his first book *Twin in the Clouds* [*Bliznets v tuchakh*, 1914]. His friendship with Mayakovsky and the fascination he found in Mayakovsky's poetry are to be discussed later. But there was one other Futurist from whom, like Mayakovsky, he may have learned something, if only in the use of complex rhymes. Igor-Severyanin, whose book *A Bowl Seething with Thunder* [*Gromokipyashchiy kubok*[23]] came out in 1913, is now forgotten, and his perfumed, voguish self-regarding 'poetries' – he invented the word *poezy* as a brand name – look so factitious that it seems only the most expert showmanship could have collected an audience for them. His 'Egofuturism' has sunk with the ego that puffed it. Yet Blok, Gumilyov and Mandelstam were all prepared to see something in him, though

Blok, having praised his 'real, fresh, child-like talent',[24] is said after hearing him declaim the poetry to have remarked on his 'greasy barrister's voice'.[25] Igor-Severyanin's control of set forms may have helped Pasternak, and his often trivial virtuosity can occasionally be seen reflected in the younger poet's earliest verse. But if Pasternak was for a while counted among the Futurists, he would never have accepted for himself the prefix 'Ego'.

Though he shared the wide culture of the Acmeists, and particularly admired Anna Akhmatova, their way could not be his. To begin with, it seemed too closely bound up with St Petersburg, the natural adversary of Pasternak's Moscow. In a poem of 1928 he seeks to emulate the 'primordial' quality [*pervozdannost'*] of Akhmatova's verse. It is a set of eight quatrains (about twice the length usual with her) which makes a tribute to the 'grains of intent prose' [*prozy pristal'noy krupitsy*] in her first volumes of 1912, 1913 and 1917. But the attempt to evoke her St Petersburg scene betrays his own sense of confinement within its streets: 'Around is spring, but beyond the city you may not go' [*Krugom vesna, no za gorod nel'zya*]. St Petersburg was complete, artificial, detached from the surrounding marshes; and quite unlike the homely growth of Moscow, which had wooden streets and was still half-buried in gardens among the palaces and new tenements.

Eventually it would be Mandelstam and Akhmatova whose purgatorial journey [*khozhdenie po mukam*] Pasternak would find himself sharing. But in 1913 there was everything to draw him towards Futurism, its novelty, its daring, its expansive freedom – everything except its eagerness to jettison the past.[26]

II

The group he joined bore the name of Centrifuge [*Tsentrifuga*]; it held together for some four years; and its programme was less clearly defined than those of more conspicuous Futurist formations with their manifestos, the militant declarations of intent, the lists of proscribed classical poets, and theories about language.[27] Apart from the fact that another good poet besides Pasternak, Nikolay Aseev, later to be the associate of Mayakovsky, belonged to this Moscow group, Centrifuge is noteworthy for certain shadings in its complexion. The ties it had with *avant-garde* painting were not unique, nor its awareness of European developments. However, two features distinguish it from the rest of Futurism: an interest in

German poetry (Anisimov with whom the circle began was the first Russian translator of Rilke): and, no doubt as a consequence of this, a much closer affinity with the Symbolists than might have been expected in an avowedly Futurist movement. Anisimov had originally brought together poets, writers, artists and musicians; and Pasternak gained entry as an improviser on the piano.[28] All this would have made Centrifuge the natural poetic home for Pasternak at a time when Futurism was triumphing in Moscow. His first volume of poetry, *Twin in the Clouds*, was published by Lirika, an enterprise under the direction of Anisimov; his second, *Above the Barriers* (1917), appeared as one of the last books to be published by Centrifuge. Up to 1917 when he wrote his third volume *My Sister Life* (which had to wait another five years for printing) Pasternak can be described as a Futurist of the Centrifuge persuasion. This allegiance did not exempt him from certain mannerisms which he later regretted, the 'flourishes' [*vykrutasy*] and 'trinkets' [*pobryakushki*] common to all Futurist writers, in verse or prose.[29] It encouraged in one or two polemical essays that strain of arrogance which Scriabin's example had seemed to legitimise. However, Pasternak's commitment – which continued with weakening ties through the 1920s – never betrayed him into taking up the common Futurist stance of total contempt for the past.

III

Twin in the Clouds has been overshadowed by the volume of three years later *Above the Barriers*, in which Pasternak first began to emerge as a fully individual poet with his unmistakable accent and with special gifts that brought special temptations. The wife of the poet Baltrushaitis told him that one day he would regret having published this immature book,[30] and afterwards he preserved only fourteen poems from it, and these were heavily revised, when he reissued *Twin in the Clouds* and *Above the Barriers* as a single volume in 1929. However, immaturity can take more than one aspect. Although Pasternak was reading Tyutchev at the time he composed *Twin in the Clouds*, he did not write pastiche of Tyutchev; and if his work has affinities with that of Blok and Annensky, these are a means of growth, not a kind of sleepwalking as so often happens with young poets. He had no more than begun to find his own resources, his own reading of life, and his characteristic measures and syntax. But it should have been plainer than it was to the reading public which virtually ignored *Twin in the Clouds* that here was an original mind at work, however strained the results and insecure the few (but by no means negligible) successes.

The title *Twin in the Clouds* later seemed to him 'stupidly pretentious' and it was supported by a number of Gemini-ridden lyrics which show that Pasternak was in part a covert Symbolist. Afterwards he allowed them to drop out.[31] The poems that remained in later editions are already attempting to seize those moments of apprehension which would be the subject of Pasternak's lyric poetry until the end. He wanted to render with an exact notation the feeling that dislocates – his own term[32] – a particular scene, which thereby becomes new and astonishing. This is the poetry of the unguarded instant when meaning miraculously appears to hang in the space between the self and what surrounds it. Those who call Pasternak merely an impressionist do him less than justice. Hemingway is an impressionist, baring his senses to heat, cold, hunger, panic; but such a willed scaling-down to the primitive has nothing in common with the Tolstoyan transcendence sought by Pasternak. The impressions that Pasternak only just gets into focus are singular and, when he succeeds in realising them fully, they compel assent and wonder. In these early poems the difficulty of making out what he sees through the corner of his eye – the turning of surmise into genuine discovery – too often overtaxes his powers. He is unequal to the effort of fending off unwanted additions: the poem lurches under a burden of images that almost break its back. In one short (uncollected) poem of four stanzas, he compares his sadness to a captive Serbian girl who tries to explain herself in her native language [*Grust' moya, kak plennaya serbka,/Rodnoy proiznosit svoy tolk*]; his eye becomes a hard-driven weather vane [*zagnannyy flyuger*], his sigh the bellows of an organ [*mekhi u organa*]; the girl's outline suggests an eel [*slovno ugor'*]; and he is left at the end like 'a burdock meaningless in the steppe, like a crane at the tub' [. . .*kak repeynik, bessmyslen/ V stepi, kak zhuravl' u bad'i*].[33]

The conceit is always prominent in Pasternak's writing, both verse and prose. Even during the last two decades of his life, when a conscious simplification had become the rule, he still found the conceit a necessity, however sparing its use. Bizarre and daring combinations abound in Futurist poetry as a whole; they are the repeated shock tactics that assail the poetic decorum of the Symbolist school; the available topics for poetry, the range of its operation, must now be unrestricted. Outrageous rhyme not only flaunts the new freedom of reference, it often seems to act also as a rudder to the imagination. One or two poems in Pasternak's first volume, and particularly 'The Twins' ['*Bliznetsy*'],[34] have such ingenious and restive rhymes that the poem appears to have been bent into the shape they impose. Did its fourth stanza allow a place for 'fuchsias in the window' following the *fait accompli* of an extraordinary rhyme for Pollux [*okonnykh fuksiy; na Pollukse*]? In 'Night Panel' ['*Nochnoe panno*'], where the rhymes without a single exception are arresting they would seem to have taken control in this stanza:

> Чтобы с затишьями шоссейными
> Огни перекликались в центре,
> Чтоб за оконными бассейнами
> Эскадрою дремало джентри.[35]

> [So that with the calm of the highways
> The lights should accord at the centre,
> So that beyond the window pools
> In a squadron should doze the gentry.]

(*Dzhentri* is a word with no rights of domicile in Russian.) Since Pasternak left this poem out of the 1929 collection, he may have come to see it rested solely on verbal cleverness.

The *Essay in Autobiography* claims that all his 'care was directed to content'; that the poems 'Venice' ['*Venetsiya*'] and 'The Railway Station' ['*Vokzal*'] should the one of them 'contain the city of Venice', the other the 'Brest, now Byelorussian–Baltic, station'.[36] This concern with a responsible meaning probably accounts for his having excluded ten poems from the revised volume. It will also explain why, dissatisfied though he was with most of his writing until 1940, Pasternak did not abandon the earlier work, but sought to strengthen it by revision, often on a large scale. We should never assume that any poems which he saw fit to keep in the canon were just exercises in wordplay, as an impatient critic might well protest. He says in *Safe Conduct* that 'fifteen years of abstention from words', when he gave himself up to music, had 'condemned [him] to originality, as some mutilations condemn to acrobatics'.[37] This originality comes from a delight in the resemblances between words, which at one time almost threatened to smother Pasternak's writing with sequences of near-puns and associations through sound alone. And yet though he seems often to commit himself to the medium – words generating other words, syntax becoming the arbitrary determinant of sense – the effect is scarcely ever what was known to the Futurists as *zaum'* – a dance of language away from all referents.

What any poet sees is at least partly given him through the telling. Pasternak's ostensibly verbal conceits and his well-nigh obligatory assonances are the means – treacherous if not handled with extreme care – to establishing what he sees.

The poem 'Venice' tells, obscurely enough in its original form, of an early awakening to a mysterious sound which is expressed – a chord not made with hands – in the trident of the sign Scorpion. At this hour when morning is born the poet feels he has 'grasped' [*postig*] 'the secret of existence that has no root' [*taynu bytiya bez kornya*].[38] The second version acquires new images which occupy the final couplets of the first and last stanzas respectively:

> Размокшей каменной баранкой
> В воде Венеция плыла.[39]
>
> [A sodden ring-roll of stone
> In the water Venice floated.]

(The *Essay in Autobiography* paraphrases this as 'the city on the water stood before me and the circles and figures of eight of its reflections floated and multiplied swelling like a rusk in tea'.)[40] The second image is this:

> Венеция венецианкой
> Бросалась с набережных вплавь.[41]
>
> [Venice like a Venetian girl
> Threw herself from the quays to swim.]

These two changes make the poem more visual: at first it had little for the eye. Thus the original fourth line 'Absence of men hung from the oar' [*Bezlyud'e vislo ot vesla*], even though it follows the evocation of a 'sleepy mooring-place' [*sonnoyu stoyankoy*], is too elusive, and it seems to have been mainly determined by the assonance of *vislo*, *vesla*. In the final version the Venetian girl's dive from the quay is anticipated by another new image:

> Большой канал с косой ухмылкой
> Оглядывался, как беглец.
>
> [The Grand Canal with a sidelong smirk
> Glanced back like a fugitive.]

Here a fleeting and troubled perception has 'dislocated' the scene. All the poem is dependent on the sound, apprehended through sleep, at its opening which the final version attributes 'perhaps' to 'an outraged woman far away':

> И женщиною оскорбленной,
> Быть может, издан был вдали.

There is less play with astrology in the poem now, and it has become a controlled and unified statement, though the impression remains, as it was intended to be, highly subjective and tenuous. But Pasternak no longer claims to have caught the secret of existence.

More was changed in 'The Railway Station'. The pathos of the poem remains as before, and it sets the tone from the opening couplet, unaltered in revision:

> Вокзал, несгораемый ящик
> Разлук моих, встреч и разлук. . .[42]

> [Station, fireproof safe
> Of my partings, encounters and partings. . .]

The replacement of certain images in the final version does not augment or clarify the meaning, but it makes the station itself and the train pulling away at the close more visible, audible, charged with life. And the syntax now gains a still greater naturalness. In a poem like this Pasternak comes near to Annensky of whom Gumilyov wrote: 'Annensky's verse is flexible, it has all the intonations of colloquial speech, but no singing effect [*net peniya*]. His syntax is as nervous and rich as his temperament [*dusha*].'[43] Here it may be that 'nervous' [*nerven*] has its meaning as a rhetorical description 'sinewy' rather than that also expressed by *nervoznyy*, 'nervy, irritable' – though this adjective is appropriate enough for Annensky's temperament. At any rate, in the former sense it applies well to Pasternak, who later in *Above the Barriers* was to develop a syntax of unparalleled vigour and complexity. The 'singing effect' is more noticeable in his verse than Annensky's, though 'The Railway Station' shows it less markedly than 'Feasts' ['*Piry*'][44] or the afterwards rejected 'At Night' ['*Noch'yu*'].[45]

A student friend first introduced Pasternak to the poems of Innokenty Annensky in the belief that these early efforts had something in common with them.[46] (This was at the time when Pasternak still belonged to the artistic group with a nonsense name, Serdarda, as a pianist.) For young poets wanting to break away from the routine of Symbolism Annensky, whose verse only became at all widely known not long before his death in 1909, did more to help them by example than any of their immediate predecessors. It was particularly the Acmeists who admired him. Gumilyov considered himself Annensky's pupil in poetry just as he had been his pupil in academic learning at the *gymnasium* of Tsarskoe Selo. Annensky for him, and for Mandelstam who quoted this opinion, was a great

European poet.[47] Akhmatova even in 1945 dedicated a poem to Annensky that calls him her teacher.[48] But Mayakovsky too shared the Acmeists' regard for him. The critic N. I. Khardzhiev explains what made Annensky congenial to a Futurist poet: 'Characteristic of Annensky are syntactical tension in the line, the unexpected train of impressionistic metaphors and comparisons dislocating the usual relations to objects, the interruptions of lofty poetical diction by prosaisms and words from specialised technical language.' He adds what the word 'dislocating' might have led us to expect: 'All these elements of construction have had development in Pasternak's poetry.'[49]

The impress of Annensky can be seen most clearly upon the first poem of Pasternak's book:

Февраль. Достать чернил и плакать!
Писать о феврале навзрыд.
Пока грохочущая слякоть
Весною черною горит.

Достать пролетку. За шесть гривен,
Чрез благовест, чрез клик колес,
Перенестись туда, где ливень
Еще черней чернил и слез.

Где, как обугленные груши,
С деревьев тысячи грачей
Сорвутся в лужи и обрушат
Сухую грусть на дно очей.

Под ней проталины чернеют,
И ветер криками изрыт,
И чем случайней, тем вернее
Слагаются стихи навзрыд.[50]

[February! Get ink and weep!
Write of February in sobs.
While the rumbling slush
Burns with black spring.

Get a droshky. For sixty copecks
Through the church-bells, through the cry of wheels,
Be carried where the downpour
Is yet blacker than ink and tears.

Where like charred pears
From the trees thousands of rooks
Break into puddles and bring down
Dry grief to the bottom of eyes.

Under it the thawed patches are black
And the wind pitted with cries,
And the more accidentally the surer
Verses are formed in sobs.]

40

The phrase 'black spring' in the first stanza, as Dale Plank has observed, evokes a well known poem by Annensky of 1906 about a funeral procession; and he notes Pasternak's indebtedness to the following lines among others:

> Да тупо черная весна
> Глядела в студень глаз. . .[51]
>
> [And dully did black spring
> Gaze into the jelly of eyes. . .]

The notation of 'black spring' turns into an elaborate conceit sustaining the whole poem, and Pasternak takes advantage of the fact that *chernila*, ink, is cognate with *chornyy*, black, to 'collate' [*slichit'*] as he put it in the first draft 'ink with the grief of tears' [*chernilo s gorem slyoz*].[52] This conceit is made visual in the emended version: 'where the downpour is yet blacker than ink and tears'. The third stanza has another image of blackness – rooks 'like charred pears', and in the fourth the thawed patches show blackly. Originally it was 'the cries of spring' that became 'black as water' [*Kriki vesny vodoy cherneyut*] – that is, they took the form of dark pools. This brings an odd resemblance to Blake's lines in 'London':

> And the chimney sweeper's cry
> Every black'ning church appals

since the cries in both poems are metamorphosed into blackness, just as in Blake's next couplet 'the hapless soldier's sigh' runs as red blood. Pasternak then followed this line by another that carried on the conceit: 'And the city is pitted with cries' [*I gorod – krikami izryt*]. Later this was improved by substituting 'the wind' [*veter*] for the city. It may be that *izryt*, 'pitted', owes its inclusion to the last rhyming word of the poem, *navzryd*, 'sobbingly', which survived from the first version though everything else was changed.

The derivation here seems obvious enough. In his general mood, however, Pasternak is very different from Annensky, the master of resignation. The poem about February may seem close to his work, with its themes of melancholy and sleeplessness. But the true notes of Pasternak were to be joy, astonishment, and an impatient eagerness to take life at the full.

V

They are heard more distinctly in *Above the Barriers* [*Poverkh Bar'erov*, 1917], a collection of some fifty poems written between early 1914 and the end of 1916. These bring him up to the threshold of his first triumph, *My Sister Life* [*Sestra moya zhizn'*], the poems which were his response to the year of revolutionary hope 1917. *Above the Barriers* had an epigraph from Swinburne, who appealed to Pasternak in much the same way as Keats and Shelley did.[53] The impetuous movement of certain poems in *Above the Barriers* – to become more general in *My Sister Life* – may have been inspired by the onrush of Swinburne's lyric metres. The revised selection from this book published in the volume of 1929 with the same title *Above the Barriers* was dedicated to Vladimir Mayakovsky, just as the selection from *Twin in the Clouds* was to Nikolay Aseev. Mayakovsky, whom he had met in the summer of 1914, liked the poetry of *Above the Barriers* and subsequently of *My Sister Life*.[54] Despite their differences in temperament, and in the conceptions they held of what poetry should be, Pasternak and Mayakovsky were natural allies at this period. They soon discovered that their technique was very similar. Both delighted in unexpected imagery, and practised ingenious and out-of-the-way rhyming. But it became an obligation for Pasternak to suppress in his own work any striving after the effects of Mayakovsky, and to reject his heroic stance.[55]

One lyric of this collection, 'Spring' ['*Vesna*'], contains two stanzas that define the poetic imagination as Pasternak understood it:

Поэзия! Греческой губкой в присосках
Будь ты, и меж зелени клейкой
Тебя б положил я на мокрую доску
Зеленой садовой скамейки.

Расти себе пышные брыжи и фижмы,
Вбирай облака и овраги,
А ночью, поэзия, я тебя выжму
Во здравие жадной бумаги.[56]

[Poetry, be a Greek sponge with suckers
And amid the sticky greenery
I'd like to put you on the wet plank
Of a green garden bench.

Grow splendid frills and farthingales,
Absorb the clouds and ravines,
And at night, poetry, I shall wring you out
For the good of greedy paper.]

(The 'sticky greenery' seems to evoke the 'sticky little leaves opening in spring' that reconciled Ivan Karamazov to life;[57] poetry for Pasternak must celebrate growing things, and therefore its appropriate haunt is a garden bench.) The same image for poetry occurs in

an essay of 1922, 'Some Theses' ['*Neskol'ko polozheniy*'].[58] There
he insists that to conceive poetry as a fountain is wrong; it should
rather be a sponge that 'must suck in and become saturated'. The
Formalist critics always brought poetry down to the devices by
which it gained its effects; but Pasternak saw 'the organs of perception' as what really counted. However, the argument here is directed,
as it develops, more against Mayakovsky than the Formalists.
Pasternak resists the art that displays itself from a platform, when
it should seek an obscure place in the gallery. With the later poems
of *Above the Barriers* he has attained that different conception of
the self and its role in poetry which will enable him not to be swept
along in Mayakovsky's wake.

The presence of Pasternak inside these poems is purely that of the
observer and participant in what he sees. Having taken his position
above the barriers rather than behind the barricades, he allows the
surrounding world to make its disclosures to him. Mayakovsky in
A Cloud in Trousers [*Oblako v shtanakh*, 1914–15] writes a wholly
centripetal poem; his self is the constant point of return; the effect
of the poem is that he throws his grotesque and gesticulating shadow
over the whole scene. Pasternak in the poem 'Marburg', which also
has for its theme an unhappy love affair, works in the opposite
direction: his poetry is always centrifugal, and even in this most
personal of confessions Pasternak moves very quickly from the foreground. The nominative 'I' is soon replaced by oblique cases. The
last three stanzas, preserved from the original version with a few
changes in the first of them, demonstrate the impersonality of pure
receptiveness at which he has arrived:

> Чего же я трушу? Ведь я, как грамматику,
> Бессонницу знаю. Стрясется – спасут.
> Рассудок? Но он — как луна для лунатика.
> Мы в дружбе, но я не его сосуд.
>
> Ведь ночи играть садятся в шахматы
> Со мной на лунном паркетном полу.
> Акацией пахнет, и окна распахнуты,
> И страсть, как свидетель, седеет в углу.
>
> И тополь – король. Я играю с бессонницей.
> И ферзь – соловей. Я тянусь к соловью.
> И ночь побеждает, фигуры сторонятся,
> Я белое утро в лицо узнаю.[59]

[What am I scared of? Why, like a grammar-book
I know insomnia. If it happens, they'll save me.
Common sense? But that's like a moon to the moonstruck.
We are friends, but I am not its vessel.

43

Why, the nights sit down to play chess
With me on the moonlit parquet floor.
There's a scent of acacia, and the windows are thrown open,
And passion like a witness grows grey in the corner.

And the poplar is the king. I play with insomnia.
And the queen is the nightingale. I reach out for the nightingale.
And night wins, the pieces are put aside,
I recognise by its face full morning.]

In the second stanza he appears to be more conscious of night sitting opposite him at the chessboard than of his own initiative in the game (and it is night that wins). His passion has become detached – a witness turning already grey in the corner. Between these statements Pasternak's imagination follows its customary process. As he said in 'Some Theses': 'poetry looks for the melody amidst the lexical noise [*shum slovarya*] and, having picked it out as one picks out a motif, then falls into improvisation upon that theme'.[60] On a small scale this is what happens in the third line of the second stanza. The accidental play of 'lexical noise' gave him the assonance of *pakhnet* ['smells'] and *raspakhnuty* ['thrown open'], and the 'melody' thereby revealed is a correspondence and a covert rhyming of the two statements. It seems that the intervention of acacia scent and the open windows have served to distance the poet's passion from him. When the first person 'I' returns in the final stanza, the self that has been reconstituted is there first as a participant ('I play with insomnia' – they are equals); then, in the second instance, he 'reaches out for' the nightingale, the queen in this chess game, but the ultimate action of the self in the poem is merely to confront the reality of morning. A perfect equilibrium has been set up between the mind that perceives and the totality that is perceived (*beloe utro* seems to have the value of *belyy den'*, 'broad daylight', and *belyy svet*, 'all the world'). In Pasternak's most characteristic poetry subjective and objective are perfectly balanced, and the 'voice' (to use a grammatical term) is between active and passive, like the Greek middle voice.

The earlier poems, especially, of *Above the Barriers* bear the marks of Futurism. Some have an urban scene like the fragment 'The Tenth Anniversary of Presnya' ['*Desyatiletie Presni*'] which refers to the Moscow workers' rising in December 1905[61] and shows the awareness of violent change in the offing that Mayakovsky had expressed in *A Cloud in Trousers*. Here Pasternak comes quite close to Mayakovsky with the image:

44

Тревога подула с грядущего,
Как с юга дует сирокко.[62]

[Alarm blew from the future
As from the south blows the sirocco.]

The opening stanza of 'The Urals for the First Time' ['*Ural vpervye*'] in its grotesque sensationalism might have been written by Mayakovsky:

Без родовспомогательницы, во мраке, без памяти,
На ночь натыкаясь руками, Урала
Твердыня орала и, падая замертво,
В мученьях ослепшая, утро рожала.[63]

[Without a midwife, in darkness, unconscious,
Striking against the night with her hands, the Urals'
Fastness yelled and falling in a dead faint,
Blinded by her pangs, gave birth to morning.]

(One suspects that the whole elaborate image grew out of the word-play *Urala orala/utro rozhala*.) And there are the deliberate crudities that the Futurists brought into their poetry to overthrow decorum and to legitimise the modern city as theme, without any transforming haze of romantic pathos. Thus in the second stanza of 'The Yard' ['*Dvor*'] 'the frozen boil of October is picked open' [*Myorzlyy naryv oktyabrya raskovyryan*][64] – in revision it became 'the boil of the roadways' [*mostovykh*][65] – and elsewhere 'earth's Adam apple shows black through the snow' [*Skvoz' sneg cherneetsya kadyk/Zemli*];[66] 'the bay like a tick has fastened on to the meadows' [*Zaliv kleshchom vpilsya v luga*];[67] 'the sky like a dead beast has not been cleared away from the roads' [... *paloe nebo s dorog ne podobrano*];[68] 'the gardens feel sick at the stillness of the versts' [*Sady toshnit ot vyorst zatish'ya*].[69] In 'A Bad Dream' ['*Durnoy son*'], a poem of 1914 which has images from the First World War – in revision it collects 'bandages in the yolk of xeroform' [*bintami v zheltke kseroforma*] and a hospital train snorting with its brakes [*Sopyat tormoza sanitarnogo poezda*][70] – reference is made to 'the black gums of fences' and 'the gums of gap-toothed thickets' [*skvoz' chornye dyosny/Zaborov, skvoz' dyosny shcherbatykh trushchob*].[71] All this imagery has its parallels in Mayakovsky's work and that of other Futurists.

Yet the most characteristic poems in this volume, those anticipating the Pasternak whose vision from *My Sister Life* onwards would not change, seem to be no more than tinged with Futurism. Certainly they are modern – in their free associations and colloquial tone, in their complicated syntax (which may owe something to the example

of prose writers like Andrey Bely), in their very large and sometimes
recondite vocabulary, in the unexpectedness of their rhyming. Yet
these attributes do not, even when all found together, necessarily
make a Futurist. Where Pasternak is most individual in *Above the
Barriers* he often appears most traditional – as when he brings
Tyutchev into the twentieth century. This he does in such poems as
'Three Variants' ['*Tri varianta*'] and 'July Storm' ['*Iyul'skaya
groza*']. Consider these lines from the second of 'Three Variants':

Гроза близка. У сада пахнет
Из усыхающего рта
Крапивой, кровлей, тленьем, страхом.
Встает в колонны рев скота.[72]

[The storm is near. The garden smells
From its mouth drying up
Of nettle, roof, decay, terror.
In columns rises the bellowing of cattle.]

The apprehension of crisis in nature, of imminent change could be
Tyutchev's; so could the brevity of line, the simple stanza form, and
directness of statement. But the combined impression of nettles, a
roof, decay and terror in the smell of the garden belongs to a more
complicated sensibility. Tyutchev is capable of evoking a moment
in which surprise transfigures the scene; but his poetic resources are
more limited than Pasternak's; he uses the idiom of romantic
Russian poetry as written before him by Pushkin and Lermontov,
and though he sometimes achieves a real freedom within these limits,
much of his verse falls into what had become a conventional
rhetoric. The novelty of his perceptions does not extend to the daring
effect in Pasternak's last line where the bellowing of the herd rises
up from the plain like a column of dust in a whirlwind. And the two
concluding stanzas of 'July Storm' surpass the dramatic intensity
even of Tyutchev by their novelistic attention to detail:

Гроза в воротах! на дворе!
Преображаясь и дурея,
Во тьме, в раскатах, в серебре,
Она бежит по галерее.

По лестнице. И на крыльцо.
Ступень, ступень, ступень. – Повязку!
У всех пяти зеркал лицо
Грозы, с себя сорвавшей маску.[73]

[The storm is at the gates! in the yard!
Transfigured and gone wild,
In gloom, in peals, in silver
It runs down the gallery.

Up the staircase. And on to the porch.
A step, step, step. – Bring a bandage!
In all five mirrors the face
Of the storm that has stripped off its mask.]

The detail of *five* mirrors not only multiplies the effect of the lightning flash but also makes this a unique moment in a particular house.

Pasternak's greatest achievement in *Above the Barriers* is to have brought off so many subtle notations, as of the star in the poem 'On the Steamer' ['*Na parokhode*'] which looks like the wick in the river's icon-lamp [*svetil'ney plavala/V lampade Kamskikh vod – zvezda*], or the fireflies that appear on the water at the height of a candlestick [*V reke, na vysote podsvechnika,/Kishmya-kisheli svetlyaki*].[74] The one indubitable triumph of the volume was the confessional poem 'Marburg', though it gained immensely from revision. One stanza came to Mayakovsky as an example in his essay 'How to Write Verse' ['*Kak delat' stikhi?*', 1926]:

В тот день всю тебя, от гребенок до ног,
Как трагик в провинции драму Шекспирову,
Носил я с собою и знал назубок,
Шатался по городу и репетировал.[75]

[That day all of you from the combs to the feet,
Like a tragedian in the provinces with a Shakespearian play,
I carried round with myself and knew by heart,
I strayed about the town and I rehearsed it.]

'Marburg' stands on the brink of *My Sister Life*, in which Pasternak finds his own voice outside the Futurist movement.

4
'My Sister Life': The Summer of 1917

I

The above is the full title of Pasternak's most celebrated book of poems. In the selected editions of his verse published in 1933 and in 1935 he placed *My Sister Life* at the beginning,[1] an order which the Michigan editors have retained. This seems right: the Pasternak we know starts with the book, and he never forgot that summer. As he said in *Doctor Zhivago* (which is about the brother of life) and in a note prepared for the abortive 1957 edition of his poems, the interval between the two revolutions of 1917 was a moment that transformed everything and opened up hearts and minds.[2] They are very romantic terms in which he speaks of 'roads, houses and stars' that 'held meetings and orated' along with human beings.[3] Yet there have been occasions – like the year 1789 in France, or 1968 in Czechoslovakia, or 1974 in Portugal – when, for a brief while, human energies are miraculously increased, hope seems credible, and a spirit of renewal appears to have swept over an entire nation. The outcome is too often darkness and cruelty; but Pasternak did not retreat from his conviction that the summer of 1917 had been a golden date for Russia. He saw the life of the ordinary man and the life of the artist in that hour as indistinguishable. The experience gave him absolute faith in the romantic vision. It is a faith that sustains and permeates the poetry of *My Sister Life*. The revolution for Pasternak (meaning February and its aftermath, not October) was more than anything else an escape from political necessity. The people of Russia were living that summer in a trance when there seemed a real possibility of throwing off those 'mind-forged manacles' which Blake had denounced.

It is not the accuracy of Pasternak's judgment that need concern us here. Poets can offer a different kind of history: they prove the potential, rescuing the past from itself. Nor did Pasternak alone make this judgment. 'There wasn't a man alive', Viktor Shklovsky has said with some hyperbole, 'who didn't experience periods of hope in the revolution.'⁴ Such hope is valuable, since without hope human life deteriorates. There would seem to be a profound craving in our nature for the romantic impulse that seeks renovation. *My Sister Life* records the joy of a few exceptional months when the horizons became limitless. Its poems do not try to interpret the revolution, as Blok did a little afterwards in *The Twelve* [*Dvenadtsat'*, 1918]. They stand obliquely towards it, and what they do is to record with the most delicate needle the atmospherics of the time. As Marina Tsvetaeva says, 'In the summer of 1917 he kept pace with [the Revolution]; he was listening attentively.'⁵

II

The volume is dedicated to Lermontov. As Pasternak explained many years later to his American translator: 'What was he [Lermontov] to me, you ask, in the summer of 1917? – The personification of creative adventure and discovery, the principle of everyday free poetical statement.'⁶

At first sight Lermontov may seem an unlikely poet to have inspired Pasternak. Blok had written in 1906, when attention to Lermontov was growing, and all were reading him 'fitfully, and feverishly, and tacitly, and in trembling': 'The notes of Lermontov found an echo in the most "nocturnal" spirit of Russian poetry – Tyutchev.'⁷ Lermontov's Demon had become even more familiar to the Russian public through the many illustrations to the poem of that name by Mikhail Vrubel. (They had appeared in an edition of 1891 to which Leonid Pasternak had contributed the greatest part of the drawings.)⁸ Marina Tsvetaeva saw this attraction of light to dark as natural, and compared Lermontov to two wings balanced in tension.⁹ But it is Mayakovsky rather than Pasternak who shares the pride, the concentrated will to self-definition, and to the engrossment of all other minds, that made Lermontov much closer to Byron than ever Pushkin was. While Lermontov's Demon stands as prologue to *My Sister Life* and promises to 'come back like an avalanche' [*lavinoy vernusya*],¹⁰ his shadow scarcely falls over the poems.¹¹ The avalanche sweeping through this volume is one of light, not darkness; when there are moments of pain and frustration, they meet with an acceptance that is almost joyful. The exhilaration of *My Sister Life* recalls the carefree excitement of Pushkin's earliest poems, before repression followed the Decembrist fiasco of 1825.

Pasternak chose Lermontov as mentor for a less obvious reason than romantic self-regard. He had already decided that the idea of 'biography as spectacle' which prevailed in his time must be left to those who had need of it and could not escape from its temptations.[12] Lermontov, however, anticipated for Pasternak a more hopeful development in modern poetry. The particular kind of realism that Pasternak had admired in Tolstoy, Verlaine and Chopin, whereby the biography of the artist becomes a history of the artist's own time, had its Russian origins, so he believed, with Lermontov: 'Pushkin erected the house of our spiritual life, the edifice of Russia's historical awareness. Lermontov was its first tenant.'[13] *My Sister Life* is autobiographical in recording the love affair of a particular summer; but, the summer being what it was, the poems contain much besides. The love affair, which can be traced through them and is annotated here and there with precise detail, inevitably colours all Pasternak's feeling about the summer of 1917.[14] But the much wider experience brought to him by those months is reflected upon the personal story, and what he tells could only have happened, with that special awareness on his part of a world in motion around him, during the revolutionary summer. The 'everyday free poetical statement' he achieved at that time was possible only because he saw and felt himself as belonging entirely to a people suddenly liberated and overwhelmed by new realities.

His poem celebrating above all others the participation of man and nature in one and the same renewal is 'Spring Rain' ['*Vesenniy dozhd'*'][15] of which more later. But most readers looking for Pasternak's full originality would turn to the lyric from which the whole series took its title, the one beginning 'My sister life is today in flood' [*Sestra moya zhizn' i segodnya v razlive*].[16] Here a spring rain overflows and transfigures the world, so that 'in the storm eyes and lawns are violet and the horizon smells of damp mignonette':

> Что в грозу лиловы глаза и газоны
> И пахнет сырой резедой горизонт.

This answers to the lover's own state of mind when his heart 'scatters train carriage-doors over the steppe' [*Vagonnymi dvertsami syplet v stepi*]. Indeed, it more than answers to his state. We are given not so much a correspondence as a merging. In the note Pasternak had intended for the 1957 edition he declares that the common mood during this summer 'effaced the boundary between man and nature';[17] he was enabled to read the one in terms of the other; and what had become for personal poetry a habit of his imagination now seemed to find warrant in the whole situation of Russia. The railway journey of this poem remains a private experience; the *fata morgana* he sees (or imagines) in the last stanza is the girl he loves – not to be compared with the 'new constellations' in a poem by Akhmatova of 1921 which 'shine in the depth of transparent July skies', for these, in a context of general ruin and deprivation, carry a clear political meaning.[18] If Pasternak in his poem was 'listening to the revolution', it would be with an ear, preternaturally keen perhaps, but intent mainly on the beating of his own heart.

Things are quite otherwise in 'Spring Rain' which takes over from the former poem its sense of joy and release, and then proceeds to express that sense as a general one, shared by roses, eyelashes and clouds, and finally given specific meaning by the events of the hour in Russia. No other passage in *My Sister Life* so unmistakably points to the Melyuzeevo chapter of *Doctor Zhivago*.[19] The moon is moulding people, dresses, 'the power of enraptured lips', into 'an epic in plaster, moulding a bust never moulded by anyone':

> Впервые луна эти цепи и трепет
> Платьев и власть восхищенных уст
> Гипсовою эпопеею лепит,
> Лепит никем не лепленный бюст.[20]

And the conclusion sets down what Pasternak never ceased to think about the summer of 1917:

> Это не ночь, не дождь и не хором
> Рвушееся: «Керенский, ура!»,
> Это слепящий выход на форум
> Из катакомб, безысходных вчера.

> Это не розы, не рты, не ропот
> Толп, это здесь, перед театром – прибой
> Заколебавшейся ночи Европы,
> Гордой на наших асфальтах собой.

> [This is not night, or rain, or in chorus
> Bursting out 'Kerensky, hurray!'
> This is a blinding emergence on to the forum
> From catacombs yesterday with no way out.

> These are not roses, not mouths, not the murmur
> Of a crowd, but here before the theatre is the surge
> Of Europe's tottering night
> Full of pride in herself on our pavements.]

The emergence is 'blinding' [*slepyaschchiy*], a word used again in 'A Storm, Instantaneous For Ever' ['*Groza, momental'naya navek*'][21] where the thunder takes 'a hundred blinding snapshots at night as record' –

> Сто слепящих фотографий
> Ночью снял на память гром.

That is to say, revolution dazzles like the storm.

III

Life is the poet's 'sister'. Thus the inner relationship of the cycle – his feelings for a particular woman which are linked inseparably with certain villages of the Saratov region – gives way to another relationship that transcends it. And this is expressed in the wholly characteristic phrase 'my sister, life'.[22] What does Pasternak imply when he claims kinship in this way? 'Life' is perhaps a word that comes too readily to Russian lips, although in Pasternak's use of the term it never suffers devaluation. What he meant by such intimacy with life can be understood from a passage in *Doctor Zhivago*:

Lara walked along the railway track down a path trodden by pilgrims and the devout, and she turned into the meadow way leading to the forest. Here she stood still and half-shutting her eyes drew in the confusedly fragrant air of the surrounding expanse. It was closer to her than father and mother, better than a beloved and wiser than a book. For one instant the meaning of existence was again disclosed to Lara. She was here, she realised, to make sense of the wild fascination of the world and to call everything by its name, and if that was not within her powers, then out of love for life to bring forth for herself successors who would do this in her place.[23]

Pasternak in *My Sister Life* seeks the appropriate form of kinship with the phenomenal world that will suggest not a dependence – as when Dante speaks of *la commune madre*[24] – nor wedded love, as when Blok calls Russia his wife (*O, Rus' moya! Zhena moya!*).[25] Rather he wants one that will allow the freest companionship, with a large element of play and discovery. The English reader will think of Wordsworth addressing his sister Dorothy, by whom, as the last long paragraph of *Tintern Abbey* proclaims, the sense of 'former pleasures' is kept alive for him – of joy leading to joy, and of 'wild ecstasies'. Pasternak had not Wordsworth's need to shake off a burden of past care or guilt at the time he began *My Sister Life*. It is a work that exists wholly in the present, or more accurately in the presence of a continuous emotion. Not until a dozen years later would he separate the past from the experience of the moment, when he wrote the poems later to be published as *Second Birth* [*Vtoroe rozhdenie*, 1932]. *My Sister Life* records a bond not unlike that of Saint Francis for whom sun and wind were his brothers, the moon and the stars his sisters.[26] Though Pasternak makes no mention of God the common Father, his relationship with life seems to fall under the broad designation of 'creatural'. His celebration of life is also a celebration of the creative principle which has made his mind what it is, and enabled it to discover its likeness in the world he observes.

Modern poetry has an inescapable concern with the creative process. Pasternak says in *Safe Conduct*: 'the best of the world's productions, while telling of the most diverse things, are in fact recounting their own birth'.[27] The first fully achieved work by him would seem to be doing this, and it declares that the imagination and the world represented by the imagination are united in the closest kinship. As Wordsworth could recognise his most spontaneous being in the younger Dorothy, so the imagination for Pasternak could see its own features and find the reflection of its own impulses in life the sister of art.

IV

Pasternak's method, in these poems and in those of the following year, was to rely on immediate inspiration. So he explained in 1957 to his Georgian friend Simon Chikovani: 'I wrote down only what by the stamp of its language, by the turn of its phrase came out as it were of its own accord, involuntary and indivisible, unexpected and not to be gainsaid.'[28] The work was little revised, as he remarks in the same letter and as the text shows.[29] It has not been established that all the poems were written in the summer of 1917, nor can we be sure that the order in which they are printed corresponds with the order of their appearance. However, the series has been so laid out that it presents a narrative, with each group of poems under its separate title forming a chapter in the romance; there are indications of a progressive change in season, from early spring to autumn; and, what seems more important, the experience is cumulative, with a deepening of awareness, and at the close a resolution of discord and pain, in the acceptance and new discoveries of the 'Afterword' ['*Posleslov'e*']. These final poems have won through to a calm restraint and, by comparison with what preceded them, a simplicity of form and expression which anticipates the style of *When the*

Weather Clears [*Kogda razgulyaetsya*, 1956–9]. One critic in 1922 saw here even an approximation to Pushkin, and admired their 'strenuous attention' [*pristal'noe vnimanie*] resulting in such clarity.[30] Everything goes to suggest that the order of the poems is faithful to the experience they record.

It was an experience primarily of the imagination – to use Pasternak's own phrase quoted above,[31] of 'creative adventure and discovery'. The love poems are submerged in this larger enterprise. They have not the sufficiency, the exclusive concern with a painful and chastening ordeal, that makes the poems Tyutchev wrote about Elena Deniseva between 1850 and 1865 a complete cycle and the incontrovertibly just statement of their disastrous love. Tyutchev may well have achieved a greater mastery than he ever had before in these poems – to that extent they too, like all excellent work, share the excitement of 'creative adventure and discovery'. But this excitement has been subdued to the necessities of his pain. Thus the experience recorded in the Deniseva poems does not resemble Pasternak's in the love poems of *My Sister Life*. Tyutchev explores primarily his condition, and incidentally the resources of his art; Pasternak, one might say, explores the resources of his art through his condition. To find in Pasternak's work some counterpart of the anguish in the Deniseva poems we need to consider, for instance, the lines he wrote early in 1959 under the title of 'The Nobel Prize' ['*Nobelevskaya premiya*'], beginning 'I am finished like a beast at the kill' [*Ya propal, kak zver' v zagone*]. Here too the situation is paramount, and the poet, somewhat unusually for Pasternak, has written six stanzas that do not have anything to say directly or otherwise about the nature of art, except that it has the power to make all the world weep over the beauty of his homeland:

Я весь мир заставил плакать
Над красой земли моей.[32]

As Dale Plank has shown in minute detail, the process of discovery can be followed in these poems by attending to the evolution of their sound patterns. Like Khlebnikov, Pasternak developed an extreme and almost morbid sensitivity to the formal relations between words, as shown in their derivation from a common root, or in the chance entanglements of alliteration and assonance. Khlebnikov actually sought to determine the laws of primal utterance which he supposed to be hidden in families of words with similar sound and cognate meaning (this being at times conjectural).[33] Pasternak can often in his earlier poetry be said to advance through assonance and rhyme; the logic of this device becomes irresistible, and a whole stanza can fill up with tendrils growing out of a few words. Plank has analysed most fully of all a poem that surpasses every other in the book for its dependence on this method – 'Our Storm' ['*Nasha groza*'].[34] He is able to trace sound 'formulas' which seemingly control a stanza, or more stanzas than one. Pasternak yields apparently to the arbitrary play of words, and yet (though Plank feels doubtful about the third and fourth quatrains of this poem) it is demonstrable that mere verbal association had not shaped the course, here or elsewhere in *My Sister Life*.

Yury Tynyanov's article of 1924 on the logic of Pasternak's procedure is well known,[35] and both his examples and his formulations cannot be improved upon. Tynyanov saw the 'mission' of Pasternak as one of bringing together words and things: with Khlebnikov and other Futurists the word as itself [*slovo kak takovoe*] had gained an autonomy which allowed it to live a hallucinatory half-life, remote from verifiable experience. 'When you take to pieces any verse of Swinburne', T. S. Eliot once wrote, 'you find always that the object was not there – only the word.'[36] This is not entirely true of Khlebnikov, but it holds for some of the lesser Futurists. Eliot went on to contrast with Swinburne's language that of two prose writers, James Joyce and the earlier Conrad, which was 'struggling to digest and express new objects, new groups of objects, new feelings, new aspects'. And that applies fully to Pasternak. The interlocking of words in his poetry is a means of connecting images, of perceiving new relations between things which are then seen as logically inseparable. What had first seemed fortuitous. Tynyanov maintains, has turned into a link of extraordinary strength which is put by the critic above 'the strongest logical connection'.[37] If logic is indefeasible, it makes no sense to claim a higher authority for poetic statement. Yet the authority of classical logic has been questioned by the so-called intuitionist or constructive logicians who reject the law of excluded middle and other principles of classical logic. A statement which is valid in the context of one logical system may thus not be valid in the context of another. But no change of the context can undo poetic statement. Its connections are unique; once a poem has achieved the necessary form, the work is final. The poem 'An Even More Stifling Dawn' ['*Eshcho bolee dushnyy rassvet*'][38] expresses unappeasable yearning [*toska*] in which the murmuring of a dove, the drizzle, a dusty market, clouds, a dispute in the bushes, the conversation of prisoners all build up inexorably into a sultry greyness. The impetus to do this may come from the association of words, yet the images they evoke are held together in a visual and auditory design, just as visually the fragments of reality are held together in a cubist picture by Picasso or Braque. But here the poem had the advantage of being able to add a sound track and present a fusion of sight and hearing:

> Рассвет был сер, как спор в кустах,
> Как говор арестантов.

[The dawn was grey, like a quarrel in the bushes,
Like the talk of prisoners.]

By the last movement of the poem, these images have proliferated into a new series:

> Я их просил –
> Не мучьте!
> Не спится.
> Но – моросило, и топчась
> Шли пыльным рынком тучи,
> Как рекруты, за хутор, поутру.
> Брели не час, не век,
> Как пленные австрийцы,
> Как тихий хрип,
> Как хрип:
> «Испить,
> Сестрица».

[I begged them –
Do not torment me.
I can't sleep.
But it drizzled, and stamping
The clouds went through the dusty market,
Like recruits, beyond the farmstead, in the morning.
They shuffled not an hour, nor an age,
Like captured Austrians,
Like a low wheeze,
Like a wheeze:
'Drink please,
Sister.']

From the recruits to the Austrian prisoners taken on the Galician front[39] the sequence returns to the misery of the first lines in this passage ('Do not torment me. I can't sleep') and we are standing by the bed of a parching man in a hospital ward, whose wheezing dominates the last four lines, and has already been foreshadowed in the stressed syllable of *avstríytsy*, the Austrians. But it is not only the wounded (possibly dying)[40] man who appeals to the nursing sister, it is also the poet calling for relief to his sister life.

V

Several poems in the volume are programmatic – 'Definition of Poetry' ['*Opredelenie poezii*'],[41] 'Definition of Creative Work' ['*Opredelenie tvorchestva*'],[42] and immediately following the lines 'In Memory of the Demon' ['*Pamyati Demona*'] the piece that might be expected to make the most explicit statement, 'About These Verses' ['*Pro eti stikhi*'].[43] In fact, *My Sister Life* nowhere contains a declaration of intent similar to Verlaine's 'Art Poétique' (which Pasternak afterwards translated).[44] Not one of the three poems just mentioned lays down a prescription like 'Rien de plus cher que la chanson grise / Ou l'Indécis au Précis se joint', or the famous 'Prends l'éloquence et tords-lui son cou!' Instead, Pasternak writes a poem 'About These Verses' which refuses to formulate any principles in abstract terms such as might clarify his procedure throughout the book. The two opening quatrains, like the rest of the poem, are in the future tense, announcing what will happen; but immediately it becomes clear that the poetry is going to take over, and will involve the poet in a world where all is changed, the snow-storm will obliterate ends and beginnings [*Kontsy, nachala zametyot*], and the sense of time will be lost:

> В кашне, ладонью заслонясь,
> Сквозь фортку крикну детворе:
> Какое, милые, у нас
> Тысячелетье на дворе?

> [In a muffler, screening myself with my hand,
> Through the ventilation pane I'll call to the children:
> 'Tell me, my dears, what
> Millennium have we outside?']

Inside, the poet is occupied with Byron, Poe and Lermontov – three figures who might seem more appropriate to Mayakovsky, but may have been chosen because they all stand in opposition to a commonplace bourgeois routine with its assurance of the calendar. For him a moment will come when he recognises 'the world has long been different' [*Uvizhu: svet davno ne tot*].

> Галчонком глянет Рождество,
> И разгулявшийся денек
> Откроет много из того,
> Что мне и милой невдомек.

> [Like a young jackdaw Christmas will glance
> And the day having cleared up[45]
> Will reveal many things
> That hadn't occurred to me and my beloved.]

Christmas eyes the world like a jackdaw on the look-out for bright trinkets. By a favourite device of Pasternak's – though to call something so fundamental to his art a device is failing to recognise its inevitability – here Christmas has become the agent of the poet's perception. A shift [*sdvig*] has occurred; and the play of his own mind is now not so much reflected as encountered in what he sees: the reality of his experience is such that feeling dislocates the object,[46] and seems less to impart movement to things than to be caught up in a movement it has not initiated. In this poem he will almost at once stand aside for the verses to perform:

> На тротуарах истолку
> С стеклом и солнцем пополам.
> Зимой открою потолку
> И дам читать сырым углам.
>
> Задекламирует чердак
> С поклоном рамам и зиме.
> К карнизам прянет чехарда
> Чудачеств, бедствий и замет.

> [On the pavements I shall pound out
> With glass and sun in equal measure.
> In winter I shall open to the ceilings
> And allow the damp corners to read.
>
> The garret will begin to declaim
> With a bow to the window-frames and winter.
> Up to the cornices will leapfrog away
> Eccentricities, disasters and signs.]

There is no object to the verbs in the first and third lines, unless one assumes that it is 'these verses'.[47] Once the poet has 'opened' them to the ceiling, the damp corners can read (*chitat'* also means 'recite', and leads on to *zadeklamiruet*, 'begins to declaim'). He has flung open the still unwritten book of his poems (not, as one translator assumes,[48] the window to let in air) and from that instant he loses his active role in this poem, except to ask about the millennium. In those first two stanzas the only reality is that of his verses: they are mixed up with winter pavements, the damp room. Then the snow-storm blurs all awareness of time and connection (ends, beginnings) until suddenly he awakes to a change in the weather: *Vnezapno vspomnyu: solntse est'* ['Suddenly I shall recall: the sun is there']. Somebody outside has beaten a path [*tropku k dveri protoril*] to the house in which he lived with his poetry. *Solntse est'*: 'the sun is' (Wordsworth's most expressive verb, and the Bible's): the reality of his verses has now been overtaken by that of the universe that exists, no matter in which millennium, and reveals the 'many things that hadn't occurred to me and my beloved'. Life doesn't replace poetry here but augments it, and leads it on to new discoveries.

VI

Pasternak's achievement, first realised in *My Sister Life*, has been to make discoveries through language which are then ratified by nature. He is always the highly conscious artist, however simple, even naive, his feelings may be; the master of an elaborate syntax, an almost reckless aptitude for rhyme, and a startlingly rich vocabulary. His poetry and his prose lend themselves to technical discussion of the kind exemplified by Roman Jakobson in a well known essay of 1935 which Davie and Livingstone have translated as 'Marginal Notes on the Prose of the Poet Pasternak'.[49] Whereas Mayakovsky depends for his effect chiefly on metaphor, this counts for less with Pasternak. There are, needless to say, some striking metaphors in *My Sister Life*, as in the lines

> Грех думать – ты не из весталок:
> Вошла со стулом,
> Как с полки, жизнь мою достала
> И пыль обдула.[50]

> [It's a shame to think you are no Vestal:
> You came with a chair,
> As from a shelf you took down my life
> And blew off the dust.]

And he has the power of inevitably right comparison always at hand:

> Как в неге прояснялась мысль!
> Безукоризненно. Как стон.
> Как пеной, в полночь, с трех сторон
> Внезапно озаренный мыс.[51]

> [How tenderness clarified thought.
> Irreproachably. Like a moan.
> As the foam at midnight on three sides
> Suddenly lights up a headland.]

But his main resource is not metaphor so much as metonymy: 'using an action instead of an actor, a man's condition, or one of his remarks or attributes, rather than the man himself, and the consequent separating off and objectifying of these abstractions'.[52] The abundant life in his poetry comes from the actualising of such things through language at play. The syntax builds up, new images are released as words escape from the entanglement of sounds approximating to them, and a continual work of creation goes on. It all originates in language: there the discoveries are made, but they arise from a wholly serious kind of word-play:

> Попытка душу разлучить
> С тобой, как жалоба смычка,
> Еще мучительно звучит
> В названьях Ржакса и Мучкап.[53]

[The endeavour to separate my heart
From you, like the complaint of a fiddle bow,
Still agonisingly sounds
In the names Rzhaksa and Muchkap.]

Rzhaksa and Muchkap are villages in the Saratov region, where the main episode of *My Sister Life* happens. As the stanza says, these names have become identified with the pain of separation which still can be heard in them. The dominant vowels in this quatrain are *a* and *u*, which occur in the two place-names. Rzhaksa takes up the sound of *zhaloba*, 'complaint' (and perhaps has echoes of derivatives from *plakat'*, 'to weep', like *plaksivyy*, 'piteous', and *plaksa*, 'cry-baby'); Muchkap rhymes with *smychka*, 'of the fiddle bow'. Thus the two names embody the comparison in the second line: the metaphor is made actual in their sound. Muchkap also concludes the series *razluchit'*, 'to separate', *muchitel'no*, 'agonisingly', and *zvuchit*, 'sounds'. In this way the two place-names emerge from the verbal texture of the stanza with a new meaning, and the discovery of 'About These Verses' has been repeated: *svet davno ne tot*, 'the world has long been different'. The means to discern this psychological truth was originally linguistic. So Pasternak finds and locks into position a whole range of insights, which have dislocated the world of normal perception by the intensity of feeling that accompanies them.

This is apparent in the poem called 'Looking-glass' ['*Zerkalo*'].[54] Here the opening stanza presents a customary paradox in this poetry: the looking-glass pursues the garden (just as at the end of the poem the garden storms up to the looking-glass, raising its fist). Perception here, as so often with Pasternak, reverses the normal order of things. What could be more passive than a looking-glass? It is the time-honoured image for quiet and steady contemplation, in which appearances are brought to the mind. But in this poem the mirror goes rushing out into the garden:

В трюмо испаряется чашка какао,
Качается тюль, и – прямой
Дорожкою в сад, в бурелом и хаос,
К качелям бежит трюмо.

[In the pier-glass evaporates a cup of cocoa,
The tulle sways and by a straight
Path into the garden, the wind-fallen boughs and the chaos
To the swing runs the pier-glass.]

At first the mirror is passive. It absorbs the steaming-away of the cocoa-cup, but this action within the mirror leads to another, also reflected there – the swaying of the tulle (a curtain, one assumes). The connection is made good through word-play: *chashka kakao*, 'a cup of cocoa', seems to generate *kachaetsya*, 'sways', which incidentally rhymes with the earlier verb. Once the tulle has been set in motion, the path to the garden is suddenly revealed – and inevitably it seems that *kacheli*, 'swing', must be the destination of the looking-glass. The movement of a swing controls the poem: in its final stanza the garden comes back to the looking-glass. Note that the first stanza begins and ends with the same word, *tryumo*, from the French *trumeau*, 'pier-glass' – its case oblique at the start, nominative at the close. All the action is contained in the looking-glass. It has borrowed speed from the poet's eye that catches sight of the garden, wind-fallen boughs, and swing once the tulle has moved; and this is a kind of metonymy, the man's attribute of vision (represented by the mirror) being endowed with an independent life.[55]

The word that gains the next most emphasis after *tryumo* through positioning and syntax is *khaos*, 'chaos', and this confusion is kept alive by the central image of the second stanza:

Там сосны враскачку воздух саднят
Смолой; там по маете
Очки по траве растерял палисадник,
Там книгу читает Тень.

[There the pines swaying abrade the air
With resin; there worried and worn
The front garden[56] has come to lose its spectacles in the grass,
There Shade is reading a book.]

The swaying motion has passed from the tulle via the swing to the pines. It would seem that the image of the front garden searching for its spectacles in the grass may be suggested by the groping movement to and fro of shadows from the pine trees, which contrasts with the fixed calm of Shade (motionless shadow), represented as one reading a book – that is, reading steadily page after page. The front garden cannot do this. Having lost its spectacles it cannot focus in the imperturbable manner of Shade.

Perhaps this brief analysis of two stanzas will show how Pasternak's verse retains its momentum and orders the perceptions in a firm and significant pattern. The poetry is remarkable for many things: for its wide variety of metres, for its inventiveness in rhyme (internal as well as external), for its boldness of association which requires a corresponding boldness of vocabulary, and above all for its syntax. Here pre-eminently Pasternak demonstrates his control. The poems are extremely resourceful in their syntax, which keeps close to common speech but can become highly elaborate, like that of Tolstoy when he is trying to pin down an elusive impression:

> Чтобы, комкая корку рукой, мандарина
> Холодящие дольки глотать, торопясь
> В опоясанный люстрой, позади, за гардиной,
> Зал, испариной вальса запахший опять.[57]

> [So as, crumpling peel in the hand, to swallow
> The cooling segments of a mandarin, hastening
> To – girdled with a chandelier, back there behind a curtain –
> The hall, beginning to smell once more with the perspiration of a waltz.]

This stanza pivots on the word *zal*, 'hall' which is placed between two adjectival clauses. The first of these describes the approach to the hall, the second the impression it gives when you arrive, a faint odour of sweat from the waltzing bodies. And the syntax is knit more closely by assonance – *pozadi, za gardinoy/Zal...zapakhshiy...* There is almost a stammering excitement to reach the hall, the actuality of which is confirmed by the assonance of the verbal adjective *zapakhshiy*.

Mandelstam described Pasternak's syntax as that of somebody who talks with conviction, and is carried away by the heat of his argument.[58] Pasternak's everyday habit of speech, according to many witnesses including Shklovsky,[59] was vehement, a confused gesticulating towards the point he was getting at, an inarticulate abundance. In the poetry his voice is no less animated, but it gains steadiness through his attention to syntax. Every shift of tone, every glancing thought, is held in a balance. The individual poem finds very quickly its syntactical mould, and trusts to it until the design has been perfectly rounded out.

VII

One of the earlier poems in this series, 'Balashov',[60] ends with a Mayakovskian image, followed by a statement that could only be Pasternak's:

> Юродствующий инвалид
> Пиле, гундося, подражал.

> [The disabled soldier turned idiot
> When he spoke through his nose, imitated a saw.]

Such a debased and sickening apparition belongs to the urban poetry of Baudelaire; it could well have appeared in Mayakovky's *A Cloud in Trousers*. The broken soldier is playing the part of a holy fool (*yurodstvuyushchiy*), and this would seem naturally to prompt a question about the purpose of things (the *yurodivyy* was traditionally 'God's fool' sent into the world as a prophet). So Pastnernak addresses the girl:

> Мой друг, ты спросишь, кто велит,
> Чтоб жглась юродивого речь?

> [My dear, you will ask, who ordains
> That the fool's speech should burn?]

No doubt he recalls here Pushkin's prophet who in the poem of that name ['*Prorok*'] is sent to 'burn the hearts of men with his word' [*glagolom zhech' serdtsa lyudey*].[61] This would appear to be confirmed by the two final lines which give the poet's answer:

> В природе лип, в природе плит,
> В природе лета было жечь.

> [It was in the nature of lime-trees, of flagstones,
> In the nature of summer to burn.]

The burning natural to this idiot cannot, like that of Pushkin's prophet, be called vocation. His speech burns in the general heat of summer, along with lime-trees and flagstones; every living and inanimate thing is affected by the dog-days. The last line may bear a further implication: not only the usual conflagrations of a hot summer came in 1917, but also the torch set deliberately to manor houses. The triple repetition of *priroda*, 'nature', is incantatory; it seems like a ritual movement of acquiescence. The three nouns qualifying nature – lime-trees, flagstones, summer – lead on to one another in sound – *lip, plit, leto*. Once again through the verbal pattern an inevitable connection has been established.

The first two lines of this final quatrain were used by Pasternak
as the epigraph (afterwards removed) to a later poem in the series,
'*Davay ronyat' slova. . .*' ['Come, let words fall'] which appears as
the second lyric of the 'Afterword' ['*Posleslovie*'].[62] Here the formula 'you will ask, who ordains' [*Ty sprosish'*, *kto velit*] is repeated
three times, and it gets a different answer. The metre has been
reduced by two syllables; its cadence seems quieter and more deliberate than that of the earlier poem. This passage forms the second
half of a lyric celebrating autumn with a resignation that grows out
of natural piety:

Ты спросишь, кто велит,
Чтоб август был велик,
Кому ничто не мелко,
Кто погружен в отделку

Кленового листа
И с дней Экклезиаста
Не покидал поста
За теской алебастра?

Ты спросишь, кто велит,
Чтоб губы астр и далий
Сентябрьские страдали?
Чтоб мелкий лист ракит
С седых кариатид
Слетал на сырость плит
Осенних госпиталей?

Ты спросишь, кто велит?
– Всесильный бог деталей,
Всесильный бог любви,
Ягайлов и Ядвиг.

Не знаю, решена ль
Загадка тьмы загробной,
Но жизнь, как тишина
Осенняя, – подробна.

[You will ask who ordains
That August should be large,
To whom nothing is slight,
Who is immersed in the finishing

Of a maple leaf
And from the time of Ecclesiastes
Has not abandoned his post
Shaping alabaster?

You will ask who ordains
That lips of asters and dahlias
In September should suffer?

'MY SISTER LIFE'

That the slight leaf of the willows
From grey caryatids
Should flutter on the dampness of flagstones
Of hospitals in autumn?

You will ask who ordains?
– The almighty god of details,
The almighty god of love,
Of the Yagaylos and Jadwigas. [63]

I do not know if they have solved
The riddle of darkness beyond the grave,
But life is like the stillness
Of autumn – detailed.]

Now that summer has gone and the romance is finished, when the flagstones have exchanged heat for dampness, and instead of the blazing lime their neighbour is the willow shedding its leaves, Pasternak has returned to his question. At the end of the poem 'Balashov' it comes directly after the disabled soldier has appeared. He is an emanation of the wearying heat; in accounting for him, the poem accounts for the experience of a July day in this small town on the steppe. 'It was in the nature of summer to burn.' The poem goes no further than this; it is folded back upon itself. But in the later poem from 'Afterword' the question virtually forms the whole argument. It is answered in a way that looks beyond the poem, to reveal the place of suffering and decay in the natural order – they were already familiar to Ecclesiastes – and, more centrally perhaps, to describe (not for the first time in this volume) a poetic. The problem of life after death is brushed aside in a phrase that refuses to be more than nonchalant. Pasternak does not concern himself here with metaphysical issues. The task he sets before poetry is to recognise particulars, and to harmonise them through the imagination. *My Sister Life* has room for an astonishing variety of detail. It brings together the most diverse conditions and categories:

Топтался дождик у дверей,
И пахло винной пробкой.

Так пахла пыль. Так пах бурьян.
И, если разобраться,
Так пахли прописи дворян
О равенстве и братстве.[64]

[The shower was stamping at the doors,
And there was a smell of wine corks.

So smelt the dust. So smelt the tall weeds.
And, to be precise,
So smelt the copy-book maxims of the gentry
About equality and fraternity.]

All the barriers are down in this volume. He explains what has happened in the poem called 'Afterword' ['*Posleslovie*']:

> Это солнце горело на каплях чернил,
> Как в кистях запыленной смородины.[65]

[It was that the sun burned in the ink drops
As in the clusters of the dusty blackcurrant.]

5

Poetry under the Soviets:
'Themes and Variations'

I

Pasternak's reputation as a poet became firmly established with the appearance of *My Sister Life* in 1922 and of its successor *Themes and Variations* [*Temy i variatsii*] in 1923. The former year is remarkable for other publications: Joyce's *Ulysses*, T. S. Eliot's *The Waste Land*, Rilke's *Duinese Elegies* and *Sonnets to Orpheus*, César Vallejo's *Trilce*, Mandelstam's *Tristia*. The list could be extended, and its effect is one of rebirth after the war – a resumption along the lines of discovery first plotted a decade before.

Themes and Variations was published by Helikon in Berlin, and there too in 1923 Grzhebin reissued the earlier volume which he had originally brought out in Moscow. At that time Berlin, with its vast influx of Russian refugees, and the coming and going of those who had taken Soviet citizenship, rivalled Moscow as a centre of Russian publishing. Pasternak had previously been known for his infrequent public readings in Moscow.[1] Like most writers during the years of War Communism that followed the October Revolution he had lacked opportunity to publish. One result of newsprint being in scant supply was that poetry tended to flourish more than prose: a generally compact and more memorable form, verse at the beginning dominated Soviet literature.[2]

Henceforth, these two volumes by Pasternak were to ensure that he could count on a public – fairly small perhaps but highly appreciative, and one that included among his admirers the best Russian poets of the time. Nadezhda Mandelstam's testimony can be supported: 'For many years Pasternak held undisputed sway over all other poets, and none of them was immune to his influence. Akhmatova used to say that only Tsvetayeva came through this trial with honor.'[3] Osip Mandelstam in 1922 had singled him out from all the Moscow futurists as combining 'invention and memory'.[4] In an

67

essay of 1923 he linked Pasternak's name with that of Khlebnikov for their achievement in freeing the Russian language so that it might realise in poetry its full native genius: 'After Khlebnikov and Pasternak Russian poetry again puts out to the open sea, and many of the customary passengers will have to say goodbye to its steamer.'[5] He compared Pasternak's poetry with a series of breathing exercises to regulate the true voice of expression; and described it as 'a brilliant *Nike* [statue of victory] transposed from the Acropolis to the Sparrow Hills' outside Moscow.[6] Marina Tsvetaeva, of whom Akhmatova further said that 'Pasternak enriched her and perhaps thanks to him she not only kept her true voice but even found it in the first place',[7] wrote in lavish praise of his poetry in the same year 1923.[8] Her addiction was shared by Mayakovsky, who used very often to repeat Pasternak's verses, and particularly, with such feeling that he might have written them himself, the first two stanzas of the 'Afterword' to *My Sister Life*.[9]

Lilya Brik, who records this last detail, has described how Mayakovsky in those years was 'saturated with Pasternak', talking of him incessantly. Pasternak had been aware from their first meeting in 1914 of Mayakovsky as an exemplar whom it was hard not to accept totally. He explains in *Safe Conduct*: 'When they asked me to tell something of myself I would speak about Mayakovsky... I worshipped him. I embodied in him my own spiritual horizon.'[10] But after the appearance of *My Sister Life* it became clear to Pasternak that their basic approaches to poetry were altogether different. Mayakovsky, engrossed in himself and in the revolution which he had unwisely made his own, tried for as long as possible to ignore the gulf between them. Every writer in those days had to ask himself where he stood in relation to the new order which was often as arbitrary and jealous in its dealings with the bourgeois artist as the God of the Puritans had been with the individual sinner. Mayakovsky knew the initial joys of the converted: his way had been marked out for him as a Soviet poet. Pasternak never became a Soviet poet in the true sense: he was more accurately a poet living under the Soviets, whose regime he could accept not as a mere *fait accompli* but as the fulfilment for that hour of Russia's destiny. But to recognise the Soviet order was not to abandon the sovereignty of art. Mayakovsky must have hoped that 'the social demand' would positively enhance his powers as a poet. He needed the revolution to save him from the anarchy of his temperament, counting on Bolshevik discipline to regulate his artistic conscience. But evidently he looked with some envy on Pasternak's freedom. Once after hearing Pasternak read, Mayakovsky on his way home suddenly came out with the comment, made in an unusually wistful and subdued tone: 'Lucky Pasternak! See what lyric poetry he writes. While probably I never shall again.'[11]

For a little while Pasternak contributed to Mayakovsky's journal *Lef* – three poems in all. In one of these he allows that public events will change him:

> За морем этих непогод
> Предвижу, как меня, разбитого,
> Ненаступивший этот год
> Возьмется сызнова воспитывать.[12]

> [Beyond the ocean of these storm spells
> I foresee how, shattered as I am,
> The year still to come
> Will take in hand my education anew.]

The year still to come was 1919. He refers, one would think, not to party directives but to the ordeals of common life as the source from which that teaching will flow. At times during the next decade, the 1920s, Pasternak wanted very definitely to write such poetry as would honour the revolution. He had no wish to stand aside from the Soviet people. But for him they were still the Russian people who found themselves in the Soviet epoch rather than a new species whose highest motivation must be political.

II·

Themes and Variations has in many ways a resemblance to *My Sister Life*. Although it lacks a narrative frame, it adopts a similar division into cycles, of which there are six. These, however, serve principally to group poems which were written at different times. The volume does not bear the impression of a single continuing experience in the manner of *My Sister Life*, except in its fourth section 'The Break' ['*Razryv*']. This sequence, dated 1918, surpasses in passionate feeling anything the earlier book has to show. Pasternak wrote many of the poems collected in *Themes and Variations* during 1917 and 1918 when inspiration was running high and he 'wanted to bring his testimony as near as possible to the extemporised'.[13] It carries forward the momentum of *My Sister Life*. As he explained in the letter to a Georgian poet from which I have just quoted, the principle behind both volumes of trusting to the immediate, natural

69

and spontaneous phrase prevailed with him only during those two years. Yet there are some distinctions to draw. Certain emphases become more conspicuous in the second volume. Thus, its final section *Neskuchnyy sad* (the name of a Moscow park meaning 'the garden that isn't dull') consists for the greater part of impressionistic poems about the seasons in a country setting; and perception of this kind, original, momentary and intense, would continue throughout his work, being further refined and set down with an effect of unforced simplicity in his poems of the last decade. After *Themes and Variations* a new phase of imaginative effort begins when Pasternak attempts to write on an epic pattern. *Themes and Variations* twice appeared (in 1929 and in 1930) with *My Sister Life* as a single volume. What I said about the previous volume needs to be amplified a little in view of certain innovations, or more successful restatements of earlier discoveries, in this sequel to his first wholly authentic work.

Here perhaps even more than in *My Sister Life* there is apparent on every page a virtuosity not unlike that of the extemporising pianist elated by his audience. This virtuosity plays with syntax and form, with conceits caught in mid-air, with splendidly improvised rhymes, and with many changes of tone, from the colloquial or proverbial to an urgent complexity in which language, while not divorced from the speaking voice, enters into unprecedented relations. An example of this personal usage is the well known definition of poetry in the lyric by that name ['*Poeziya*']:

> Ты не осанка сладкогласца,
> Ты – лето с местом в третьем классе,
> Ты – пригород, а не припев.[14]

> [You are not the posture of the euphonist,
> You are summer with a seat travelling third,
> The edge of town, not a refrain.]

Pasternak may, as one contemporary critic said, have passed through the Futurism with which he began;[15] but he remained Futurist enough to prize novelty. In this Pasternak did not stand alone: the desire to shock and surprise by novelty was prominent in much poetry of that time, and T. S. Eliot and García Lorca escaped from it no more than he did. But they reveal an alert sophistication quite alien to him. Pasternak's elaborate mastery of technique went with a *naïveté* of feeling. Much of his subtlety rests at the level of very fine sensuous notation. He had the mind to discriminate between impressions, and to organise them beautifully. But sophisticated (in the tradition of Laforgue for Eliot, of Góngora for Lorca) he never became. And indeed that quality of mannered self-possession does not belong to any of the most considerable Russian writers.

Yet the poetry is self-conscious at least in technique, for all its freshness and innocence. The series entitled 'A Theme with Variations' ['*Tema s variatsiyami*'] might at a first reading suggest Picasso's game of parody and subversion with, for instance, a canvas by Velázquez. The whole sequence revolves round certain poems by Pushkin – the start of *The Bronze Horseman* [*Mednyy vsadnik*], 'The Prophet' ['*Prorok*'] and *The Gipsies* [*Tsygany*] – and it evokes the well known painting of him on a rocky coast by Ayvazovsky and Repin. One passage ('Imitation') ['*Podrazhatel'naya*'][16] not only adopts the movement of Pushkin's verse in *The Bronze Horseman*, but begins with the two opening lines of its Prologue. Instead of Peter by the Neva contemplating his future city, Pushkin stands by the sea contemplating the novel he will write. The conclusion of this passage, as Dale Plank has noted,[17] acquires a density that is Pasternak's own, when the hero seems to merge with the landscape. There are ambiguities that Plank points out, and the texture of the verse thickens. Then, in the following section, where the metre has changed, the manner becomes wholly Pasternak's:

> Мчались звезды. В море мылись мысы.
> Слепла соль. И слезы высыхали.
> Были темны спальни. Мчались мысли,
> И прислушивался сфинкс к Сахаре.[18]

[The stars were rushing. In the sea washed the headlands.
Salt was blinded. And tears dried up.
Dark were the bedrooms. Thoughts were rushing,
And the sphinx listened to the Sahara.]

All this series of 1918 is an engaging improvisation, but hardly more. Once the musical reference of its title has been taken, the object could no longer be supposed that of Picasso (wilful appropriation, mockery, almost a visual punning). This set of poems following the line of an improviser who makes up variations on a theme, does not, of course, remain merely an exercise. It explores, as so many of Pasternak's writings do, the process of creation. His poetry, like much modern poetry, watches itself in motion, whereas Pushkin, even when in 'Autumn' ['*Osen'*'][19] he describes the act of composition, cannot be said to show Pasternak's awareness of the description itself. Perhaps it is only in the modern age that a poet could say 'the best of the world's productions. . . are in fact recounting their own birth'.[20]

Are the other series in this book virtually doing the same thing? The title might indicate that Pasternak was engrossed with technical problems and the delight of solving them. In the final section one poem is called 'In the Forest' ['*V lesu*'], another group of poems 'Winter Morning' [*Zimnee utro*'], a third group 'Spring' ['*Vesna*'] – all of them subjects that are familiar enough from Tyutchev and Fet. The poems under these headings, or at least some of them, look very much like variations on Tyutchev or Fet by a poet who has formed his sensibility in the era of modernism. Those who value only the older poetry are going to complain that Pasternak has allowed his ingenuity to run away with him, so that the details get out of hand, and a restless ambition to innovate and to startle changes the mode of Tyutchev and Fet into a glittering mass of conceits. That is to put the case in its most hostile form, as Wladimir Weidlé did in an essay of 1928.[21] He did not deny the talent of Pasternak, for him a genuine poet who had been spoiled by the age. When Weidlé came, thirty years later, to reconsider his views, in the light of all Pasternak had done since, he still regretted the one-sidedness that modernism had fostered in the poet's development, and which it took so many years to overcome.[22] Here Weidlé, of course, gains support from the disenchanted comments made subsequently by Pasternak on his earlier work.

Themes and Variations is a more obvious target for such criticism than *My Sister Life*. It lacks the loose unity of the latter, and this causes the individual poems to stand out more on their own, sometimes rather showily. In the opening section 'Five Tales' ['*Pyat' povestey*'] each separate lyric is a virtuoso piece. The second of these, 'A Meeting' ['*Vstrecha*'], may be taken as representative. Its action is very slight. The poet makes his way home from a gathering just before daylight in March, while the wind tears the puddles like sacking [*vretishche*]; we overhear the goodbye:

> В шестом часу, куском ландшафта
> С внезапно подсыревшей лестницы,
> Как рухнет в воду, да как треснется
> Усталое: «Итак, до завтра !»[23]

> [At six o'clock, like a bit of landscape
> From the staircase suddenly grown damp
> How it crashes into the water and how it thumps,
> A weary 'Well then, till tomorrow!']

As the poet walks in the company of the March night, he is seen as belonging to the landscape: all this poem has been conceived in terms of a picture:

И мартовская ночь и автор
Шли рядом, и обоих спорящих
Холодная рука ландшафта
Вела домой, вела со сборища.

[And the March night and the author
Went side by side, and both of them quarrelling
The cold hand of the landscape
Led home, led from the gathering.]

So they are met by the new day which is propelled towards them:

И мартовская ночь и автор
Шли шибко, вглядываясь изредка
В мелькавшего как бы взаправду
И вдруг скрывавшегося призрака.

То был рассвет. И амфитеатром,
Явившимся на зов предвестницы,
Неслось к обоим это завтра,
Произнесенное на лестнице.

[And the March night and the author
Went fast, glancing now and then
At a phantom that glimmered as if real
And suddenly hid itself.

That was the dawn. And like an amphitheatre
That had appeared at the harbinger's call,
There was borne towards both that tomorrow
Uttered upon the staircase.]

Dale Plank has commented on the ingenuity of the ending to this poem, when trees and buildings are displaced as in a three-tiered hexameter (the line being echeloned, with its second and third clauses dropped in a descending sprawl):[24]

Оно с багетом шло, как рамошник.
Деревья, здания и храмы
Нездешними казались, тамошними,
В провале недоступной рамы.

Они трехъярусным гекзаметром
Смещались вправо по квадрату.
Смещенных выносили замертво,
Никто не замечал утраты.

[It came with a baguette, like a picture-framer.
Trees, buildings and fanes
Seemed not to belong here, but there
In the gap of the inaccessible frame.

73

Like a three-tiered hexameter
They were shifted to the right along a quadrat.
Shifted they were carried out for dead,
Nobody remarked the loss.]

Plank takes the morning with its baguette or moulding-frame to be a stage-hand; and he translates the word *proval* in the last line of the penultimate stanza as 'pit' – the part of a theatre behind the stalls. For him the poet has now stepped on to the stage. However, despite the appearance of an amphitheatre, this poem is placed rather in a pictorial frame, as Plank also observes. The 'cold hand of the landscape' seems to conduct it all the way through.

'Meeting' is a difficult poem, with the features of a cubist painting, and its final dislocation [*smeshchenie*] relates to the cubist manner. Pasternak's highly-wrought idiom needs very close attention:

> Автоматического блока
> Терзанья дальше начинались,
> Где в предвкушеньи водостоков
> Восток шаманил машинально.

[The automatic pulley's
Torments further began,
Where foretasting the gutters
Dawn played the *shaman* mechanically.]

We can see that *mashinal'no* grew out of *shamanil*, and *vostok* from *vodostokov*. But the adverb *mashinal'no* has to be explained by the presence of an automatic pulley in the previous couplet. This first image – of machinery to be put in motion with the day – cannot be disentangled from that of the dawn performing its rites.

III

In poetry like this, as in the variations on Pushkin, art is in danger of becoming over-obtrusive. English readers who know metaphysical verse of the seventeenth century will understand why Mirsky, writing in the 1920s when Donne was again widely read, found it 'very tempting' to compare him with Pasternak. Each, according to Mirsky, was a poet's poet; each combined passion with ingenuity, and broke up the smooth diction of an earlier school.[25] For the Pasternak of 'A Meeting' Crashaw might give the juster parallel. Here the conceits may seem forced in the manner of Crashaw's; and yet, as we have seen, they owe to a skilful organisation of syntax and sound their convincingness, their inevitability. Another poem, 'The Break', does indeed suggest Donne, and Donne at his finest, when he is struggling to clarify and to master a complex emotion. It is a sequence of nine lyrics in different metres that moves through the conflicting passions caused by a woman's deceit. There are tones in it not far from 'The Apparition', and again others that match the tenderness of 'A Valediction: forbidding mourning'. In the second lyric pain and indignation take on a depth and vibrancy that are new to Pasternak:

> О стыд, ты в тягость мне! О совесть, в этом раннем
> Разрыве столько грез, настойчивых еще!
> Когда бы, человек, – я был пустым собраньем
> Висков и губ и глаз, ладоней, плеч и щек!
> Тогда б по свисту строф, по крику их, по знаку,
> По крепости тоски, по юности ее
> Я б уступил им всем, я б их повел в атаку,
> Я б штурмовал тебя, позорище мое![26]

> [O shame, you are a burden to me. O conscience in this early
> Break how many dreams are importunate still!
> Had I been a man – I was a void collection
> Of temples and lips and eyes, palms, shoulders, and cheeks!
> Then by the hiss of my stanzas, their cry, their sign,
> By the strong hold of my anguish, by its youth
> I would yield to them all, lead them into attack,
> And take you by storm, my humiliation.]

Mayakovsky may have recalled this image in his last considerable poem *At the Top of My Voice* [*Vo ves' golos*, 1930] in which he calls on his verses to die like the nameless ordinary soldiers storming a position:

> умри, мой стих,
>   умри, как рядовой,
>   как безымянные
>   на штурмах мерли наши![27]

Changes of inflexion and speed in Pasternak's sequence are beautifully calculated:

> Пощадят ли площади меня?
> Ах, когда б вы знали, как тоскуется,
> Когда вас раз сто в теченье дня
> На ходу на сходствах ловит улица!»[28]

> ['Will there be pity for me in the city squares?
> Oh, if only you knew my anguish
> When some hundred times in the course of a day
> The street catches on the move your likeness!']

No mood is held for long. The note here between regard and insecure resignation turns rapidly in the next lyric to one of frenzied appeal to have his grief smothered. From the hurrying excitement of a passage that describes Actaeon in pursuit of Atalanta, the voice changes to an elaborate slow irony:

> Разочаровалась? Ты думала – в мире нам
> Расстаться за реквиемом лебединым?[29]
>
> [You are disillusioned? You thought in peace
> We should part over a swan requiem?]

The poem's last quatrain (often quoted like the first lines of the series, and the second excerpt above, by Mayakovsky[30]) places the personal disaster in a context of public confusion. The note is very restrained, and the final simile has a Roman ring: these are the times of Tacitus.

> Я не держу. Иди, благотвори.
> Ступай к другим. Уже написан Вертер,
> А в наши дни и воздух пахнет смертью:
> Открыть окно, что жилы отворить.[31]
>
> [I don't hold you. Go, do good works.
> Be off to others. *Werther* has already been written,
> And in our days the very air smells of death:
> To open the window is to open your veins.]

It is natural to set 'A Break' over against 'Marburg', the poem of an earlier separation. A line such as *Poshchadyat li ploshchadi menya?* ['Will there be pity for me in the city squares?'] can be compared with this from 'Marburg':

> Плитняк раскалялся, и улицы лоб
> Был смугл, и на небо глядел исподлобья
> Булыжник. . .[32]
>
> [The flagstone glowed, and the street's forehead
> Was swarthy, and at the sky glowered up
> Cobblestones. . .]

The tone of 'Marburg', however, is ecstatic: the poem flowers into fantasies more vivid than the grief it purports to express. In 'The Break' an irrepressible feeling shapes every line. Not until *Second Birth* in 1931–2, and especially the love lyrics of its third section, does Pasternak write so evidently from the heart. The other poems of *Themes and Variations* are endlessly inventive, and they certainly cannot be called hollow. Yet their success is mainly a matter of technical triumph. They achieve a fusion of energy and control which only in 'The Break' are used to articulate and make bearable a moment of intense passion.

More usual with Pasternak are those moments in which dislocation results not from emotional shock, the sudden reversal of
feelings, but rather from what he has called in the *Essay in Autobiography* a 'passion of creative contemplation' [*strast' tvorches-
kogo sozertsaniya*]. There he applied the words to Tolstoy, who saw
everything 'in its original freshness, newly, and as it were for the
first time'.[33] Tolstoy stripped away the conventional associations: he
looked at the world with a deliberate *naïveté*, a dogmatic innocence.
The *naïveté* in Pasternak is not something assumed: his self-consciousness is different from Tolstoy's, an artistic rather than a
didactic need. But in the later as in the early poetry, he does
resemble Tolstoy, whenever a whole scene is illuminated by 'the
passion of creative contemplation'. The most striking example of
this can be found in a short and very well known poem of 1918,
which appears as the first one in a sequence entitled 'Spring'
['*Vesna*']:

> Весна, я с улицы, где тополь удивлен,
> Где даль пугается, где дом упасть боится,
> Где воздух синь, как узелок с бельем
> У выписавшегося из больницы.
>
> Где вечер пуст, как прерванный рассказ,
> Оставленный звездой без продолженья
> К недоуменью тысяч шумных глаз,
> Бездонных и лишенных выраженья.[34]

[Spring, I've come from the street, where the poplar is amazed.
Where the distance is scared, where the house fears to fall.
Where the air is dark blue, like the bundle of linen
Of one discharged from hospital.

Where evening is empty, like a broken-off story,
Left by a star without continuation
To the perplexity of a thousand loud eyes,
Fathomless and devoid of expression.]

Tolstoy will interpret a scene in terms of a man's feeling: Prince
Andrey sees the pledge of his own restoration in the old oak tree
which has put forth leaves,[35] Levin on his way to Kitty's house as
her affianced lover is met by new and astonishing sights on every
hand.[36] In Pasternak's poem the speaker, at the moment he enters
from the street, vanishes.[37] The action takes place in the street where
the poplar is amazed, and four times more the conjunction 'where'
recurs. There, in the scene that has suddenly closed for him on
leaving the street, his excited apprehensions live on, transferred to
their objects. The novelty of vision here has not been contrived by

syntax, although syntax, with the gradually lengthening adverbial clauses, has realised the vision in its singularity. The poem catches the sense of a spring evening, the emptiness in the air, the feeling of convalescence after a long winter, the unfulfilled hopes and inexpressible excitement. It builds up with a gathering momentum. The opening has the directness of Blok's famous lyric *Noch', ulitsa, fonar', apteka. . .*[38] [*Night, the street, a lamp, the chemist's*]. In both poems the first word states the essence of the scene (it is spring or night); then the local particulars emerge (the street, houses, the quality of the lighting – in Blok's poem, 'meaningless and dull light'[39] from a street lamp, in Pasternak's, the dark blue of the sky, the single star at the approach of evening). But whereas Blok's poem, also in two quatrains and eight lines, is locked into a circle of despair, ending with the same everlasting scene –

Ночь, ледяная рябь канала,
Аптека, улица, фонарь.

[Night, icy ripple of the canal,
The chemist's, the street, the lamp]

– Pasternak's with its expanding syntax follows an expanding movement that proceeds even when the story is broken off. There are two conceits in the poem (apart from that of the astonishment and fear that assail poplar, view and house): first, the comparison with a discharged patient from a hospital, the blue of whose bundle is the same colour as the evening sky; the second, the comparison of this moment with a story that is interrupted (and as Plank has suggested, the star that 'leaves it without continuation' may also be an asterisk).[40] The first image of the discharged patient reflects back on the poplar's amazement (trembling of its leaves?), and the fear of the distance and the house that feels near toppling: they too share the surprise at recovery and the apprehensions of the invalid. In the second image Pasternak, as so often, merges nature and art: an experience for him exists through its telling. (Thus, in the last stanza of 'The Break', he protests '*Werther* has already been written':[41] the pains of today are different and demand another form for them to be realised.) The 'thousand loud eyes' are perhaps the stars that come out in what should have been the continuation of the story, when darkness falls. They seem to bear some relation to Lermontov's figure – itself derived from Goethe's 'Willkommen und Abschied' – in *Mtsyry*:

THEMES AND VARIATIONS'

И миллионом черных глаз
Смотрела ночи темнота
Сквозь ветви каждого куста. . .[42]

[And with a million dark eyes
The obscurity of night looked
Through the twigs of every bush.]

The eyes are at once 'loud' and 'devoid of expression' — that is to say, not expressionless because they have nothing to declare but the opposite, *deprived* [*lishonnykh*] of expression. They are also described as *bezdonnykh*, 'fathomless' — the ordinary romantic term for the eyes of a mistress deep in significance.[43] (Pasternak uses the phrase *zharkiy, bezdonnyy belok* ['hot, fathomless white of eye'] for Pushkin's Zemphira in *The Gipsies*,[44] though the adjectives would be more appropriate to the pupil.) There is a fathomless depth of meaning in the spring nightfall which cannot be put into words because the poet has left the scene.

IV

Pasternak wrote in *Safe Conduct* that the effect of art is to give all things an equal status in the eye of the impassioned artist.

Focused upon a reality that is dislocated by feeling, art is the record of that dislocation. . . Particulars gain in vividness, while they lose their independent meaning. Each may be replaced by another. Any one is valuable. Any one you may choose serves as evidence of that condition in which reality is held after being shifted around.[45]

Poetry so conceived will move easily from the palpable to the notional:

ясен, как мрамор,
Воздух рощ и, как зов, беспризорен.[46]

[clear as marble
The air in the woods and like a call forlorn.]

(*Besprizoren*, here rendered 'forlorn', means 'neglected' and was the word applied to the thousands of homeless and fatherless children in the civil war. The poem dates from 1917; six years later, on its publication in 1923, this overtone would have been unavoidable.) Nothing in Pasternak's view need be excluded from poetry; and everything it draws upon may be read in terms of something quite different: 'Art is realistic as an activity, and symbolic as a fact. It is realistic in that it did not invent a metaphor but found it in nature and piously reproduced it.'[47] So in 'Poetry' ['*Poeziya*'], a statement about his art written in 1923, Pasternak offers four metaphors that he has found in nature to express what poetry is:

> Поэзия, я буду клясться
> Тобой, и кончу, прохрипев:
> Ты не осанка сладкогласца,
> Ты – лето с местом в третьем классе,
> Ты – пригород, а не припев.
>
> Ты – душная, как май, Ямская,
> Шевардина ночной редут,
> Где тучи стоны испускают
> И врозь по роспуске идут.[48]

> [Poetry, I shall swear
> By you and end up wheezing out:
> You are not the posture of the euphonist,
> You are summer with a seat travelling third,
> The edge of town, not a refrain.
>
> You are Yamskaya Street,[49] stifling sweet like May,
> The Shevardino redoubt[50] by night,
> Where the clouds utter moans
> And go their ways like drifting lumber.][51]

He disclaims a mellifluous poetry that carries itself with a conscious dignity and grace,[52] and here Pasternak is still the Futurist. Instead, poetry becomes a matter of overwhelming sensation, close to humanity: in a hot third-class railway carriage during summer, in a city suburb, or among the scents of a street crowded with prostitutes, or at night on the field of Borodino among the wounded and dying.

Characteristically at the head of these four incarnations there is an image from the railway. Journeys by train occur everywhere in Pasternak's art. The title poem of *My Sister Life* ends with a scattering of carriage doors over the steppe;[53] the volume has many references to branch lines and stations in the Saratov region; another poem describes the rail journey back to Moscow. Every one of his first four stories in prose features the railway; a volume of poetry published in 1943 was called *On Early Trains* [*Na rannikh poezdakh*]; and the first part of *Doctor Zhivago* concludes with a memorable rail journey from Moscow to the Urals, while from the very start of the novel trains have been present, their whistles sounding in Yura's ears after his mother's funeral, and his father committing suicide on the 'five o'clock express'. And Pasternak has a love of wayside halts, and all the paraphernalia of railways; he is a master of the technical terms, so that one recalls Kipling in ·*007*. But Pasternak's interest takes another form than Kipling's: it is not as a way of life, another manifestation of human skill, that the railway fascinates him, but rather as a means to that 'dislocation' in which art consists. Roman Jakobson has suggested that the railway journey appeals to him as bringing a rapid change of place to the passive observer.[54] Thus the girl Zhenya, in *The Childhood of Luvers*, looks out of the train window while 'the Urals goes on shaping and reshapes itself';[55] and thus in *Safe Conduct* the train (at the beginning) circles round and the wayside halt is 'turned over slowly like a page that has been read', before disappearing from view.[56] The train becomes emblematic of his poetry, in which the writer himself is often an excited and seemingly helpless observer. At the same time, with its chance meetings of strangers, 'a seat travelling third' allows a small-scale experience of city life, the main inspiration of Pasternak's poetry.[57] In the carriage as in the street all is momentarily brought together, like Zhenya's mother and the fat man with asthma.[58]

His strange formula in the next image, 'the edge of town, not a refrain' [*prigorod, a ne pripev*] is repeated in almost the same words two stanzas on: *Predmest'e, a ne perepev* ['A suburb, not a repetition']. The second term on each occasion (*pripev, perepev*) refers back to the mellifluous poetry of the third line, and the variation *perepev* makes it clear that such poetry repeats itself (like much work of the Symbolists in their decline). *Prigorod, predmest'e* both mean 'suburb'; but I have translated the first 'edge of town' since Pasternak's Moscow was not encircled by Wokings and Wembleys. The borderland of the city attracted him because, as he wrote in *Spektorsky*, it is the place

> Где кругозор свободнее гораздо,
> И, городской рубеж перебежав,
> Гуляет рощ зеленая зараза.[59]

> [Where the horizon is far freer,
> And running across the border of the town
> Freely roams the woods' green contagion.]

(This is the feeling of the city in the *Zhivago* poems.) The words *prigorod* and *predmest'e* (that which is beside or before the town or place) imply a nearness of relations such as he figures in a poem of 1931: '*Tesney, chem serdtse i predserd'e*'[60] ['Closer than heart and auricle']. Poetry is that which surrounds the city, and mediates between it and the countryside.

81

About the 'diverse community' [*pyostroe obshchestvo*] in Yam-skaya Street, near which Pasternak was born, he speaks in *Safe Conduct*. What he met there filled him with 'a pity for women frightening him out of his life'[61] and Strelnikov denounces the conditions of the exploited in that quarter during his last talk with Zhivago.[62] The note of pity becomes clear in the final image, recalling the night after the slaughter of Borodino, and with its evocation of *War and Peace* pointing the road for poetry to its fulfilment in epic.

This was the road that lay ahead of Soviet poetry in the 1920s, when there was a general turning towards narrative and an 'epic' breadth of conception. Nadezhda Mandelstam has written slightingly of this 'gigantomania', when the novel and the play – and outside literature the epic film – appeared the necessary forms in which to celebrate Soviet life.[63] Pasternak could not remain indifferent to this call, which Mayakovsky had rushed to answer. At least one poem written by Pasternak in this period, 'Sailor in Moscow' ['*Matros v Moskve*', 1919][64] looks in this direction, and was eventually published with half a dozen other poems mostly dating from the earlier 1920s, under the heading 'Epic motifs'. *The High Malady* [*Vysokaya bolezn'*, 1924] which first appeared in *Lef* is preoccupied with an assault on the 'fortress' of epic; *Spektorsky*, a long narrative in verse which he had difficulty in shaping – it took six years to complete – began that same year, 1924. A lyric of 1921 opens the new perspective. Having described the life of a poet in Russia as going on

> Под серой бегущей корою
> Дождей, облаков и солдатских
> Советов, стихов и дискуссий
> О транспорте и об искусстве.

> [Under a grey moving crust
> Of rains, clouds and soldiers'
> Soviets, of verses and discussions
> On transport and on art]

he continues

> Мы были людьми. Мы эпохи.

> [We were people. We are epochs]

and there follows the image of a train whirling them across the tundra.[65] More than one poem of *Themes and Variations* bears the traces of that period when private citizens were swept into a new and terrifying era. Pasternak, a lyric poet by vocation, gave much time to both prose and narrative verse, the latter particularly in the 1920s. The prose, as we shall see, remained at this stage an extension of the lyrical voice. But the narrative poetry, whatever the result, aimed to escape from the lyrical mode.

Themes and Variations is thus at the crossroads. On the one hand it recognises even in 1917 that a change must come –

> Я скажу до свиданья стихам, моя мания,
> Я назначил вам встречу со мною в романе.[66]

[I shall say *au revoir* to verses, my passion,
I have arranged you should meet me in a novel.]

But a poem of the same year calls childhood 'a ladle for the depths of the soul' [*Kovsh dushevnoy glubi*] and owns it to be 'my inspirer, my choirmaster' [*Moy vdokhnovitel', moy regent*].[67] And one of the most memorable achievements in this volume is the lines of 1919 that tell how the imagination grows with the growing child:[68]

> Так начинают. Года в два
> От мамки рвутся в тьму мелодий. . .

[Thus they begin. At about two
From the nurse they rush into a swarm of melodies.]

There is nothing here to adumbrate the civic poet, who was to write of the 1905 revolution. It goes on to describe how 'they begin to understand' [*nachinayut ponimat'*] and this is through the familiar process of alienation, childhood fears, Faustian exaltation. The poem, in its final stanza, arrives at a position that recalls Mayakovsky:

> Так затевают ссоры с солнцем.

[So they start quarrels with the sun.]

Then a single line follows:

> Так начинают жить стихом.

[So they begin to live by verse.]

What this meant Pasternak came fully to realise in the next decade.[69]

6

Pasternak and the New Russian Prose

I

When in 1923 Zamyatin surveyed the 'new Russian prose'[1] he reserved consideration of Pasternak to the end, after making shrewd and often merciless comment on the Proletkult writers, on the Serapion Brothers[2] (to whom, with Shklovsky, he had acted as mentor – they included Mikhail Zoshchenko and Vsevolod Ivanov), and on Pilnyak and Leonov. 'Pasternak', he observed,

has chosen the most difficult but also the most promising path: this is a writer entirely by himself [*bez rodu i plemeni*]... The change [*sdvig*], the novelty he brings is not in the subject (he is without a subject) and not in vocabulary, but on a plane where almost nobody else is working: in syntax. However he has symbolism too – very effective and all his own [*ochen' ostraya i svoya*].[3]

Zamyatin was able to judge Pasternak as a prose writer simply on the evidence of one short story – this was probably *Letters from Tula* [*Pis'ma iz Tuly*] published in 1922 – and one longer fiction that came out in the same year, *Detstvo Lyuvers*, known to English readers as *Zhenia's Childhood* (in Alec Brown's translation) or *The Childhood of Luvers* (in Robert Payne's). Both these stories had been written in 1918, when the creative energy released for Pasternak with *My Sister Life* was still at its height.

The others who came under Zamyatin's scrutiny differed from Pasternak in having concentrated on prose. They broke into the new Soviet literature, when books were again published after the time of shortages in the civil war, as the precursors of a generation for whom prose was to be the dominant medium. Symbolist poetry had arrived at a visible end with the death in 1921 of its greatest exponent, Blok; and after some twenty-five years that supremacy of the lyric poem which the Symbolists had brought about in Russian literature was challenged and overthrown. The poets often turned

84

during the 1920s to narrative forms in verse, as did Pasternak; but to resurrect verse narrative, in a language and a culture that had seen prose fiction developed to such a pitch by the great nineteenth-century masters, was bound to be very difficult. The young men who followed the pre-revolutionary generation – Zoshchenko, Babel, Yury Olesha, and countless others of lesser talent – were convinced of the need to devise a new prose drawing on common speech and looking to journalism as its arena and as the discipline that would dictate its practices. Babel, for instance, greatly admired Kipling. It was remarked by Zamyatin in his essay that 'the language of our epoch [is] rapid and pungent, like a code'.[4] With the methods of a prose fiction that accepted this language, and worked towards the perfecting of a journalistic medium, Pasternak's own procedure had nothing in common. His prose writings, from *Apellesova cherta* [*Il Tratto di Apelle*, or *The Line of Apelles*, 1915] to *Safe Conduct* at the end of the next decade, supplement the poetry of those years. Sometimes, as *Povest'* [*A Tale*, 1929][5] does in relation to the verse narrative *Spektorsky* (1924–30), the prose organises more elaborately and on a larger scale the same kind of impressions. *The Childhood of Luvers* actually forms part of a lost novel;[6] but even had it been published in full, this would certainly not have put his poetry of the same years into the shade. However, Pasternak's prose is no less accomplished than his verse during this period – Weidlé actually finds it more satisfying[7] – and in reading the stories and the auto-biography one recognises that the medium comes naturally to him, and serves particular purposes more appropriately than verse. The various short or longer prose fictions in this period constitute an overflow from Pasternak's poetry: they deal with the predicament of the artist (as in *The Line of Apelles, Letters from Tula*, and *A Tale*), or they explore more persistently than a lyric can, and over a period of time, the sensibility of a child, Zhenya Luvers, which is clearly akin to the sensibility of the artist.

Zamyatin is wrong when he states that Pasternak in these stories has no subject. Even the slightest of them – the opening pair, *The Line of Apelles* and *Letters from Tula* – are not the flimsy web of impressions that he seems to imply. It is true that, in the former, descriptive writing gets out of hand, just as in Pasternak's verse of that time conceit bred conceit to the detriment of coherence. The leaning tower invades Pisa with an army of shadows that are resisted by the last rays of sunset like partisans in the streets.[8] This image has no bearing at all on the adventure of the poet Heinrich Heine (a modern namesake); and similarly the bravura passages on the heat of a Tuscan evening, or on the sunlight that plays on the floor of the hotel room in Ferrara where he sleeps, can only be justified as attempts to make the Italian scene overwhelmingly actual. They are travel notes, impressions of Pasternak's journey to these places a few years before, that he cannot exclude. His eye is caught by the thickening patterns of sunlight as it passes through the Venetian blinds. These patterns are not symbolic; they do not subtly indicate the tone of the experience which awaits Heine. Pasternak blends all the powers of his syntax to fix that impression of the room's secret life, its changing activity all round the immobile Heine. But in this passage the only hero is syntax, the victorious power of expression. Heine becomes a device: the phrase 'Heine sleeps' merely punctuates the unfolding paragraph three times.

Yet, as Michel Aucouturier has shown,[9] *The Line of Apelles* should be taken seriously for what it is – a first essay in clarifying the nature of the poet's art, and especially the relation between spontaneity and the playing of a role, like an actor's.[10] Heine has received a challenge from the Italian poet Relinquimini. He is to prove his genius by a statement on love no less distinctive in its brevity than the single line Apelles once drew as his signature, or visiting-card, on the wall of a fellow painter. In Ferrara Heine summons by a ruse Relinquimini's mistress. He sets himself to seduce her, and then, unexpectedly for him, they fall in love. The moment of recognition on Heine's part occurs between two paragraphs. In the manner of Sterne, the narrative falters at the words 'he notices that...' and crossing the boundary of feeling into a new section of the story (IV) resumes '... that this woman is really beautiful'.[11] The miracle takes place: Heine who was acting a part now becomes genuinely creative, the artist whose love engulfs and bears up the woman like a wave. Similarly in *Letters from Tula* the poet separated from his mistress recognises himself miserably in the third-rate actors who have come to Tula in order to take part in an historical film. Counterposed to his discovery is that of the retired actor who by rehearsing a former role has found the inner peace ('physical silence') sought by the poet and found it in 'making another person [*postoronnego*] speak through his lips'.[12] Pasternak, it is clear from *Safe Conduct*, was troubled by the affinities between actor and poet, and did not approve the way in which his contemporaries accepted 'the idea of biography as spectacle'.[13] This illumination at Tula takes place *'on the territory of conscience'*:[14]

Tolstoy had lived in those regions. The story shows an awareness of Tolstoy's demands upon art – that it should not trifle, or
seek display, but communicate true feeling directly, as the poet
in this story communicates his sense of self-disgust and humilia-
tion.

Both of these stories are concerned with the themes that form
the titles of lyrics in *My Sister Life*: they can be described as working towards a 'Definition of Poetry' and a 'Definition of Creative
Work'. The narrative prose form enables Pasternak to dramatise
the poet's self-recognition as it arises from a social relationship, and
to reveal the shift from everyday life to the life of the imagination as
a process sudden and unforeseen like the leap from play-acting to
serious engagement in *The Line of Apelles*. On the evidence of these
two initial stories he does not promise to develop into a novelist.
They are spirited pieces, the first in its dialogue, the second in the
monologue of the letters. They move confidently, the narrator's
voice holds the ear, the phases of each story are well controlled.
Weidlé suggests that both *The Line of Apelles* and *Letters from
Tula* are no more than trials of the pen.[15] While the former still
belongs to the experimental era of *Above the Barriers*, the latter
reflects its proximity to *My Sister Life* and the poems of 1918. It
seems to be a part of the poet's lightly disguised autobiography,
which is also there in the fragment *Lovelessness* [*Bezlyub'e*], dating
from November 1918 – a chapter from some missing novel. This tells
of a journey in March 1917 from the Urals on the way to Moscow,
which is also described in the *Essay in Autobiography*.[16] Some
incidents from Pasternak's life appear in the poetry (the school scene
from *Nineteen Five*); but a great deal of the prose writing, and not
only that which announces itself as autobiography, draws freely upon
his own experience. Zhenya's childhood is no nearer to his own than
Ursula Brangwen's in *The Rainbow* is to Lawrence's; but both
writers have recovered the quality of their self-awareness as children
through imagining the early years of an isolated girl. *A Tale*, as
Pasternak's sister testifies in her preface to the Penguin translation,[17]
borders upon his own experience as a tutor in 1914. It is not
apparent that *Aerial Ways* [*Vozdushnye puti*, 1924] does this.
Polivanov the revolutionary is there depicted as Pasternak's anti-
self, in the way that Antipov was to Zhivago. Generally the prose
fiction takes the middle ground between the poetry of Pasternak and
his autobiographical writings. Both his fiction and autobiography are
concerned above all with the poet's destiny and purposes.

II

The two episodes in *The Childhood of Luvers* are entitled 'The Long Days' ['*Dolgie dni*'] and 'The Stranger' [*Postoronniy*']. Although forming a complete story they seem to represent no more than the prelude of the novel that was lost. Zhenya Luvers is not an artist (though conceivably she might have become one). Her perceptions and interests, however, make her an unusual child. By the choice of his title for the story, Pasternak challenges comparison with the well known works by Tolstoy and Gorky called *Childhood*. These had been told in the first person: Tolstoy's story was a fictional rendering of his own earlier years, with recognisable characters but imagined incidents; Gorky's purported to be a truthful account of his own beginnings as Alyosha Peshkov. Pasternak stands much nearer to Tolstoy than to Gorky. His nature shrank from the persistent self-regard of Gorky's chronicle, which presents a little boy as untarnishable as Oliver Twist. At the same time Pasternak in his awareness of the child's mind does not look out for unconscious hypocrisy, following Tolstoy. He explores the imagination of childhood and not primarily its moral growth. The latter does indeed become prominent in the second episode, but it fails to engross his attention as it engrossed Tolstoy's throughout the trilogy of which *Childhood* forms the first part. Pasternak resembles Tolstoy in his immediate apprehension of the way a child responds to adults and to their conventions. He resembles him too in the understanding of a child's conclusions about life.

What prompted this difficult task for a man of describing a young girl's experience at the onset of puberty? Pasternak's was a genius that invariably waited upon events. In his poetry he looks on, he overhears, he is assailed by impressions. The first appearance of menstrual blood is symbolic of this condition. Zhenya has been surprised by the workings of life, about which very early in the story[18] Pasternak observes that few are initiated into its purposes. An artist is close to a child in his lack of shielding preconceptions – and these, with ideas of reward and punishment, and entry into a world of human obligations, come to children quickly enough. Zhenya must learn to accept the process of life with gratitude. The French governess and her mother do not encourage her to do this, though the following day her mother tells Zhenya there is no need for fear when it happens again. Pasternak has extended a tradition of Russian literature into the area of childhood. It had long used the consciousness of a young woman to examine the moral life. Instead he takes a little girl (more of a little girl in the 1900s than she would be now at a like age) to act as the recording intelligence. Zhenya replaces the writer himself in childish days and her attitudes move him to that special pity he felt towards women.[19] When the girl forced herself to explain confusedly what had happened, and why she wanted the governess's powder, 'her mother listened, rejoicing, loving her and tormented by tenderness for this thin little body'.[20] The tenderness Pasternak feels is not a form of narcissism, such as can be detected in the early chapters of *David Copperfield*. It attests his power to imagine the role of the other sex, and to explore a child's sensibility at its most unprotected.

Zhenya's preoccupation in the first episode, which goes on to describe how the family left Perm for Ekaterinburg on the other side of the Urals, is constantly with the significance of names. When in her infancy she heard the name of the factory across the river, 'that was all that was wanted – to know what they called the thing she didn't understand – Motovilikha. On that night this still explained all to her, because on that night the name had its full and childishly reassuring significance'.[21] Afterwards she learns that a name can hide what is most essential, when next morning she wants to know what the word 'factory' means. Most of all Zhenya finds it difficult to understand the significance of the name Asia. With her small brother Seryozha she looks out for the boundary stone between Europe and Asia; it flashes by; and the same dusty alder woods line the track in Asia as they did mile after mile previously in Europe.[22] So what is Asia? Seryozha has an answer that evades the imaginative issue. He points to the Urals on the schoolroom map, and tells her: 'They have agreed to draw the natural boundary, that's all.' The following day Seryozha wakes up in Ekaterinburg, while Zhenya, still unresolved of her difficulty, wakes up in Asia.[23] *The Childhood of Luvers* impresses by its achieved unity, the consistency of its tone – everything is brought back to the child's feeling, and through her sense of the events the narrative gains both scale and coherence. Zhenya's acuteness in weighing up what her parents mean to her (they are both inaccessible to their children) does not fall short of the little girl's in *What Maisie Knew*; but Pasternak, unlike James, won't make her a moral umpire for the adults. It is Zhenya who perceives the different qualities of her governesses: Miss Hawthorn is summed up in the cool justice of her lavender-scented hands; the Frenchwoman 'had been like a fly, and nobody cared for her. Her name was utterly lost, and Zhenya could not tell among what syllables and sounds you would happen upon that name.'[24] Later, in the second episode, it is Zhenya who observes the sexton Defendov and his family, noting how they are different from hers; who sees the effect the Akhmedyanov boys have on Seryozha; who takes an interest in the Belgian Neguerat and in his friend Tsvetkov, the lame man endued by her with such a mysterious significance for her life and eventually killed in an accident involving her parents' carriage. All the impressions of the railway journey, the Ekaterinburg boulevards with their dazzling white pavements, the new flat, and the unfamiliar maid, are hers too. There was nothing remarkable in this: any story with a child at the centre will make the child's perceptions paramount. The gain for Pasternak can be measured in terms of the control that became possible. Every image, every unusual comparison in the story arises from Zhenya's mind. They are no longer irrepressible conceits, as in *The Line of Apelles*, but the alert perceptions and combinations of a very sensitive child's understanding. *Letters from Tula* begins with an ingenious image: 'in the train from Moscow they were conveying the sun that had suffocated on a multitude of striped carriage seats.'[25] This returns in the closing paragraph: 'A train was going to Moscow and in it they were conveying a vast crimson sun on a multitude of sleepy bodies.'[26] The conceit appears to have been imposed on the story, for the sake of pattern-making. The second sentence in *The Childhood of Luvers* may look rather similar: 'As at one time her little boats and dolls, so afterwards her recollections sank into the shaggy bearskins, of which there were many in the house.'[27] Here the fusing of the material and the ideal, of toys and memories, imposes itself. The psychological fact could not be more accurately put. Her memories are confused with the toys, and both are lost in the shaggy bearskins, the first setting of childhood, beyond which a search of her past cannot go.

In the second episode Zhenya leaves her childhood behind and becomes a fully moral being, with the recognition through Tsvetkov's death that a stranger, 'without a name or with a fortuitous one, who neither provokes hatred nor inspires love',[28] can enter into her life and must be treated as a person in his own right. The tutor who proposes to read Lermontov with her suddenly realises that she has matured into a woman – and already at the sexton's house it has dawned upon her that she is '*terribly* like mamma'.[29] Thus *The*

Childhood of Luvers, although Zamyatin failed to see it, has a subject, and in its second episode the italicising of these two moral discoveries and their formulation as general truths show a dependence on Tolstoy's *Childhood, Boyhood* and *Youth*. Once again Pasternak has found his way to 'the territory of conscience'.

III

This makes his prose different from that of Andrey Bely, the starting-point for much experiment in the 1920s. Bely's writing is agile, varied and fantastic. Such mannerism has its place, in the work of Proust for example, when expressing a tortuous mind in pursuit of uncommon insights. Its affectation may even be the only way for that author of achieving sincerity. Pasternak's earlier prose, *Safe Conduct* included, falls quite distinctly and regularly into mannerism, like his earlier poetry. But his principal aim was not to dazzle the reader, any more than this was Proust's. He matched syntax to the movement of thought and feeling: the order of the sentence reproduces the order of his perceptions in time. Here too he resembles Tolstoy. When demonstrating a thesis in didactic vein Tolstoy writes almost with the baldness of Chernyshevsky, but when he registers a sensation, physical or moral, his constructions can be elaborate, and sometimes indeed top-heavy. Pasternak needed a similar complication to keep up with the variety of his intuitions, which were psychological quite as often as aesthetic. It has to be admitted that *The Childhood of Luvers*, in view of its difficult subject, is straightforwardly written. As the drama of a child's consciousness, it can have no room for display or sophistication.

Weidlé quotes with approval of its 'limpid charm' [*bezoblachnoy prelesti*] a short paragraph that compares the tinkling of a soldier's balalaika with the sound of gnats in the yard.[30] But 'it was even subtler and gentler. It sank lower than the gnats towards the ground and without getting dusty more lightly than any swarm could it returned to the height, twinkling and breaking off, with momentary falls [*s pripadan'yami*], unhurried.'[31] This sudden realisation of the music and the midges in terms that become interchangeable is entirely characteristic of Pasternak. It also bears the stamp of a child's imagination. What follows in the next paragraph, as Zhenya reflects on the significance of the lame man she has just seen, is remarkable in another way:

Zhenya went back to the house. 'Lame', she was thinking about the stranger with the album, 'lame, and a gentleman, without crutches.' She went in by the servants' entrance. In the yard there was a smell of cloying camomile infusion. 'It's some time now since Mamma got together a whole pharmacy, a lot of dark blue bottles with yellow tops.' Slowly she mounted the stairs. The iron rails were cold, the treads gnashing in answer to her scraping. All at once there came into her head an odd thought. She strode over two steps and paused on the third. It came into her head that recently there had begun to show between Mamma and the yardman's wife an unaccountable resemblance. Something most elusive. She stood still. It must be, she pondered, the kind of thing people mean when they say: we are all human beings. . .or all tarred with the same brush. . .or fate is no respecter of rank – she pushed away with the point of her shoe a medicine bottle that had rolled there, the bottle flew down, dropped on to the dusty sacks and was not broken – in a word it's something very very common, common to all people. But then why not between herself and Aksinya? or Aksinya, say, and Ulyasha? This seemed to Zhenya all the odder because it was difficult to find two women more unlike: Aksinya had about her something earthy, as of kitchen gardens, something that brought to mind the swelling of a spud, or the primal green of a squash melon, while Mamma. . .Zhenya laughed at the very thought of comparing them.

But meanwhile it was just Aksinya who gave the tone to this comparison that forced itself on her. She came out on top when they were brought together. It wasn't that the peasant woman gained, but the lady lost. For a moment Zhenya had a glimpse of something crazy. She fancied that the spirit of the ordinary people's life had taken possession of her mother [*vselilos' kakoe-to nachalo prostonarodnosti*], and she thought of her mother [speaking broadly like Aksinya] – and suddenly it came to her in a flash there'd be a day when in her new silk housecoat without a sash, sailing by, she would go and blurt out: 'stand by the door!'

The corridor smelt of medicine. Zhenya went to her father.

Here Pasternak renders the full experience of Zhenya's discovery, the physical movements and sensations that accompany her thought. The medicine bottle evokes her mother, when she is already aware of the lame man as a gentleman and preparing her mind unconsciously for the contrast between that fact and the servants' entrance she is using. And suddenly she sees her mother's position in the household as undermined by this inexplicable likeness to Aksinya. The medicine bottle that she kicks in the moment of speculation falls to the ground but is unbroken, just as her thought plunges into a void but arrives whole at a formulation. Pasternak in his prose as in his poetry recognises the way the mind working under stress of emotion grasps at and weaves into the process whatever comes before the eye. Here Zhenya seems to be helped by the bottle's safe landing to her thought, but scarcely registers any connection. On another occasion earlier at Perm when resolving to explain all to her mother, she had looked out at the night and the cold river 'and – flung herself in'.[32] The duty of confession became for her merged entirely with the imagined sensation of the darkness outside and the icy waste. And she took the plunge.

In the passage that has been quoted one phrase – 'the spirit of the ordinary people's life had taken possession of her mother' – obviously could not belong to Zhenya, though it explains in the author's own language what she had divined. And two other phrases – 'something most elusive', 'the primal green [*prazelen'*] of a squash melon' – also belong to adult speech, and the second to Pasternak's idiosyncratic vocabulary. He crosses the limits of a child's lexicon whereas Mark Twain, for instance, avoids crossing them in *Huckleberry Finn*. These occasional sorties into adult expression do not, however, impair the convincingness of what Zhenya sees. It is noteworthy that Maxim Gorky, who could not make sense of Pasternak's verse, was entirely won over by *The Childhood of Luvers*, and astonished that its author had been able so successfully to 'reincarnate himself as a thirteen-year-old girl'.[33] (Gorky even wrote a preface for a proposed translation to come out in New York.[34]) Nadezhda Mandelstam finds the realisation of Zhenya more complete by far than that of Lara in *Doctor Zhivago*.[35] *The Childhood of Luvers* is flawless in its rendering of an innocent and unspoilt awareness as this grows into a fuller knowledge of life. The prose is exploratory in the same way as the verse of Pasternak at this time, a mastering of new perceptions through experiment with the medium. He learns about Zhenya and about the advantages of prose simultaneously.

IV

Two other stories must be considered before we turn to the longer poems of the 1920s. The first, *Aerial Ways*, was published six years after Pasternak had written *The Childhood of Luvers*. Thus it not only appears at a time when the new Soviet literature had taken root; its third and final part has a manifest connection with that literature, since it describes the contemporary scene and presents the revolutionary ethos. There Polivanov, the actual father of the child whom his friends have lost in the scene before the war, once again meets the mother of the boy, fifteen years later, in a world that has utterly estranged them. He is an overworked functionary of the new regime; matters of life and death are, if not actually in his hands, very close to them. She comes to him as a bedraggled 'former person' whose son has been involved in a plot against the Soviet state. Critics point out that Polivanov anticipates Pasha Antipov,

subsequently known as Strelnikov, in *Doctor Zhivago*. The personal
no longer has claims on him; and he now feels more closely linked
with the sentry, whose weary indifference had been opposed to the
questioning Lelya, than with Lelya herself. Polivanov talks like a
newspaper article, putting in all the formal syntax and even the com-
mas.[36] His office momentarily recalls the lost world of St Petersburg,
but this is an illusion. Outside the yard is piled with litter; normality
has broken down. Their scene ends with Polivanov's total nervous
prostration, and her seeming disappearance. 'Then he found her.
Like a huge unbroken doll she was lying between the underpart of
his desk and the chair in that very layer of shavings and rubbish
which in the darkness, and while still conscious, she had taken for
a carpet.'[37] The telephone line from his room communicates with
the outer darkness through which pass the aerial ways carrying the
ideas of Lenin, Liebknecht and the Third International. These ideas
have driven Polivanov to the verge of breakdown, like that of the
country itself; they have converted his former love into a clumsy
unwanted doll; they have imposed a merciless order. All this is
shown, but it is also accepted. The self-engrossment of Lelya's
husband, long ago, boasting of a paternity that was not his; the
hysteria of Lelya herself, and the fury with which she turned on the
negligent nurse; the dwarfish insignificance of their movements as
they search for the child, over a widening area, in the night – all
these are now doubly distanced. The whole episode had been unreal
to Polivanov in its final moments when he shook off the responsibility
of his parenthood by walking down to the sea. The story balances
the two worlds, and it finds the later one genuinely terrible, a melodrama in which the son's return, so easily putting an end to that
earlier scare, can no longer be entertained. Both Lelya and Polivanov are caught in a process that has no respect for their former
relationship. The carpets have been stripped away; only shavings
and litter remain. *Aerial Ways* is not a story of protest, or even of
regret – at least on its surface. It reveals the new situation, indelibly;
and in the desire to deal honestly with fact it neither grieves nor
exhorts.

V

The other story, *A Tale*, published in 1929, has a degree of
entanglement with the verse narrative *Spektorsky* (1924–30) which
Pasternak says in the opening paragraphs of his prose fiction is best

put out of mind. (The relation between the two works will be examined in the next chapter.) *A Tale* is the recollection of a young tutor's experiences in 1914, the last summer 'when life still apparently took note of individuals',[38] and the story begins and ends at his sister's house in the Urals, two years later. This work derives in some parts closely from Pasternak's own circumstances before the Great War, and Seryozha, not surprisingly, is a poet. Yet a further inset into the already framed narrative is made with the presentation of the scenario that Seryozha writes for a verse drama. Pasternak describes the process of creation in a passage that anticipates the famous account in *Doctor Zhivago*.[39] His hero like the author himself is overcome by a feeling of pity for women that leads him to cast round for ways of making money to liberate them. In his verse drama a young poet and musician sells himself to the highest bidder, at a country house where he recites poetry and extemporises on the piano to the curious who have come to witness this strange transaction. His benevolent purchaser does not know what to do with him, and the huge sum the young man has spent as the proceeds of his sale to relieve the sufferings of women only brings on disorder.

A Tale is written with the same accomplishment as *The Childhood of Luvers*, and the writer's resources are more varied. He shows a considerable fluency in dramatic dialogue (anticipated in the earlier stories), and there is a scene in which Seryozha realises the full human predicament of a prostitute that takes Pasternak into a region similar to Gorky's 'lower depths'. Seryozha's sensibility is more complex than the child Zhenya's, and therefore the writing becomes in places more baroque, as in the passage where Anna is identified with the Moscow scene on a summer morning: 'he saw how, surrounded with poplars like frozen towels, she was swallowed up by the clouds and slowly tossed back her Gothic brick towers'.[40] This returns to the manner of *Themes and Variations* at its most elliptical. But generally the notation is, though full of novelty, clear and no more complicated than the subject demands. To give one instance: Seryozha has found Anna lying on her bed in a faint.

He gasped for breath, and was himself not far from fainting. Suddenly she came round.
'You, friend?'[41] she murmured indistinctly and closed her eyes.
The gift of speech returned not to human beings alone. Everything in the room began to talk. It was filled with noise, as though they had let children in. First of all, jumping up from the floor, Seryozha shut the door to. 'Ah, ah', aimlessly tramping round the room he repeated in something like a state of monosyllabic bliss, rushing continually now to the window, now

to the chest of drawers. Although the room which faced north swam in lilac shadow, yet the medicine labels could be made out in any corner, and there was no need in deciphering phials and bottles to run with each of them separately to the window. That was done only to give vent to his joy which demanded noisy expression. Mrs Arild was fully conscious, and simply to gratify Seryozha she yielded to his insistence. To please him she agreed to sniff smelling-salts, and the pungency of ammonium chloride penetrated her in a moment as it does any healthy person. Her tear-stained face was overspread with creases of astonishment, her eyebrows were sharply pointed upwards, and she pushed away Seryozha's hand with a movement full of recovered strength. He also made her take valerian. When drinking the water she knocked her teeth against the rim of the glass, and then uttered the mooing sound with which children express the complete satisfaction of a need.[42]

These four or five minutes of her restoration to the world, and of the world's restoration to itself, are finely imagined. The intimacy between the pair is expressed in terms that have strong sexual overtones, and it is ironic that Seryozha and Anna will have to accept this surrogate for love-making. When she comes down for their promised walk, he has already forgotten her in the fever of writing his scenario.

VI

With *A Tale* Pasternak ends the first phase of his fictional writing. Ahead lies the autobiography *Safe Conduct*, and already in the decade that follows he will begin to make drafts for his one completed novel, *Doctor Zhivago*. The prose of a poet usually impresses by its singularity and attention to detail. Mandelstam's is a case in point. Those who are accustomed to using charged language and to the renovation of meanings will, when they leave poetry at intervals for prose, come to it with a nervous intensity that produces a prose somewhat oblique, looking towards the poetry from which it has been separated. Prose for Pasternak is truly an alternative medium to verse. He writes indeed at the opposite pole from an expert in traditional novelist's prose such as Bunin, who adds nothing to the possibilities of expression, but has schooled his mind and senses to work within the limits reached by Turgenev and Goncharov. The achievement of Pasternak in his earlier prose was to increase its range of perception and to devise an elaborate and varied syntax closely related to that developed in his poetry. He aimed to recover for verse in the 1920s its amplitude as a medium for describing man in society. The experiment, as we shall see, was no more than partly successful; and clearly it did not persuade him that for a major statement about his time poetry could dislodge prose, the medium of the classical Russian novelists. Pasternak was able to conceive poetry and prose as equal partners in the enterprise of his imagination. For a Russian poet following Tolstoy, Dostoevsky and Chekhov – the dramatist who showed with Ibsen that prose in the modern theatre could serve poetic ends – there was every reason to make trial of prose. The stories that Pasternak wrote between 1915 and 1929 even without the poetry make Pasternak a significant artist. But they could not have been written without the poetry.

7

'From Lyrical Thinking to the Epic'

I

Early in 1927 Pasternak reported on his work in progress through a Soviet journal,[1] as he had the previous year. At this time the narrative poem *Lieutenant Schmidt* [*Leytenant Shmidt*] was nearing conclusion; and he had already published *Nineteen Five* [*Devyat'sot pyatyy god*] which occupied him from the autumn of 1925,[2] and which would be further revised before appearing in book form with *Lieutenant Schmidt*. The brief note he contributed makes one crucial statement: 'I consider that the epic is what our time inspires, and accordingly in the book *Nineteen Five* I move across from lyrical thinking to the epic, although this is very difficult.' And he announces: 'Subsequently I mean to work at prose.'[3] His experiments in prose during this decade have already been discussed;[4] they too were an attempt to free himself from 'lyrical thinking', although the result was merely to give the same process a wider scope. The stories in prose could be described as sustained 'lyrical thinking'. As we have seen they are for the most part deeply personal. But the situations presented by them receive a firm outline, whereas those of *My Sister Life* or 'The Break' have to be inferred from hints in the poetry. However, Pasternak as a writer of prose fiction ventures very seldom into the public world before *Doctor Zhivago*. Only the last episode in *Aerial Ways* can be said to have much in common with the long poems he was to write during the 1920s. This story appeared early in 1924, at almost the same time as *The High Malady* [*Vysokaya bolezn'*], and the scene in which Lelya meets Polivanov, now working for the Bolsheviks, is similar to the poem both in its passages of rhetoric (the aerial ways crossing 'the sky of the Third International'[5]) and its uneasy acceptance of a harsh new order hostile to the personal life. *The High Malady*, as first printed in *Lef* without the concluding tribute to Lenin and with a number of indiscreet comments that were later removed, could not in its ambiguity achieve the epic vision Pasternak sought. If the age inspired 'epic', the term had to mean a confident poetry of celebration, such as Mayakovsky aimed at in *150,000,000* (1919–20), although this work should be called a strip cartoon rather than a serious attempt at epic. The task before Soviet poets in the 1920s as many of them saw it was to chronicle the rise, progress and achievements of the first workers' state, and for that theme nothing but an epic treatment would do.

II

Of this need Pasternak was almost comically aware in the line (afterwards to go out) that opened *The High Malady*, much to Mayakovsky's amusement:[6] 'The Achaeans show staunchness' [*Akheytsy proyavlyayut tsepkost'*]. The paragraph following this unexpected echo of Mandelstam's classical manner in *Tristia* (1922) evokes the siege of Troy and the birth of its epic (presumably the events that will inspire Homer). Pasternak is discontented with the lyric poetry he and others had written – 'song' [*pesn'*] the 'high malady' of his inspiration, which seems to be irrelevant in the Soviet epoch. 'Song' or 'lyrical thinking' could have no place in a world that had 'flung itself from books on to lances and bayonets' [*brosavsheysya ot knig / Na piki i na shtyk*].[7] The role that this statement demands from the poet would seem to be the one recorded a few years later by Mayakovsky in *At The Top of My Voice* [*Vo ves' golos*]:

> Но я
>   себя
>   смирял,
>   становясь
> на горло
>   собственной песне.
> Слушайте,
>   товарищи потомки,
> агитатора,
>   горлана-главаря.[8]
> [But I
>   subdued
>   myself,
>   standing
> On the throat
>   of my own song.
> Hear,
>   comrade descendants,
> An agitator,
>   a bawling ringleader.]

99

Pasternak could claim, though with a different emphasis from Maya-kovsky, that he too was 'a living man who spoke to the living' [*zhivoy/s zhivymi govorya*], but agitation, the call to emulate invari-ably found in 'epic' as understood by Soviet writers, could never become the nerve of his poetry. A few dozen verses added at the end of *The High Malady* to praise Lenin (who is made virtually an artist, a 'genius' able to express 'the bare essence' [*golaya sut'*] of the moment) – these mark the nearest step Pasternak could take in the direction of epic, and it was not taken for some years.[9] He wrote instead a strange lyrical monologue on his own position. The metre is principally that of Russian narrative verse in the classical period (iambic tetrameters), as it had been used by Pushkin in *Poltava* (1829) or more recently by Blok in *Retribution* [*Vozmezdie*, 1910–21]. This is a good metre for relating action in straightforward, vigorous terms; but already by the time of *Poltava* the epic element had to coexist with lyrical passages, and the experiment Blok made in *Retribution* of reviving Pushkin's narrative manner and form all too easily led him into confessional verse (the third, Warsaw, chapter). *Retribution* becomes a personal myth given as the key to history; and Blok was unable to finish his poem. Andrey Sinyavsky is right in pointing to Blok's example as decisive for Pasternak when he came to write narrative poems on the events of his age, and in quoting particularly what Blok said in the Foreword to *Retribution* of 1919 about the way in which he understood history: 'All these facts' – and Blok had cited for the years 1910 and 1911 the deaths of Tolstoy, the actress Kommissarzhevskaya and the painter Vrubel; the 'crisis of Symbolism'; the strikes in England, Agadir, the vogue for French wrestling at the circus – 'all these facts, seemingly so different, have for me a single musical sense. I have grown used to juxtaposing the facts from every area of life that has been accessible to my vision at a given time, and I am convinced that together they form a single musical drive [*napor*].'[10] In *The High Malady* Paster-nak first tries out this method though it had been implicit even in *My Sister Life*, which succeeds in catching what Blok calls 'the rhythm of the age'. This for Blok involved the use of a particular metre, one based on the iamb; just as, in the age of Catiline, he argued that the complicated metre of Catullus' poem *Attis*, which is written in galliambics, expressed its peculiar rhythm.[11] Pasternak's choice of Pushkin's iambic tetrameter as the principal measure for *The High Malady* was inappropriate. It brought back too strongly the voice of Pushkin himself, which had also been heard somewhat incongruously in *Retribution*. The true rhythm of the epoch, as Blok later discovered when he came to write *The Twelve*, was a mixed one, which could relate and harmonise its many voices. *The High Malady* is equivocal, rather than polyphonic.

Afterwards the initial line about the Achaeans gave way to another: 'The shifting rebus is seen by glimpses' [*Mel'kaet dvizhush-chiysya rebus*]. It is a poem about things noted sharply, and felt, as always with Pasternak, vividly; but their meaning remains obscure to him. As an essay in political understanding it could only disappoint even those readiest to indulge the fellow-travelling writers of the 1920s. The tone is one that betrays an acute discomfort turning to dismay when the poet considers the Ninth Congress of Soviets at which he was present:

С стенных газет вопрос Карельский
Глядел и вызывал вопрос
В больших глазах больных берез.[12]

[From the wall newspapers the Karelian question
Looked and provoked a question too
In the large eyes of the sick birches.]

There is opposition between the nature they disregard and the men who are called upon to restore a country laid waste by famine and terror:

и все окрест
Смотрело полным погорельцем,
Отказываясь наотрез
Когда-нибудь подняться с рельс.

[all around
Had the look of one burnt out of house and
In downright refusal
Ever to get up from the rails.]

The poet calls 'blasphemous' the propaganda message wired by the Congress to survivors of the Japanese earthquake. *The High Malady* is not, however, a disaffected work. It indicates plainly enough the distance at which its author stands from any committed supporter of the revolution:

А сзади, в зареве легенд
Идиот, герой, интеллигент
В огне декретов и реклам
Горел во славу темной силы,
Что потихоньку по углам
Его, зазнавшись, поносила
За подвиг, если не за то,
Что дважды два не сразу сто.

101

А сзади, в зареве легенд
Идиот, герой, интеллигент
Печатал и писал плакаты
Про радость своего заката.
Над драмой реял красный флаг.
Он выступал во всех ролях
Как друг и недруг деревенек,
Как их слуга и,как,изменник.[13]

[And behind, in the glow of legends
The idiot, hero, intellectual
In the heat of decrees and posters
Burned to the glory of the dark power
That secretly in the corners
Filled with conceit abused him
For his heroic act, if not because
Two and two weren't at once a hundred.

And behind, in the glow of legends
The idiot, hero, intellectual
Printed and designed placards
About the joy of his own decline.
Over the drama flew the red flag.
It appeared in every role,
As friend and enemy of the villages,
As their servant and their betrayer.]

The High Malady is the unhappy utterance of a poet who cannot see that he matters to the new dispensation:

Я говорю про всю среду,
С которой я имел в виду
Сойти со сцены, и сойду.[14]

[I speak of the whole milieu
Together with which I had it in mind
To quit the scene, and I shall quit.]

He is alienated, and feels the world is alienated with him: it shares the 'high malady':

Всю жизнь я быть хотел как все,
Но век в своей красе
Сильнее моего нытья
И хочет быть как я.[15]

[All my life I wanted to be like everyone,
But the age in its beauty
Was stronger than my moaning
And it wants to be like myself.]

There is a longing to unite poetry and the social purpose; and Pasternak's interest in the epic further attests this. But as Sinyavsky says, *The High Malady* is an unachieved epic: it seeks to fulfil its

aim strictly by way of style' [*sobstvenno yazykovym putyom*].[16]
Another critic, A. M. Ripellino, has called it 'an attempt at the epic
without a frame' and makes a comparison with the annelida, a
worm whose body is composed of annular segments.[17] To succeed
in narrative verse Pasternak needed the support of a body of facts
that must be organised. *Nineteen Five* and *Lieutenant Schmidt*
could depend on such a framework.

III

Pasternak's difficulties in writing *Nineteen Five* were not at base
ideological, for the poem, unlike *Doctor Zhivago*, nowhere enters
upon an argument about politics or political attitudes. The revolution of 1905 appealed to his imagination in the same way as the
February Revolution of 1917.[18] It had for him the character of some
great irresistible change or upheaval in nature. Seen as if for the
first time the coming of snow is like that – winter, creative and
astonishing, 'from October strays into our prose with its ugliness'
[*V nashu prozu s eyo bezobraz'em/S oktyabrya zabredaet zima*]. So
the prologue to *Nineteen Five* states, continuing with a whole-
hearted affirmation:

В неземной новизне этих суток,
Революция, вся ты, как есть.[19]

[In the unearthly newness of these days and nights,
Revolution, you are there, completely.]

Pasternak's subject was one he could take up with a good will. It
was an assignment put in his way by the time itself, when a poet
could feel it his duty to confront the immense changes in Russian
life, and their origins. He wanted to break free from what seemed to
him, as they had finally seemed to Blok, the limitations of the lyric.
But the consequences were twofold, and here the difficulty began. On
the one hand, he must move out of lyrical timelessness – the
'momentary for ever' seized in the storm, for example [*Groza,
momental'naya navek*[20]] – and contemplate instead the process of
history, its sequence in time. On the other hand, he must turn away
from the refracted lights of the revolution, from the wholly personal
world lit up by the glare behind his back, and face the full dazzling
experience. Being a lyric poet does not necessarily doom a writer to
failure when he tries to encompass historical events. Donald Davie
names in this connection Hart Crane,[21] whose long poem about

America, *The Bridge*, has the amplitude of epic, and breaks down in the end not because Crane was a lyric poet out of his element, but because he was a poet who could not think things through. Pasternak, however, had up to this point always preferred the sidelong glance [*kosoy vzglyad*].[22] His eye was rapid and ranging; it attended to all the signs and intimations of the weather, the street, the garden. He did not place man at the centre; his poetry is centrifugal, and its human interest appears everywhere, in the mind's awareness of kinship with whatever lives, moves, and so crowds into Pasternak's picture. It now became necessary to change his priorities. For a Soviet poet human concerns were everything, and they received their true focus in the revolution. Pasternak, we can foresee, would not be able – 'else sinning greatly', in Wordsworth's phrase[23] – to adopt this perspective altogether. But the first requirement of epic is that humanity should be placed in a heroic light; that the destiny of men belonging to a particular nation (or in the new circumstances a particular class) should matter pre-eminently to the poet; that the excellence of life should consist in achievement and in the activity of the human will. How was he to meet this demand?

In the proper sense, he would meet it scarcely at all. A modern Joan of Arc from the Siberian prisons, 'a woman convict among the leaders' [*katorzhanka v vozhdyakh*], is invoked in the prologue to personify revolution (which also has the severity of an exacting artist).[24] But to this heroic image giving the dimensions of myth no actual hero in the poem itself corresponds, unless it be the sailor Matyushenko who makes his brief appearance in the naval mutiny scene, striding 'like a giant' [*Gigantom/Proshol/Matyushenko*] to bawl the news of victory down into the engine-room.[25] Briefly here, and in the decision that follows at dawn to weigh anchor, Pasternak writes on the approved pattern. However, such heroism and such decision as the poem will show are elsewhere the work of masses. If this were a film – and the comparison is unavoidable with Eisenstein's *Battleship Potemkin* appearing at almost the same time[26] – the camera would close in only now and again. There are countless individual moments, but very few individual men. (Bauman, for example, whose name opens the fifth chapter, 'Students' ['*Studenty*'], has already died. What counts in the poem is the funeral procession and the clashes that followed, and the chrysanthemums on Bauman's grave relinquished to the night and the stars.[27]) The action of men takes place in a setting of ocean and sky, overlooked by the frozen moon working spells [*vorozhit zamoro-*

zhennyy mesyats][28] or the sun that 'watches through binoculars/
And listens/To the guns' [*Solntse smotrit v binokl'/I prislushivayet-
sya/K orud'yam*][29] To this extent nature might seem dependent on
man, but really sun and moon are here because they impinge on the
awareness of actors in the human drama. Pasternak's imagination
looks out on the total scene. It stands on high, in the manner of
Pierre Bezukhov at the inception of Borodino.[30] And the final movement of the poem is away into space:

Простор
Открывался бежавшим героям

[Space
Opened before the heroes in flight]

– and as the weapons are laid out on white sheets for the surrender,
action comes to a close, and we are aware, as at the chapter's beginning, of the great distances beyond.[31]

Eisenstein said of *The Battleship Potemkin* that 'it looks like a
chronicle (or newsreel) of an event, but it functions as a drama', and
he went on to claim for his film 'a severely tragic composition',
falling into five acts.[32] Pasternak also styled his poem 'a chronicle',
in verse form; but, at any rate while the work was still in composition, he admitted that the 'fragments' he had so far done 'still
wanted an internal link'. At that stage he had written on the Potemkin mutiny (Chapter 4), Gapon and the Ninth of January (Chapter
2), and the December rising in Moscow (Chapter 6).[33] Each episode,
as the series developed, would be superbly controlled, and the same
kind of analysis that Eisenstein applied to the scene before the fusil-
lade on the Odessa steps (when the yawls go out to the battleship)[34]
could, in literary terms, be made of any sequence from *Nineteen
Five* and no less satisfactorily. Indeed, as a film scenario Pasternak's
poem would probably need little change, at least in its main episodes. He has achieved the able film director's command of varying
distances, with sudden sharp focus on telling detail. Thus, as the
procession of Bauman's funeral goes by:

С высоты одного,
Обеспамятев,
Бросился сольный
Женский альт.
Подхватили.
Когда же и он отрыдал,
Смолкло всё.
Стало слышно,

Как колет мороз колокольни.
Вихри сахарной пыли,
Свистя,
Пронеслись по рядам.³⁵

[From the height of one (balcony),
Losing all sense,
Flung itself in a solo
A woman's alto voice.
They caught it up.
When it ceased sobbing
There was total silence.
One could hear
How frost shivered the belfries.
Whirls of sugary dust,
Whistling,
Swept down the ranks.]

However, no such rigour of total design can be found in Pasternak's poem as Eisenstein claimed for his film. 'Here are individual scenes' [*Vot otdel'nye stseny*], he says at one point in the last chapter,[36] and it is a series of scenes that he has given, advancing on a strong rhythmic flow from the Ninth of January in St Petersburg to the December insurrection in Moscow. The course of the year 1905 itself provides the dynamic. Apart from establishing this pattern of a wave that spreads and towers and finally crashes down before ebbing away, the poem provides no dramatic nexus, no plot in the full sense, for its narrative. *Lieutenant Schmidt* was to be different, because the central role of Schmidt himself would find expression in tragic terms, and thereby Pasternak could engage directly with the revolution. In *Nineteen Five* he writes more under the influence of LEF which prescribed the rendering of fact, reportage. It is, nonetheless, reportage such as only a poet, and only one of Pasternak's inescapable bias, could have conceived.

The revolutionary year 1905 came when he was just turning fifteen.[37] After the encounter with Scriabin, it was probably the greatest experience of his boyhood, and even a lonely middle-class child, who spent the holidays at home improvising on the piano,[38] could share the national excitement, when the troubles reached Moscow and he felt the blow of a Cossack on his shoulder during a demonstration. And thus *Nineteen Five* in its second chapter, 'Childhood' ['*Detstvo*'], becomes part of that dispersed autobiography which Pasternak was to write, disguised in his fiction and explicitly in *Safe Conduct* and its successor of twenty-five years later. 'Childhood' is preceded by an introductory chapter, 'Fathers' ['*Ottsy*'], but here the traditional theme of fathers and children throws up no conflict between the generations. The personnel of these two chapters (excluding the Ninth of January episode which was inserted in the second) belong almost entirely to the intelligentsia: 'students in pince-nez' [*Studeny v pensne*], 'our mothers or the women friends of our mothers' [*Nashi materi/Ili/Priyatel'nitsy materey*],[39] and the boys of his Greek class at the Moscow Fifth *Gymnasium*.[40] In this way the events of 1905 relate to a datum point in his own memory, 'This happened in our time' [*Eto bylo pri nas*], the first chapter begins.[41]

The year which had seemingly gone without trace and 'turned into a nought between the nine and the five' [*Stal nulyom mezh devyatki s pyatyorkoy*[42]] first comes alive for Pasternak in Moscow. To Moscow in the autumn and winter it circles back. The insurrection of the Presnya workers won Moscow the right to stand as the scene of the poem's climax. It also allowed Pasternak to round off the chronicle within his own experience. He had not himself gone through the ten days of carnage in December, but all this happened in his own city, and at no distance from where he lived. Thus of the six chapters in the poem four are virtually part of his own life or what had led up to it, the time of 'the fathers'. Only two chapters deal with events he could not have witnessed. The third, 'Peasants and Factory Workers' ['*Muzhiki i fabrichnye*'] begins with a picture of landowners in flight from their burned out manor-houses, then shifts to Lodz in Congress Poland during its 'June days' of struggle between railway workers and troops. The fourth, 'Naval Mutiny' ['*Morskoy myatezh*'], is set in Sevastopol. To these must be added a section that belongs to the second chapter on Father Gapon and the Ninth of January massacre in St Petersburg. The Lodz and Sevastopol incidents took place at midsummer, which falls in with the design of the poem, so that, like the other alien episode of Gapon, they can be surrounded by the personal elements of the narrative. Pasternak's 'chronicle' thus lends itself easily to a lyrical treatment.

Apart from the Prologue, all six chapters of *Nineteen Five* are written in the same metre. Their regular stanzas consist of four anapaestic lines with five stresses each, and these lines are broken up into smaller units (two or more often three) on the page. The effect is of rapid and ceaseless advance, until the chapter draws to a measured close. The subtlety of the rhythm, and also this final quiescence, can be appreciated in the last stanza of 'Naval Mutiny':

107

День прошел.
На заре,
Облачась в дымовую завесу,
Крикнул в рупор матросам матрос:
– Выбирай якоря! –
Голос в облаке смолк.
Броненосец пошел на Одессу,
По суровому кряжу
Оранжевым крапом
Горя.[43]

[The day passed.
At sunset,
Arrayed[44] in a smoky curtain
He shouted through the megaphone, a sailor to the sailors:
'Anchors aweigh!'
The voice in the cloud fell silent.
The ironclad went to Odessa,
On its grim bulk
The orange flecks
Burning.]

The spacing of these lines is far from mechanical. It separates the units of meaning, and as always with Pasternak syntax is played against rhythm. There are two instances here where the normal triple division of a line has been waived, and in each more emphasis is gained by the sense. The first occasion marks an extraordinary event – the giving of an order to the seamen by one of their comrades – which also imparts a new and dramatic turn to the action: the battleship is set on a new course, to the last phase of the mutiny in Odessa. The clause stretches out to the brief command:

Крикнул в рупор матросам матрос:
– Выбирай якоря! –

[He shouted through the megaphone, a sailor to the sailors:
'Anchors aweigh!']

In the second example, the unbroken sentence mirrors the direct course of the ship:

Броненосец пошел на Одессу,

[The ironclad went to Odessa.]

Then, in the final three segments, it seems to die away in the sunset, to the single word 'burning'. The *Potemkin* had the previous evening been touched prophetically by this orange light, but then it no more than 'speckled' the hull – *Oranzhevym krapom/ryabya.* Now, at the finish of the episode, the warship fades away; but the glare of its revolutionary ardour persists.

The metre chosen by Pasternak is well suited for gathering up a host of miscellaneous objects – names, impressions, memories, as in

> Это – народовольцы,
> Перовская,
> Первое марта,
> Нигилисты в поддевках,
> Застенки,
> Студенты в пенсне.[45]

> [It is the members of People's Will,
> Perovskaya,
> The First of March,
> Nihilists in close-fitting tunics,
> Torture chambers,
> Students in pince-nez.]

Sinyavsky quotes in his discussion of *Nineteen Five*, to illustrate 'how heterogeneous objects and ideas are brought under one and the same signification [*pod edinyy priznak*]',[46] a few lines from the third chapter:

> Снег лежит на ветвях,
> В проводах,
> В разветвлениях партий,
> На кокардах драгун
> И на шпалах железных дорог.[47]

> [Snow lies upon boughs,
> Upon wires,
> Upon branches of parties,
> On the cockades of dragoons,
> And on sleepers of railroads.]

This is an important device in the poem, and it reveals, in keeping with the earlier lyric poetry, Pasternak's synthesising imagination at work. Here rhythm and syntax once more carry the burden. The flowing and capacious rhythm draws into itself and subdues all the confused variety of the revolutionary year. The resultant poem is impetuous in its forward sweep almost after the fashion of Shelley's 'Ode to the West Wind' – a work that Pasternak admired, and afterwards translated.[48] *Nineteen Five* differs from 'The West Wind' in scale, in metre, and in substantiality; it takes along with it a much greater mass of accurately observed detail; it achieves at its finest a breadth of view and a precision that recall Tolstoy. All the same, the tone, the pathos of the poem connect it firmly with the revolutionary rapture of the previous century. Its derivation is not from Ryleev or the civic line in Russian poetry which continued with Mayakovsky. Somewhere at the origins of *Nineteen Five* are Shelley and Swinburne. To make this observation is not to detract from its success in the mode Pasternak had adopted. 'These days are like a diary', he says [*Eti dni, kak dnevnik*[49]]. Because of his lyrical presence throughout the poem, it reads often like the diary of that spontaneous but self-critical artist – so she appears in the Prologue – the 1905 revolution herself.

IV

When *Lieutenant Schmidt*, the successor to *Nineteen Five*, is considered, Pasternak appears to have both gained ground and lost it. *Lieutenant Schmidt* has a plot, the absence of which in Pasternak's prose and verse narrative alike had often troubled the critics. This plot can be followed, though with occasional difficulty as to the details, in the text published by the Michigan and the 1965 Soviet editions.[50] As originally serialised in 1926 and early 1927 it was fuller and clearer, and there were titles given to the sections or 'chapters'. Pasternak had found in an episode of November 1905 which he did not use for his previous poem the most satisfactory means at that time of projecting an attitude towards the revolution (1905 or 1917, it is all the same in essentials) which prepares for *Doctor Zhivago*. The sudden rise to prominence of a naval lieutenant, Pyotr Petrovich Schmidt, in the November mutiny at Sevastopol, his readiness to accept a burden which he had not sought and which he could not sustain, his heroic behaviour at the trial that followed and at his execution – already in this Pasternak had to hand the situation, so strong in its appeal for him, that is expressed by Yury Zhivago's poem 'Hamlet'.[51] After the completion of *Nineteen Five* it must have seemed that Schmidt's story would carry Pasternak much nearer to the goal of writing a genuine epic for the times. The 'chronicle' had become immediate through the recollection of his own schooldays and his proximity to the events in Moscow. Lieutenant Schmidt, natural orator and reluctant man of action, could be presented almost without disguise as the artist or at any rate the contemplative intellectual drawn into politics.

Thus far the obvious gain and the opportunity. Where Pasternak loses ground is in the handling of his poem. There are three parts corresponding to the three acts of a drama – one prepares for the main action, a second describes the mutiny and its debacle, the third Schmidt's trial and death. The stanzas and the line length do not remain regular. In a lyrical monodrama like Tennyson's *Maud*, which expresses one character's shifting and unstable emotions, such variety makes for no disorder. It would be too strong a criticism of *Lieutenant Schmidt* that the poem is chaotic. A narrative line emerges; the transitions, however abrupt, are musically right. Pasternak's procedure follows that used so effectively in his lyrical sequence 'The Break';[52] but in this poem the scale has to be much larger, and the passages often bring a sudden shift of focus which at least momentarily can perplex. There are blocks of description like the opening scene at the Kiev trotting races; brief dramatic episodes like those in Schmidt's apartment before he decides to lead the mutiny; letters to his sister and to his confidante; narrative passages; and Schmidt's speech at the trial, an impassioned lyric in quatrains (based on his actual words to the court). It is clear enough what the poem gains in economy and directness; and the modulations are skilful. Yet its lyrical impulse conflicts with the epic intention. The diversity of form is also inappropriate.

Pasternak could not solve satisfactorily this problem of bringing together public and private interests until he wrote *Doctor Zhivago*. To do so required a long adjustment to the perspective that first showed in *Lieutenant Schmidt*. The poem took him farther in the direction he wanted to go than any previous work. But it suffers from the strain of trying on the one hand to celebrate the revolution and on the other to give a central importance to the dilemma of Schmidt, for which responsibility lies with 'the blind whim of chance' [*sluchaya slepoy kapriz*[53]]. Schmidt explains to his judges that he was 'singled out from the ranks / By the elemental wave itself' [*iz ryada vydelen / Volnoy samoy· stikhii*[54]], and earlier it is stated that the silence and loneliness that surround Schmidt while he writes to his confidante will have to accept the choice of this hero for want of a better [*Za neimen'em luchshego / On ey v geroi prochitsya*[55]].

Lieutenant Schmidt reveals its author's inability to think and feel as a proletarian would. Probably anyone who has grown up in the middle classes will find himself debarred from making in any real sense such an identification. He can like Lenin read the expression of the people; or again like Mayakovsky simulate their tones and attitudes, confused by him too often with the brutality of the mob. Pasternak chose to depict in Schmidt a man who was far removed from working-class life. As the sailor visiting him reflects, 'Schmidt has a nice place' [*Khorosho u Shmidta*[56]] with his *portières* and books. Marina Tsvetaeva (to whom the work was dedicated secretly in an acrostic poem[57]) found him altogether too much the intellectual

– 'an inspired student from the end of the nineties' and not a seaman at all. In the letter of 1926 conveying this comment she says that Schmidt reminds her of Blok: 'The same awkwardness in his joking, the same mirthlessness in it.' And also of Chekhov to whose facetious tone she had taken a dislike from childhood. She makes here the point that the elemental is what most inspires in Pasternak's treatment: 'The poem sweeps past Schmidt, he is a brake.'[58] Her essay 'Art in the Light of Conscience' ['*Iskusstvo pri svete sovesti*'] elaborates this view:

Boris Pasternak in utter purity of heart, having surrounded himself with all the materials, writes, copies from life – even to its blunders – Lieutenant Schmidt, while his principal character is the trees at the meeting.[59] Above Pasternak's square they are the leaders. Whatever Pasternak writes – it is always the elements, and not the people, as in 'Potemkin' the *sea* and not the sailors.[60]

Her reference to the 'blunders' [*oploshnosti*] recalls what Henry James said in his preface to *The Spoils of Poynton*: 'I saw clumsy Life again at her stupid work.'[61] It was Schmidt's letters that she particularly resented: 'I am convinced that the letters are almost word for word, they are so unlike yours. You have given a human Schmidt, in the weakness of nature, touching but so hopeless.'[62] Two of the letters, one that describes how earlier he lost some money which belonged to his ship, the other boasting that he had become famous as the delegate of the Sevastopol workers, were both dropped from the poem: Tsvetaeva had written scathingly of the first 'Only a document could be so improbable.'[63] It is, of course, mainly in the letters that Pasternak develops the private side of his narrative, and Tsvetaeva exposes the weakness that results. Clough in his poem *Amours de Voyage* had been able to mediate historical events wholly through letters. But his detached and sceptical hero who describes the agony of the Roman Republic in 1849 is a more interesting correspondent than Schmidt, and one who can allow Clough to use all the resources of his own style. Pasternak has to be documentary – it was almost inescapable for the 'epic' poem at that time – and Schmidt, though not unlike Pasternak in his political stance, was no poet. Clough could relate a chapter of history entirely through the impressions of an individual onlooker:

> I, who avoided it all, am fated, it seems, to describe it.
> I, who nor meddle nor make in politics.[64]

But Pasternak seeks also to describe the Sevastopol rising at times impersonally; and the outcome gives the impression of wavering

between epic and novel. In Part Three, for example, the second
section describes a journey by mail train which a woman is making.
Her identity is disclosed after fourteen lines: 'You have guessed
who she is: his correspondent' [*Vy dogadalis', kto ona. - Ego
korrespondentka*[65]]. Later he refers to the 'tale' [*povest'*[66]]. His
exclamation that the prison island of Ochakov has been 'rendered
freshly in Dante' [*kak svezho Ochakov dan u Danta!*[67]] is followed
by a passage relating the woman's thoughts which belongs wholly
to the nineteenth-century novel. The interview she then has with the
commandant (in the same section) seems distantly to recall that of
Nekhlyudov in Tolstoy's *Resurrection* with the old general,[68] and
the description of Schmidt's trial (III, 7) again suggests the same
novel. The affinities are a matter of tone – the implied senselessness:
while the reading in court goes on and on 'without end or pauses'
[*bez kontsa i pauz*] we are informed that a similar occasion, with the
roles reversed, awaits the judges. Inevitably Pasternak with his life-
long enthusiasm for Tolstoy would have been reminded of *Resurrection* when he came to the prison scenes. Nor is there any reason
why Tolstoy's example should not have been appropriate for an
'epic' poem. But the main interest in *Resurrection* is a private one,
the moral dilemma of Nekhlyudov wishing to make amends to the
prostitute Maslova whom he had originally seduced. So too the
main interest in *Lieutenant Schmidt* centres on the predicament of
Schmidt himself.

He is a victim of his age, and so, he tells his accusers, are they
[*Vy tozhe: zhertva veka*[69]]. 'Like you, I am part of the great/
displacement of periods' [*Kak vy, ya – chast' velikogo/Peremesh-
chen'ya srokov*[70]]. Schmidt recognises that it is for him 'to end in
Golgotha',[71] or as he has written to his confidante: 'I have lived and
yielded up/My spirit for my friends' [*Ya zhil i otdal/Dushu svoyu
za drugi svoya*[72]]. The archaic form of the last phrase underlines the
scriptural reference: 'Greater love hath no man.'[73] His final words
in the courtroom are an ecstatic affirmation of the meaning his life
has acquired through sacrifice:

«Не встать со всею родиной
Мне было б тяжелее,
И о дороге пройденной
Теперь не сожалею.

Поставленный у пропасти
Слепою властью буквы,
Я не узнаю робости,
И не смутится дух мой.

Я знаю, что столб, у которого
Я стану, будет гранью
Двух разных эпох истории,
И радуюсь избранью».[74]

[Not to rise with the whole motherland
Would be to me more grievous,
And for the road I have gone down
Now I feel no regret.

Set on the precipice edge
By the blind power of the letter,
I shall not recognise fear
And my spirit shall not be troubled.

I know that the pillar against which
I shall stand will be the boundary
Of two unlike epochs of history,
And I rejoice in my election.]

The elemental force to which he has willingly surrendered the chances of personal happiness is depicted, in the scene of the oath-taking (I, 4), as 'a whirlwind that tears away phrases/Like maples and elms' [*vikhr', obryvayushchiy frazy/Kak klyony i vyazy!*], so that 'only interjections' [*odni mezhdomet'ya*] are left.[75] The excitement of the sailors listening to Schmidt's harangue is such that 'it wants to live and breathes/Not by words, but by the utter loss of them' [*Ne slovami, – polnoy ikh utratoy/Khochet zhit' i dyshit ikh vostorg*[76]]. At this point the spoken word abdicates; but it returns with full power in Schmidt's address to the attentive courtroom. His 'election' to stand between two historical epochs was that of Pasternak and the generation to which he belonged. The new epoch is dominated by elemental chaos and by the inarticulate masses; but the individual who has lived through the earlier epoch must at the end remain alone with his conscience and speak in his own voice. Schmidt does not clearly understand the process of history: Pasternak in this poem still seems close to the response of Blok in *The Twelve*.

V

During the 1920s Pasternak also wrote his 'novel in verse', *Spektorsky*. The first parts of it were published before anything from *Nineteen Five*; the middle span follows *Lieutenant Schmidt*; the last two parts, which form its Epilogue, appeared in the year of his prose fiction, *A Tale* [*Povest'*, 1929], with which *Spektorsky* shares the hero and several characters more. In the first paragraph of *A Tale*

Pasternak states that the story, later to be developed both in prose and verse, had been with him for ten years. He explained elsewhere[77] in 1929 that it had become necessary to substitute prose for verse when taking up 'that part of the story which fell in the war years and the revolution'; and that he could then proceed to write the conclusion to his novel in verse. However, *A Tale*, although it begins and ends in the start of 1916, has little to say of the war years, and most of its action takes place in the summer of 1914 (whereas that of *Spektorsky* mainly happens at the close of 1912 and in the spring of 1913, with its Epilogue in 'the days of famine', 1919).[78] Accordingly, neither the novel in verse nor the prose tale stands in the same line of development as *Nineteen Five* and *Lieutenant Schmidt*. The original epigraph to *Spektorsky* consisted of three words from *The Bronze Horseman* – *Byli zdes' vorota* ['Here were the gates']. They were spoken by Evgeny, the distraught lover in Pushkin's poem, when he crosses the Neva after the flood and finds that Parasha's home has been swept away. Spektorsky in Pasternak's poem after the revolution comes upon a memento of the girl he had formerly loved. He is one among a group of writers entrusted with cataloguing and sorting out sequestered property. The revolution, like the Neva inundation of 1824, it is implied by the epigraph, left no more than the pitiful debris of that domestic comfort taken for granted in the earlier scenes of Pasternak's poem.

Spektorsky is a novel in verse. This means that its hero is descended from Eugene Onegin, and still recognisably belongs to his family; that he feels a similar detachment from the society in which he moves, and a similar closeness – though this may be undergoing rejection through irony – with his author. The hero of a modern novel in verse will bring to a focus his particular time, of which, in a sense more often than not ironic, he is the hero too. Pasternak, when he named his novel in verse after Spektorsky, accepted this tradition (just as later he did in naming his much more comprehensive novel in prose after Doctor Zhivago).[79] Seryozha Spektorsky is a writer, and certainly in *A Tale*, as we have noted,[80] his circumstances are not far removed from those of the young Pasternak. He could scarcely have been otherwise than he is, since the fictional characters that are central for Pasternak must see and think as a poet does. Through this sensibility of a youthful writer he made it his purpose 'to depict the sudden change in what lies before us [*perelom ochevidnosti*], to give a general composite picture of the time, the natural history of a way of life'.[81]

Spektorsky is much more the kind of poem we should have expected Pasternak to write in this decade than *Nineteen Five* or *Lieutenant Schmidt*. On his own testimony he had carried round its idea from the time of *Themes and Variations*. By developing it as a novel in verse he showed that there still seemed to him possibilities of finding a verse form which could reflect the age without recourse to an epic setting or to deliberately chosen public themes. There were some drawbacks to the form, as he had discovered by 1929 when, in the statement already quoted,[82] it seemed to him that the 'descriptions and formulations' needed for the war and the revolutionary periods were 'beyond the powers of verse'. This would suggest that he was dissatisfied with his earlier attempt in *The High Malady*; but there is little in *A Tale* to indicate how he could have coped better in prose, unless one or two passages of analysis (on the belief, for instance, of Natasha and her friends that the revolution was simply a play temporarily suspended, in which all would resume their parts[83]) may be taken as pointing to new opportunities. The verse form he chose, after a brief experiment with quatrains in the iambic tetrameter[84] and with a long anapaestic line again in quatrains,[85] represents a middle course between these two. He uses the five-beat iambic line arranged in quatrains, which also appears in the first two sections at the opening of *Lieutenant Schmidt*.[86] It is an extremely adaptable form, and better suited to a poem about the twentieth century than either the various combinations of the iambic tetrameter taken over by Blok for his poem *Retribution*, or the seven-line stanza of Pushkin's *Little House at Kolomna* [*Domik v Kolomne*, 1830]. Both these measures are too apt to insinuate Pushkin's tone. Pasternak in the 1920s wanted to avoid the inter-interventions of the poet himself in the work, which are so brilliantly exploited by Pushkin; and although *Spektorsky* begins with an account of its origins, when Pasternak was driven to find work in order to support his family –

Я бедствовал. У нас родился сын.
Ребячества пришлось на время бросить.[87]

[I was poor. We had had a son.
Childish things must be given up for a while.]

– very soon this Introduction turns into an apology for the kind of poem he has written. Pasternak meets Spektorsky at the end, but the purpose is not, as when Pushkin tells of his meetings with Onegin,[88] to dissociate himself in essential ways from his hero.

The verse form of *Spektorsky* is one that enables the poet to follow in Pushkin's tradition and to emulate (at times) his directness and clarity of statement, without falling into pastiche. The tone can be prosaic, or humorous, or lyrical; the verse is open to neat formulations –

А старший был мятежник, то есть деспот.[89]

[But the older was a rebel, that is a despot]

– and it can hold with elegance in the same quatrain two opposed styles, two modes of perception:

Едва вагона выгнутая дверь
Захлопнулась за сестриной персоной,
Действительность, как выспавшийся зверь,
Потягиваясь, поднялась спросонок.[90]

[Hardly had the carriage's curved door
Slammed behind the person of his sister
Than reality, like a brute that has had its sleep,
Stretched and got up only half-awake.]

A forerunner of Pasternak in the use of this verse form had been Blok, from the first of whose 'Dances of Death' ['*Plyaski smerti*'][91] Pasternak could well have derived the tone in a passage describing the Balz household:

И увидала: полукруглый стол,
Цветы и фрукты, и мужчин и женщин,
И обреченья общий ореол,
И девушку с прической à la Ченчи.[92]

[And she saw a semicircular table,
Flowers and fruit, and men and women,
And a common aura of doom,
And a girl with hair done à la Cenci.]

Spektorsky shows little respect for its hero, 'a man of no merits' [*chelovek bez zaslug*] as he is called in the Introduction;[93] and elsewhere the poem acknowledges that the day of the bourgeois individual is gone. It says of the group going to their winter retreat in pre-war days: 'Personalities are simply not in question' [*O lichnostyakh ne mozhet byt' i rechi*[94]]. Looking round at the ravaged and starving Moscow of the civil war period, the poet asks his reader:

Неужто жив в охвате той картины,
Он верит в быль отдельного лица?

[Does he surviving in a picture on that scale
Believe in the reality of the individual person?]

117

Poetry is called upon 'not to give up the broad view' [*ne postupaysya shir'yu*]; it should retain a 'living accuracy' that is concerned with 'mysteries' – the movements of history, one infers, rather than irrelevant details, 'every dot on the line':

> Храни живую точность: точность тайн.
> Не занимайся точками в пунктире. . .[95]

Spektorsky and his class are among 'the doomed', as we have learned already from the passage about Balz's household.[96] Yet the significance of Spektorsky, and his only significance, is that features of his story 'have illuminated marvellously one bit of the past' [*ozarili chast' ego na divo*[97]]. So what the poem has to offer is two contrasting scenes – before the flood and its aftermath. For the bourgeois individual, as eventually he sorts out to the advantage of another class the relics that remain from his former prosperity, it has become a bleak world indeed. Pasternak here, as in *The High Malady* five years earlier, writes of the period known as War Communism in altogether cheerless terms:

> Чужая даль. Чужой, чужой из труб
> По рвам и шляпам шлепающий дождик,
> И отчужденьем обращенный в дуб,
> Чужой, как мельник пушкинский, художник.[98]

> [Alien the distance. Alien, alien from conduits
> On ditches and hats the rain thudding,
> And by alienation turned into a block
> Alien, like Pushkin's miller, is the artist.[99]]

The story as told in the novel needs to be supplemented here and there from the prose *Tale* (about the Lemokh brothers, and Seryozha's sister). As a novel *Spektorsky* remains rather too lightly sketched in. Seryozha at the beginning has an affair with the wife of his friend Bukhteev (this is clearer from the original version). Then in Moscow he receives a visit from his sister, and at Balz's apartment he meets the woman poet Maria Ilina. (Various details, such as her subsequent fame in the emigration as a writer of epic, and the death of her father, a professor, in 1913, point to some resemblance with Marina Tsvetaeva.) She and Spektorsky fall in love, at a time when her house is undergoing repair – the disorder seems prophetic of what will follow in Russia itself. But Seryozha is called away by his mother's illness, and when he returns, Maria has gone. Years later, in 1919, he comes across this memento of her; and at the poet's flat he is brought up against Bukhteeva, now very close to the Party:

Она шутя обдернула револьвер
И в этом жесте выразилась вся.[100]

[She playfully adjusted the revolver
And in that gesture wholly declared herself.]

Her attitude to Spektorsky is still deeply maternal, but contempt is mingled with her kindliness and pity for him [*V prezren'i, v laske, v zhalosti*[101]].

In the manner of *Nineteen Five* the novel shapes itself as a collection of scenes, all rendered with a high finish; and the structure is rather musical than narrative, even though a story exists. The separate episodes, with their weather and their differences of pace and tone, correspond to the movements of a fairly elaborate orchestral work. It is a striking experiment in building a longer poem from lyrical and dramatic units, and in the end, as Pasternak had wanted, our interest is held not so much by Seryozha's fortunes as by 'the sudden change in what lies before us'. The true drama for Pasternak at this stage reveals itself not so much in action as in momentary perceptions that show what he had called in the poem *tochnost' tayn*, 'the exactitude of mysteries'.[102] These linger in the mind, and they seem to acquire a resonance beyond their moment:

Он долго в дверь стучался без успеха,
А позади, как бабочка в плену,
Безвыходно и пыльно билось эхо.[103]

[For a long time he knocked on the door without result,
And behind, like a butterfly held captive,
With no way out and dustily beat the echo.]

Spektorsky makes rueful admission that the individual no longer counts. But it is a novel in verse, and the poetry argues everywhere for the significance of the personal view, as it unfolds this record pieced together from unique observations, and ordered by the elusive intelligence:

Да, видно, жизнь проста. . . но чересчур.
И даже убедительна. . . но слишком.[104]

[Yes, clearly, life is simple. . .but in excess.
And even it convinces. . .but overmuch.]

8

'Safe Conduct', Rilke and Mayakovsky

I

For the autobiography he began to write at the end of the 1920s Pasternak took the enigmatic title *Safe Conduct* [*Okhrannaya gramota*]. A safe conduct guarantees the citizen protection from interference; and by 1929, when the first part of Pasternak's narrative appeared, the poets of Russia needed such protection. The next year Mayakovsky committed suicide. By 1931, when the second and third parts followed, both Pasternak's own life and that of his country had entered a new phase. His first marriage had broken up, and he faced problems as an artist: in the decade ahead of him it would become very difficult to retain an independent voice in literature. This was the time of collectivisation on the farms, of Stalin's growing authority, soon to be absolute, and of encroaching terror. The reader who recalls Zhivago's mysterious half-brother Evgraf, always ready to intervene in his hour of need, might suppose the title of the autobiography hints at similar protection from somebody who could do for Pasternak what Bukharin at one time did for Mandelstam. But *Safe Conduct* tells of dangers that were not directly political, and of a good genius that must be identified with the artist's own conscience, his instinct for self-preservation from the wrong forms of imaginative commitment.

Safe Conduct has an approximate counterpart in Mandelstam's autobiographical sketches, *The Noise of Time* [*Shum vremeni*] which precede it by several years, and are no less remarkable for their realisation in precise and vivid images of a poet's formative period. Yet Mandelstam's interest did not lie in the same quarter as Pasternak's. He describes his Jewish family in an alien St Petersburg that fascinated him; the school he attended; a particular teacher, V. V. Gippius; a particular friend and that friend's household; the ideology of himself and the boys he knew during the 1905 revolution. All these belong to a past he is putting away from him, and although what he depicts helped to create in Mandelstam the aloof and penetrating intelligence that shaped his poetry, he did not set out to relate 'the growth of a poet's mind'. Nor exactly in the Wordsworthian sense did Pasternak. Nothing is said here about a power that found him and saw to his spiritual development; nothing about a poetic mission for which covenant was made on his behalf; or about the visitations of glory in which he recognised his own being. It is not the growth of a poet's mind but its progress to the right orientation that Pasternak wants to explore. He produces the safe conduct that on three separate occasions guarded him from misadventure, and even from self-betrayal.

Two of these occasions have already been discussed.[1] The first part of Safe Conduct tells about Scriabin and Pasternak's renunciation of music; the second about Hermann Cohen and Pasternak's renunciation of philosophy, in order to write verse. ('Verses', he could imagine Cohen drawing the word out with scornful emphasis. Who ever believed in verses as a proper alternative to philosophy?[2]) In the third part Pasternak describes his idolising of Mayakovsky, and the resolution he soon formed to take not Mayakovsky's path but one deliberately opposed to it. Thus his autobiography is the record of three temptations successfully overcome, and each temptation was in its own hour necessary to Pasternak's self-definition. His perspective, however complicated the writing may be at times, is very simple, embracing one man's art and its problems. Pasternak excludes from Safe Conduct all that wealth of family portraiture and personal anecdote which the reader acquainted with Yeats' Autobiographies may feel cheated not to find.

I

The book is dedicated 'To the memory of Rainer Maria Rilke' who appears in its opening paragraph as a traveller in Russia 'on a hot summer morning of 1900'.[3] A few pages further on, Pasternak explains 'I am not presenting my recollections to the memory of Rilke. On the contrary, I received them myself from him as a gift.'[4] The argument leading up to this declaration turns on the familiar difficulty of writing a poet's life, which Pasternak sees as running along a different axis from 'the vertical one of biography'. What makes the poet unlike the hero whose life deserves to be narrated is that the most important things for him take place in 'the realm of the subconscious', and this 'does not submit to measurement'.

121

The real story of the poet is to be found in what his readers have gained from him – something of which he may not be aware. Here Pasternak expresses a thought that was central to the paper he read one evening in 1910, immediately before the summons came to accompany his father on a journey to Tolstoy's deathbed. He expresses it thus in a passage from the *Essay in Autobiography* describing that incident: 'although the artist is of course mortal like everyone else, the happiness of living that he experienced is immortal, and with a certain approximation to the personal and intimate form of his feelings it may be experienced by others, a century after him, in his works'.[5] So Rilke 'gave' Pasternak his memoirs by imparting to him a vision of the world, and enabling him to discover the poet he was to become.

Pasternak shared with Rilke the conviction that art is inescapably symbolic.[6] The nature of imaginative thinking, he held, is such that the images it employs are interchangeable, they are all equally aspects of the one reality. In this particular narrative the subject is the poetic vocation, and Pasternak can maintain reasonably enough: 'I am not writing my own biography.'[7] He is concerned with the one reality, in this context the art of poetry which Rilke practised with an unswerving devotion that inspired Pasternak.

Of Rilke he declared to Michel Aucouturier: 'I have always considered that in my original attempts, in all my artistic activity, I did nothing else but translate or vary his motifs.'[8] More than one critic has noted the correspondences in their thought. They had similar ideas about the impersonality needed by the artist;[9] believed alike in the transforming power of poetry;[10] and shared a 'conception of how inanimate nature yearns for the human to perfect it and preserve it'.[11] The two poems by Rilke which Pasternak translated for his *Essay in Autobiography*[12] show obvious affinities with his own work. In the first of these the poet, who has been totally absorbed in reading, is overtaken by nightfall; the world outside seems to have drawn very close to him: the power of feeling has domesticated the universe. (A star at the end of the village now resembles a light in its farthest house.) The second poem tells of wrestling with the angel in which the only real victory is to suffer defeat – much as Pasternak in one of Zhivago's poems was to proclaim that the only real victory for a Christian heart is to be overcome by 'trees, houses, stay-at-homes'.[13] There is a desire common to both Rilke and Pasternak for the poet's surrender to something greater than himself – a 'higher principle' [*vysshee nachalo*] as it is called in the Rilke translation.

Zhivago's insistence that life should be a dissolving of ourselves in others [*rastvoren'e/Nas samikh vo vsekh drugikh*[14]] recalls the Orpheus of Rilke's sonnets.[15] Both poets conceive of art as a transcendent reality. For Rilke, according to a journal entry made when he was still young, 'The artist is eternity projected into time.'[16] Half a century later Pasternak would address the artist thus: 'You are the hostage of eternity captive to time' [*Ty – vechnosti zalozhnik/U vremeni v plenu!*].[17]

Yet these convergences must not be allowed to blur the line of separation. One may conclude too easily that Pasternak and Rilke, poets who celebrate alike the artist's unique and wonder-working vision, stand together on everything. It is not so. Rilke, for instance, like the author of *Doctor Zhivago* wrote poems on episodes from the New Testament. His imagination may be termed, in much the same sense as Pasternak's, a religious one. But this did not prevent him from expressing in private what he acknowledged to be 'an almost rabid anti-Christianity'.[18] And not perhaps unrelated to that feeling are the discords within his nature which, needless to say, have no counterpart in Pasternak's. At no time did Pasternak hold the 'uncompromising belief that nothing has any real existence except in art',[19] or swing to the opposite extreme, as Rilke often would, of mistrusting the poetic vocation itself.[20] Nothing in his work corresponds to the absolutism of the *Duinese Elegies* which leaves Rilke alone with his genius, attentive to the angels while 'overleaping' humanity.[21] Rilke's self-absorption brings him closer to Shelley than to Pasternak. It is true that once Marina Tsvetaeva, infuriated by Pasternak's omission to visit his mother when passing through Germany in 1935, thought him as callous as Rilke whom she once compared with the sea, 'unloving, self-fulfilled'.[22] But neither Pasternak's poetry nor his life reveals an incapacity like Rilke's to escape from himself. On the contrary his work everywhere testifies to a generous and self-effacing temper, and in his personal relations he showed an eagerness to help others, at whatever risk, and an impatience to communicate.

III

Pasternak was overwhelmed to receive in 1926 a letter from Rilke. 'I should not have been more surprised to hear that they read me in heaven', he declared (in a reply to this letter composed when Rilke was already dead[23]). His sense that their destinies were linked in a mysterious way stayed with him throughout life. *Safe Conduct*, however, devotes far more space to another poet who had likewise overwhelmed him – Vladimir Mayakovsky.

It seems that anyway a prominent part in the narrative would have been assigned to Mayakovsky, but the shock of his suicide both for Pasternak personally and for Soviet writers in general made it impossible not to write at some length upon him. In Pasternak's view fate had picked out Mayakovsky to be the most talented poet of the Futurist generation.[24] This was, of course, the generation to which Pasternak himself belonged. The cutting off in his prime of their natural leader was something terrible, ominous and unforeseen. To Pasternak who had felt the full attraction of Mayakovsky's restless and dominating genius it was extraordinarily painful.

When they met in 1914 he was impressed to find a man playing a role like the other Futurists but determined to take it in deadly earnest.[25] Mayakovsky's histrionic challenge to the philistine world had a tragic intensity. His nature allowed him to do nothing by halves, and all the extravagant gestures of his poetry were carried over into his life. The day after their meeting Mayakovsky read to Pasternak a new poem. This was his monodrama entitled *Vladimir Mayakovsky*, sombre, grotesque, full of an ironic pathos, and in every way the ideal work with which to introduce himself to a young and impressionable fellow poet. Already he had found his distinctive voice of those days, not merely strident in the common Futurist manner, but bearing the weight of an appealing and complex personality. He was equally formidable and absurd. Pasternak instantly noted that Mayakovsky did not need any disguise (as Byron had needed to assume the mask of Manfred or Cain in his dramas). 'The poet was not the author but the subject of the lyric, which addressed the world in the first person. The title was not the writer's name, but the surname of the work.'[26] Mayakovsky on the stage reciting his monodrama and Mayakovsky when he stepped off were one and the same man. He made no retreat from his public personality. Hence Pasternak's name for this attitude (already familiar to the reader) 'the idea of biography as spectacle'.[27] He saw how such an attitude had created havoc in the lives of modern poets, and whereas Blok had managed to free himself from it, Esenin and Mayakovsky drove the idea to the very limits. By 1914 there was evidence enough in the lives of the nineteenth-century German romantics where such a commitment would end, but the eventual suicides of Esenin and Mayakovsky still lay eleven and sixteen years ahead. Pasternak knew that his own poetry at the beginning had a good deal in common with Mayakovsky's, and it could scarcely have been otherwise, given their participation in the same movement that sought to dislodge the Symbolists. However, Pasternak held out against becoming an involuntary imitator of Mayakovsky, and thus he 'renounced the romantic manner'.[28]

The cost of surrendering to the romantic manner is told in the final pages of *Safe Conduct* that describe the last year and abrupt suicide of Mayakovsky. Much later, in the *Essay in Autobiography*, Pasternak returned to the theme, enlarging upon the motives for Mayakovsky's action. 'It seems to me', he wrote then, 'that Mayakovsky shot himself from pride, because he condemned something in himself or around him to which his self-esteem could not be reconciled.'[29] It was possible in 1956 to indicate (however obliquely) that Mayakovsky could not endure any further the image of a Soviet poet which he had imposed on himself. But at the time of writing *Safe Conduct*, fresh from his initial grief at the suicide, and pained by the estrangement of recent years, Pasternak drew another moral. He presented the fate of Mayakovsky in tragic terms, with no more than a brief reference to the political disagreement between himself and Mayakovsky when the latter insisted on numbering him among the adherents of LEF. And it is in tragic terms that the life of Mayakovsky may well be seen. Pasternak in the *Essay in Autobiography* considers his suicide with that of four others – Esenin, Marina Tsvetaeva, the Georgian poet Paolo Yashvili, and Aleksandr Fadeev. Only the last of these must have felt the same dissatisfaction with a political role that Mayakovsky felt, and Fadeev had compromised in a way that was totally foreign to Mayakovsky. The tragic element in Mayakovsky's fate is not fully accounted for as the outcome of a political decision taken in good faith and persisted in when the grounds for it had been undermined. It was, even more than this decision, the romantic manner of forming it and staking his genius upon the outcome which destroyed Mayakovsky. His attitude to the revolution was in accord with the headlong self-dramatisation which had so greatly impressed Pasternak when first hearing him recite the monodrama *Vladimir Mayakovsky*. From the October Revolution until his death the spectacle that Mayakovsky made out of his biography was one in which he stood before the entire world as a militant Soviet poet. When he had to face the crisis which is inherent in the romantic manner, it was compounded by political crisis, and for Mayakovsky politics could not be detached from the personal life. There was no inner refuge. He must act out his tragedy to the finish, because without an audience he lacked identity.

IV

The appearance of *My Sister Life* freed Pasternak from doubts over the right course to pursue. He recognised that the book had been granted him by a power 'infinitely greater than myself and the ideas about poetry which surrounded me'.[30] He liked to conceive of art in this way as a natural force analogous to the notion of force in theoretical physics 'with the sole difference that it was a question not of the principle of the force, but of its voice, its presence...in the context of self-consciousness that force is called feeling'. He continues: 'Out of this theme [the theme of force] art is born. It is more one-sided than people think. It cannot be turned at will, like a telescope. Directed upon actuality which is being dislocated by feeling, art is the record of that dislocation.'[31] Such an irresistible force of feeling had assailed Pasternak on the return from Berlin to Marburg. Under its domination he recognised his need for poetry rather than philosophy. But it is in philosophical terms that he describes the state of feeling in which art is produced: 'We cease to recognise actuality. It appears in a new category. This category seems to us its own condition and not ours. Apart from this condition everything in the world has been named. The only unnamed and new thing is that. We try to name it. The result is art.'[32] In this way the experience of the artist becomes an outside reality, 'its own condition and not ours'. The artist has to name this new state of things which exists independently of himself.

Soon after leaving Marburg he discovered in Venice the 'syncretism' of great art: 'once the artist and the pictorial element have arrived at an identity, it becomes impossible to tell which of the three shows itself, and to whose advantage, as the most active on the canvas – the performer, what he has performed, or the subject of his performance'.[33]

Mayakovsky's play might be thought to have achieved this identity of writer, work and theme. As Pasternak had noted, here 'the poet was not the author but the subject'.[34] However, Mayakovsky's approach to art ruled out that impersonality which Pasternak himself practised, and without which for Mayakovsky art too easily became advertisement. The balance of the three elements in *Vladimir Mayakovsky* is less perfect by far than Pasternak's principle demands. In that play the most active force is Mayakovsky himself, who has appropriated the subject of his own life exactly as later he was to appropriate the October Revolution. So the question 'to whose advantage' – who or what gains most from the creation of his monodrama – can be answered simply. It is the poet, the personality on display: he has deliberately intensified the romantic manner, like Esenin; he has given himself to the excess of its rhetoric.[35] The native energy in his genius, that power of feeling which made the early poems so 'heavy, threatening, plaintive' (Pasternak's description of them in 1956[36]) was used for personal ends, to project the outraged and suffering antagonist of the Philistines. Mayakovsky 'selected the pose of an outward wholeness' [tsel'nost'].[37] By heroically exerting his will he tried to embody that ideal of so many writers in the nineteenth century, Turgenev, Tolstoy and Chernyshevsky among them: the 'whole man', perfectly fitted to realise his purposes. But Pasternak saw clearly a profound contradiction in Mayakovsky. His shamelessness hid an extreme sensitivity; his will had to contend with unexpected weakness. The notorious yellow blouse was put on not so much to disconcert the Philistines in their jackets, as to resist 'the black velvet of talent in himself'. It is a striking phrase, and recalls the line 'in the black velvet of the Soviet night' (v chornom barkhate sovetskoy nochi) from a famous poem written by Mandelstam ten years before.[38] The 'black velvet' of Mayakovsky's talent has not the connotations of 'worldwide emptiness' [vsemirnoy pustoty] that Mandelstam saw in the Soviet night. But it stands for something equally inexorable.

Mayakovsky's will, then, for all its tenacity was a sham. Pasternak read in his character suspicion, the failure of will. It seemed to him that Mayakovsky recognised the banality in all this passion, which was like sexual energy 'adequate to prolong the race, for art inadequate'. The passion that has to prolong an image must resemble the Passion that is celebrated in the New Testament.[39] Thus Pasternak despite his scientific analogies insisted upon the religious nature of art, in whose service is perfect freedom, without that strained exercise of the will to cover an essential lack of will that was so fatal to Mayakovsky.

V

These ideas about an opposing talent and its self-destruction may not have formed wholly in Pasternak's mind when, soon after the

shock of the disaster, he made his first response in a poem. This was
entitled 'Death of a Poet' ['*Smert' poeta*'] and it seems to derive in
some part from Rilke's poem 'Der Tod des Dichters'.[40] This is
shown in the presentation of Mayakovsky on his deathbed:

> Ты спал, постлав постель на сплетне,
> Спал и, оттрепетав, был тих, –
> Красивый, двадцатидвухлетний,
> Как предсказал твой тетраптих.[41]

[You slept having made your bed on scandal,
Slept and, all quivering done, lay still –
Handsome and twenty-two years old,
As it was foretold in your tetraptych.]

From the serenity of an image like Rilke's –

> Er lag. Sein aufgestelltes Antlitz war
> bleich und verweigernd in den steilen Kissen

[He lay. His propped up countenance was
Pale and recusant among the steep pillows]

– these lines move rapidly to the turbulent life of Mayakovsky and
here, as in the corresponding passage from *Safe Conduct*, Pasternak
quotes from *A Cloud in Trousers* [*Oblako v shtanakh*, 1915], the
defiant 'tetraptych' of Mayakovsky's youth.

> Ты спал, прижав к подушке щеку,
> Спал – со всех ног, со всех лодыг
> Врезаясь вновь и вновь с наскоку
> В разряд преданий молодых.
> Ты в них врезался тем заметней,
> Что их одним прыжком достиг.
> Твой выстрел был подобен Этне
> В предгорьи трусов и трусих.[42]

[You slept, pressing to the pillow your cheek,
Slept – with all the might of legs and anklebones
Striking through again and again headlong
Into the rank of youthful legends.
You struck through into them the more noticeably
Because by a single leap you attained them.
That shot of yours was like an Etna
Among the foothills of craven men and women.]

With the mention of 'craven men and women' Rilke gives way to
the world in which Pasternak was living. The final couplet[43] is more
memorable than anything else in the poem; it stands as a detachable
epitaph, and those two lines bring out more strongly the significance
of Pasternak's title for his autobiography.

A year later the third and last part of *Safe Conduct* was published. At the conclusion it turned to the affinities between Mayakovsky and the new Soviet state:

And then still of my own accord I reflected that this man was really perhaps the unique citizen for these civic rights. He indeed had the newness of the time climatically in his blood. Altogether he was strange with the strangeness of an epoch only as yet half realised. I began to recall traits of his character, his independence in many ways quite singular. These could all be explained by his having grown familiar with conditions which though implicit in our times had still not acquired the force of contemporaneity. From his childhood he had been the spoilt darling of the future, which was granted to him early enough and it would seem effortlessly.[44]

The tribute would have pleased Mayakovsky. But it cannot have satisfied Pasternak as being the last word on the subject, or he would not have come back to Mayakovsky's suicide in the second autobiography of 1956. It was true enough in 1931 that the 'strangeness' of the epoch had only begun to reveal itself; true also that Mayakovsky's obsession with the future did express though in hyperbolic form the driving force of the new society. But when Pasternak called Mayakovsky 'strange' he cannot have forgotten how over the years it had become impossible for them to understand each other. The paragraph has an evasive note which at the time of writing may not have been obvious to Pasternak. How exactly had Mayakovsky grown familiar with the conditions that were later to destroy him? Or had he already sensed the approaching horror? Was not his thrusting into the future with a single leap [*odnim pryzhkom*] as the earlier poem put it really an escape from the present that had become unbearable to him? In the penultimate paragraph reference was made to 'our state driving its way into the centuries and for ever accepted among them, our state without precedent and beyond possibility [*nebyvaloe, nevozmozhnoe gosudarstvo*]'.[45] The sentence harks back to the achievement of Peter the Great who also did unprecedented and seemingly impossible things. One way of accepting Soviet reality was to conceive it as a repetition of Peter's irresistible triumph. There are echoes here of the famous image used by Gogol for the advance of Russia when he compared his country to a troika at full gallop.[46] For Pasternak in this passage as for Gogol the spectacle of the Russian state is apocalyptic and awe-inspiring. At the time he could still content himself with an abstract rhetoric to provide the historical dimension for his thought.

And yet in Pasternak's occasional verse of the time there exist two poems that may be read as glosses on this account of Mayakovsky.

129

PASTERNAK

Both were written in 1931. The first, entitled 'To a Friend' ['*Drugu*'], came out in the fourth (April) number of *Novy Mir* exactly a year after the suicide. In its final stanza it takes cognisance of the difficulties facing Mayakovsky and other poets, although the general bearing of the poem is on a problem more particularly Pasternak's: how to reconcile his conception of the poet as a privileged being with the demands of an egalitarian society.

Иль я не знаю, что, в потемки тычась,
Во век не вышла б к свету темнота,
И я – урод, и счастье сотен тысяч
Не ближе мне пустого счастья ста?

И разве я не мерюсь пятилеткой,
Не падаю, не подымаюсь с ней?
Но как мне быть с моей грудною клеткой
И с тем, что всякой косности косней?

Напрасно в дни великого совета,
Где высшей страсти отданы места,
Оставлена вакансия поэта:
Она опасна, если не пуста.[47]

[Or don't I know that blundering into darkness
Ignorance would never have come to the light,
And am I a monster, and is happiness of hundreds of thousands
Not closer to me than the empty happiness of a hundred?

And don't I take my measure from the Five Year Plan,
Falling and rising with it?
But how could I manage with my thorax
And with what is more stagnant than any stagnation?

In vain on days of the great Soviet
Where the highest passion has places reserved
Is a vacancy kept for the poet:
It is perilous unless unfilled.]

'What is more stagnant than any stagnation' could be the whole milieu of official poetry, in which Pasternak's thorax could not breathe. The poet's one safety is to decline the seat that has been vainly offered – vainly, because poetry and state policy (though each, it may here be implied, should respect the other) have nothing in common.

The second poem was not published until 1932.

О, знал бы я, что так бывает,
Когда пускался на дебют,
Что строчки с кровью – убивают,
Нахлынут горлом и убьют!

От шуток с этой подоплёкой
Я б отказался наотрез.
Начало было так далеко,
Так робок первый интерес.

Но старость – это Рим, который
Взамен турусов и колёс
Не читки требует с актёра,
А полной гибели всерьёз.

Когда строку диктует чувство,
Оно на сцену шлёт раба,
И тут кончается искусство,
И дышат почва и судьба.[48]

[O had I known how it is
When I started on my debut,
That lines with blood kill,
Will rise in the throat and kill.

From jokes with that actuality behind them
I'd have turned away in blank refusal.
The beginning was so distant,
So timid the first interest.

But age is like Rome, which
Instead of silly nonsense
Demands not a reading from the actor
But total ruin in earnest.

When feeling dictates the line
On to the stage it sends its slave,
And here is the ending of art
And a breath of soil and destiny.]

In *Safe Conduct* Pasternak had spoken of renouncing the false conception that was to ruin Mayakovsky. At the time this need became clear to him such a conception 'did not presuppose heroism and still did not smell of blood',[49] though long before 1930 the situation had begun to grow threatening. Mayakovsky, as Pasternak saw him, was an actor who played out his role in earnest. Thus he foreshadows Hamlet in Zhivago's poem of that name.[50] But Hamlet is made to fulfil the part that had been written for him. Mayakovsky insisted on writing it himself to his own destruction.

VI

Nonetheless the note pervading Pasternak's first autobiography is one of celebration. He dedicated it after all to the memory of Rilke whom Marina Tsvetaeva once described as being 'not a poet but *poetry itself*,[51] and similarly the real hero of *Safe Conduct* is not the individual poet Boris Pasternak but poetry itself, which displays its character and power almost on every page. Both the autobiographical works resemble *Doctor Zhivago* in testifying to the inseparability of the poetic sense from their principal figure. In all three the progress of a poet, Pasternak or his fictional counterpart, is described; in all three the endowment of poetry manifests itself on many occasions. What he chooses to depict as well as to analyse in *Safe Conduct* is the imaginative process itself, the heightened sensation of critical moments in his life that brought him to a closer understanding of the gift he must use. When he re-creates a moment such as that of his interview with Scriabin it is the impression of enhanced spiritual activity he wishes to convey. For this every detail counts – the smoke of Scriabin's cigar, 'striated like a tortoise-shell comb', the 'circling of dazzled air, of waffles steaming away, of sugar that smoked and silver burning like paper', all of which added to his unbearable alarm, and then outside, after the verdict, the 'first current of cool air from the street', and the awareness of 'houses and distances'.[52] In this Pasternak is like Wordsworth: he dwells on every circumstance (and far more minutely and elaborately than Wordsworth ever did) which makes the setting for personal crisis. But unlike Wordsworth he was not overwhelmed by the sense of personal identity. In a manner that has become familiar from his verse he can occupy the centre of *Safe Conduct* and yet his figure casts no shadow. It is not substantially there, and only becomes visible at those points where there is a meeting in some form between himself and his poetic destiny. *Safe Conduct* belongs to the rarest kind of autobiographical writing, which is truly disinterested and deals with living ideas and the mind's allegiance to them. It was necessary for Pasternak to write such a book at this time so that he could explain to himself and to others the bias and potentialities of his poetry. It also gave him an indication of the most favourable place of entry into an eventual large-scale prose narrative. When he came to present the history of his time it would have to be approached from this angle. He would need to show the intimate connection between the spiritual health of Soviet society and the possibilities of survival for a poet.

9
'Second Birth' and Georgia

I

Second Birth was the title Pasternak gave to his next volume of poetry [*Vtoroe rozhdenie*, 1932]. The notion of second birth cannot be altogether separated from the experience of discovering Georgia, whose poets and their civilisation he came to know soon after the break-up of his first marriage. He went there in 1931, and again two years later with a 'brigade' from the Union of Soviet Writers. About Georgia and its significance for Pasternak I shall have something to remark below. The immediate question is why second birth had become a necessity.

The death of Mayakovsky may not have closed an era but indubitably it prefigured the close. Early in that era Pasternak had once or twice written verse that was acceptable to Mayakovsky's organisation LEF. He had tried to keep in touch with Soviet literature when he composed his narrative poems *Nineteen Five* and *Lieutenant Schmidt*. These were partial successes, both in themselves and as evidence that he had become a poet responsive to social concerns. However, the Pasternak whom his own percipient circle of admirers cherished was the independent creator of *My Sister Life* and *Themes and Variations*. These belonged to his youth, and at the end of this decade he had turned forty. There are signs, to be discussed later, that already he was beginning to feel the dissatisfaction with his earlier work which would eventually lead him to speak ill of it. The real second birth for Pasternak's poetry came at the beginning of the 1940s, with the Second World War and a more or less profound change in his personal beliefs, when he took a renewed interest in Christianity. But that reforming of his poetry had to follow a re-creation of the man. This was the second birth that befell him in the new decade – a time far more menacing for poets than any that had gone before, and one in which Pasternak was driven increasingly to translation, both as a livelihood and a means of keeping his hand in. There was little scope for his own verse. By 1936 he had settled down at Peredelkino, the writers' village near Moscow, had remarried, and was able to support himself with some degree of comfort and tranquillity as a translator. In that exceedingly dangerous epoch he escaped arrest, though speaking with exemplary courage at various writers' meetings.

As Eliot has made clear, second birth would seem to be the necessary condition for a poet's survival in middle age. Eliot was speaking of Yeats who when 'close on forty-nine' had at last discovered the voice of his maturity. The point is that 'towards middle age a man has three choices: to stop writing altogether, to repeat himself with perhaps an increasing skill of virtuosity, or by taking thought to adapt himself to middle age and find a different way of working'.[1] Pasternak, of course, had to adapt himself not only to middle age. Eliot says in the same essay that 'a man who is capable of experience finds himself in a different world in every decade of his life'.[2] Even those who were not 'capable of experience' had it thrust upon them in the Soviet Union as the new decade went on. But the strains of that time were made more tolerable for Pasternak by two related experiences – his passion for Zinaida Neuhaus who became his second wife (and the subject of some incomparable lyrics in this volume); and the revelation of Georgia.

II

There is a long history of encounter between Russian writers and the Caucasus. Pushkin, Lermontov and Tolstoy had found there primitive peoples and the natural beauty of its mountains. By the twentieth century intimations of Rousseau had begun to fade from that scene. Mandelstam in the early 1920s responded to the civilisation of Georgia, as later to that of Armenia, because they were ancient Christian kingdoms on classic soil, Colchis, land of the Golden Fleece. He wrote in an essay of 1922 after his first visit: 'The Georgians preserve wine in long, narrow jars and bury them in the earth. Here is the prototype of Georgian culture – the earth preserves the narrow but noble forms of an artistic tradition, it has sealed up a vessel full of ferment and aroma.'[3] Pasternak cared less than Mandelstam did about the 'Mediterranean' character of this civilisation, its tenuous link with the Hellenic past.[4] But he responded keenly to the 'ferment and aroma' he encountered in

Tiflis. Before going to Georgia he had met in 1930 the poet Paolo Yashvili, then on a visit to Moscow. Through Yashvili he met other Georgian poets when he arrived in Tiflis, and notably Titsian Tabidze. These two men in particular became his very close friends, and long after Tabidze's death Pasternak still remained on terms of confidentiality with his widow.

The Georgian poets and artists were congenial to him because they inhabited an imaginative world he knew. Like Pasternak himself they moved with the same freedom both in Russian and Western literature. Tabidze while still at the high school in Kutaisi (which Mayakovsky attended with him) had already published his own translations of contemporary Russian poets, among them Blok, Bryusov, Sologub and Annensky.[5] These (the latter two certainly) were an advanced choice for a schoolboy to make. The poetic group to which Tabidze and Yashvili belonged was known as the 'Blue Horns [*Golubye rogi* in Russian] after the drinking-horns characteristic of Georgian life, blue because this was a romantic colour – as in Wallace Stevens's 'Man with the Blue Guitar'.[6] In 1929 Tabidze wrote to Andrey Bely that all their poetic generation in Georgia had passed through Blok and through him: 'As though after you we had been born a second time for poetry.'[7] Nikolay Tikhonov spoke later of the Georgian experience as a turning-point in Pasternak's art.[8] It was so because these poets in a foreign tongue had shared in his own education and virtually restored him to his happier and freer self.

Although the year 1937 would claim both Tabidze and Yashvili among its victims, Georgia at the time Pasternak first visited it retained more of the spirit that he had known in Russia during the early twenties. He discovered there, as the *Essay in Autobiography* tells, much to refresh and excite him:

> Then the Caucasus, Georgia, individual people there, its popular life appeared to me as a complete revelation... The symbolism of folk traditions, full of mysticism and Messianic feeling, that disposed towards the life of imagination and as in Catholic Poland made every man a poet. The high culture of the progressive element in society, an intellectual life to a degree rare in those days.[9]

Mandelstam's essay quoted above maintains that Georgia had never been robbed of its national culture: 'Russification of the region never went beyond the forms of administrative life.'[10] At any rate the Georgians could meet fellow poets from Russia on a complete equality. Tabidze had no reluctance to tell Andrey Bely: 'The greatness of Russian poetry overshadows us, the tremor of which we felt as soon as we felt life.'[11] The tribute is unembarrassed, and certainly it does not suggest anything like a colonial dependence. Tabidze, Yashvili, Leonidze, Chikovani were writers with whom Pasternak could associate under no shadow of restraint. He wrote after his first visit to Yashvili: 'This city [Tiflis]...will be for me what Chopin, Scriabin, Marburg, Venice and Rilke have been – one of the chapters of *Safe Conduct* lasting for me all my life.'[12] Again in 1951 he repeated the same thought to Nina Tabidze, asking himself what had been most important in 'the book' of his life: 'The example of my father's work, love for music and A. N. Scriabin, two or three new notes in my art, the Russian night in the country, the revolution, Georgia.'[13] It was his immediate sympathy with these poets that made Pasternak such a good translator of Georgian verse. Without their free-flowing gaiety and eloquence, their inspired realisation of themselves, he would have found the new decade almost entirely discouraging. His words in a message of greeting sent to celebrate fifteen years of Soviet power in Georgia ring true despite the official occasion. Georgia, he said, 'has become a second homeland to me'.[14]

III

The Waves [*Volny*] stands as a prelude to *Second Birth* – a prelude, Sinyavsky has noted, that becomes its own theme.[15] In this lyric sequence Pasternak takes account of his position, both personal and social; he considers the past and the future; and finally prepares for the return to Moscow. There are many differences between this poem with its setting on the Black Sea and *Le cimetière marin*, yet as at the end it records the growing force of the sea wind [*Rastyot i krepnet vetra natisk*] one is reminded of Valéry's final exhortation:

Le vent se lève!...il faut tenter de vivre!

Le cimetière marin holds a more important place in its author's work than *The Waves* in that of Pasternak. Even so the latter must be reckoned a major statement, and it marks the opening of a new phase in his art. He has been able to bring together all his preoccupations and give them a single focus in a way that had not been possible for him since *My Sister Life*, in which the public world was mediated however obliquely through the personal. After *The Waves* he would no longer attempt to write verse narrative on public themes: these had been handed over to the project of his novel that became *Doctor Zhivago*. What must be noted in the poem is a new attitude towards the poetic self, the 'I' of his writing. Previously, as in 'Marburg' or again in 'The Break', though feeling had been strongly evident, it was the feeling of an immediate shock, an overpowering sensation that must be recorded as it occurs in all its intensity of anguish. But *The Waves* is not confined to the present. It looks forward and back. The opening stanza does what Pasternak's poetry had seldom done before, at least in lyric form – it enters the process of time, with all the moral consequences of living beyond the moment. Turning to the future it recognises that the future will also contain the past:

> Здесь будет всё: пережитое
> И то, чем я еще живу,
> Мои стремленья и устои,
> И виденное наяву.[16]

[Here shall be all: what has been lived through
And that by which I live yet,
My aspirations and principles,
And what has been seen in reality.]

The waves run endlessly towards him: they are his actions [*postupki*], 'the crests of experience' [*izpytannogo grebeshki*], and they bear on them the foam of change. This vision of experience moving in 'like as the waves make towards the pebbled shore' is mirrored variously: in the image of Daghestan rolling its mountain peaks towards the travellers [*On k nam katil svoi vershiny*[17]], and in the masses of Russian serfs, veterans and exiles flooding into the Caucasus a century before, 'generation by generation, step by step' [*Za rodom rod, za shagom shag*[18]]. The entire poem is penetrated by the sense of time and of journeying through time. Appropriately it returns at the conclusion to the sea with its breakers, and beyond them the horizon.

This awareness of time and the coming winter, of past mistakes and future trials, has imparted its own timbre to the poem. Pasternak writes in quatrains, nine-syllable lines alternating with eight; and henceforward the bulk of his poetry adopts the quatrain form, with slight variations. The measure here is one that Pushkin often used, though not generally in quatrains, and to a large extent Tyutchev used it also. It was taken up by Blok at a changing-point in his career (*Yamby*, 1907–14). Thus its main associations are with the classical past, and with a poetry that seeks definition and simplicity. Pasternak had occasionally employed it; indeed, his very

137

earliest pieces, 'The Station' and 'Venice', were put into stanzas identical with those of *The Waves*. However, once this form preponderates, it comes to alter the tone of his poetry in a significant way. Pasternak when he chose the form committed himself to a different relationship with the reader. Such quatrains have in their fabric the imprint of previous use: they belong to a moral tradition which also supported the Russian novel.

Whether it was his trip to the Caucasus that reminded Pasternak of that tradition is merely conjecture. In *The Waves* he mentions both Lermontov and Tolstoy who had recorded 'the feral face of conquest' [*Zverinyy lik zavoevan'ya*/*Dan Lermontovym i Tolstym*[19]], and a lyric of 1931 tells how the landscape 'rhymes summer with Lermontov, and Pushkin with geese and snow' [*Rifmuet s Lermontovym leto*/ *I s Pushkinym gusey i sneg*[20]]. Four years earlier he had written:

In my work I feel the influence of Pushkin. Pushkin's aesthetic is so broad and elastic that it permits various interpretations at various ages. The headlong inventiveness of Pushkin allows one to understand him impressionistically, as I did fifteen years ago in accordance with my own tastes and the tendencies then ruling in literature. Now this understanding has broadened in me, and there have come into it elements of a moral nature.[21]

There is no question but that 'elements of a moral nature' make their entry into *The Waves*. The lines already quoted on 'that by which I live yet,/My aspirations and principles' would be witness enough. But also he makes direct allusion to the disaster that befalls children [*K bede rodivshikhsya rebyat*] when 'the hooks of passion' [*kryuch'ya strasti*] have torn a marriage apart.[22] Regret is a note that sounds very early in the poem: regret drives on his past actions towards him like waves of the sea.[23]

These personal thoughts are inextricable from considerations on the role of the poet and the future of socialism. Pasternak chooses as the image to represent what he is doing the vast beach at Kobuleti from which at one end you can see Poti where night lingers and at the other dawn breaking over Batum. The beach is described as 'embracing, like the poet in his work, a sight that in life needs two separate men' [*Obnyavshiy, kak poet v rabote*,/*Chto v zhizni porozn' vidno dvum*[24]]. *The Waves*, in its framework of a travel poem, necessarily has to do with seeing and assaying. When it reveals the landscape, by implication the poet's own life no less than the Caucasus is spread out 'as on a palm' [*Ves', kak na ladoni*]; and when in the following line the scenery is compared with 'a rumpled bed' [*ves', kak smyataya postel'*] the allusion to a broken marriage cannot be missed.[25] But the method had declared itself before this in the second section:

> Мне хочется домой, в огромность
> Квартиры, наводящей грусть.
> Войду, сниму пальто, опомнюсь,
> Огнями улиц озарюсь.
>
> Перегородок тонкоребрость
> Пройду насквозь, пройду, как свет.
> Пройду, как образ входит в образ
> И как предмет сечет предмет.[26]

> [I want to go home, to the vastness
> Of the flat which induces grief.
> I shall enter, take off my overcoat, collect myself,
> By the street lamps I shall be lit up.
>
> The partitions' thin ribs
> I shall pass through, pass like light,
> Pass as image enters image
> And as object cuts into object.]

These eight lines in themselves carry out the process they describe at their conclusion. The vastness of the flat seems to be imposed by the three previous references to the vast beach [*ogromnyy bereg, ogromnyy vos'mivyorstnyy plyazh, ogromnyy plyazh iz golykh galek*[27]]. A sense of amplitude can be felt too in the dimensions of his grief. Then, as Plank has observed, the fourth line, translated 'by the street lamps I shall be lit up', also offers the meaning 'I shall light up like the street lamps.' Thus 'the metaphor, poet-light, has already been made in that first stanza'. The 'thin-ribbedness' [*tonkoryobrost'*] of the partitions becomes penetrable by the light of the poet's mind as his own body is by the illumination from the street. Plank notes that the intransitive sense of *ozaryus'* 'I shall light up' is prepared by the intransitive *opomnyus'* ['collect myself'] in the line before.[28]

One preoccupation shades off accordingly into another; but the dominant concern is to find a new and better way of life. The socialist future that will resolve all difficulties hovers before him as one more mountain peak; or it shows an escape 'like an outlet to light and an outlet to the sea, like the outlet into Georgia from Mleti' [*Kak vykhod v svet i vykhod k moryu,/I vykhod v Gruziyu iz Mlet*]. Through the images of light and the sea and of Georgia Pasternak attempts to read his destiny and that of his people. He would like to have his part in a future where poetry could attain its fullest significance, where 'instead of a life as scribbler of verse I could lead the life of the poems themselves' [*Ya vmesto zhizni virshepistsa/Povyol by zhizn' samikh poem*[29]]. The sense of his own inadequacy brings a dissatisfaction with the poetry he writes. This is expressed in some famous quatrains which set the direction of his art for the next three decades:

Есть в опыте больших поэтов
Черты естественности той,
Что невозможно, их изведав,
Не кончить полной немотой.

В родстве со всем, что есть, уверясь,
И знаясь с будущим в быту,
Нельзя не впасть к концу, как в ересь,
В неслыханную простоту.

Но мы пощажены не будем,
Когда ее не утаим.
Она всего нужнее людям,
Но сложное понятней им.[30]

[There are in the experience of the great poets
Features of a naturalness such
That you cannot, once having known them,
Fail to end in utter dumbfoundedness.

Your kinship assured with all that exists
And on terms with the future in daily life
You must fall at last as into heresy
Into a never heard-of simplicity.

But we shall not be spared
So long as we do not conceal it.
That is what men most require,
But complication is better understood.]

He had agreed with Scriabin that 'a spendthrift prolixity seems to be easier because it has no content'.[31] The desire henceforth grew in him to simplify his writing, though fulfilment of this desire took time. It will be necessary now to look at the lyrics that follow *The Waves*, and to ascertain how far they have slipped into the 'heresy'.

IV

There are twenty-six of these lyrics. The first four are dated 1930; one of them is the memorial poem to Mayakovsky already discussed, the other three relate to a summer spent in Kiev or its neighbourhood – Kiev with a 'motionless Dnieper' and the Jewish quarter Podol seen by night – *Nedvizhnyy Dnepr, nochnoy Podol*[32] – and the two others set in *dacha* territory at Irpen nearby – 'a Platonic feast in time of plague' [*Na pire Platona vo vremya chumy*].[33] The note here is still playful, and the menace comes ' merely from autumn. Nonetheless it seems consonant with a troubled seriousness that appears in some of the other poems.

One of the four lyrics from this time, 'Second Ballad' ['*Vtoraya Ballada*'],[34] was written at Irpen in August 1930 and dedicated to Zinaida Neuhaus. The third and fourth sections comprise a cluster of love poems all but one of which is addressed to her. This latter poem takes farewell of the wife he is leaving. It states that they now sever not their life nor the union of their hearts, but a mutual deception [*My ne zhizn', ne dushevnyy soyuz – /Oboyudnyy obman obrubaem*].[35] Only Pasternak could have consoled a wife at the final parting with these almost sophistical words that are, on the plane of his peculiar detached vision, at the same time deeply convincing to himself. He can still speak of 'our bond, our honour' as something that does not depend on a common roof [*Nasha svyaz', /Nasha chest' ne pod krovleyu doma*], and he sees her as a shoot that will now grow, lifting itself to the light [*Kak rostok na svetu raspryamyas'*]. The uglier or more painful aspects of the break are reserved for some poems in the sixth and final section.

It would seem that all the poems apart from those in the second section belong to the year 1931.[36] They thus bear witness to a sudden release which may be compared with that of fourteen years before in *My Sister Life*. The cycle they form is not on the same scale; it could scarcely recover that astonishing sense of the new and unexpected which irradiates the earlier volume; yet in the same way it presents a story through allusion, and this story has to do with the poet's finding himself once more as a man who in the transport of his love reads the universe.

These lyrics resemble *The Waves* in the blending of images or at least in the way the poet's concerns interpenetrate. He praises her because her 'purport is like the air, disinterested' [*beskorysten*], while in another 'once more Chopin seeks no gain for himself' [*Opyat' Shopen ne ishchet vygod*[37]]. The air, in the poem to his former wife, is called

My brother and hand. It is such
That like a letter it has been addressed to you

[*On mne brat i ruka. On takov/Chto tebe, kak pis'mo, adresovan.*[38]]

141

This is 'the exemplary air of wide spaces' [*vozdukh shirot obrazt-sovyy*[39]]. And a poem acknowledging the presence of her successor begins:

> You are here, we are in one and the same air
>
> [*Ty zdes', my v vozdukhe odnom.*[40]]

Although several of these poems reveal pain, their prevailing note is one of freedom and innocence. When Pasternak describes love for a woman, he confidently assumes the complicity of nature. This was recognised by Lara when meditating beside the coffin of Zhivago: 'They had loved one another because all things around had wished it so: the land beneath them, the sky over their heads, the clouds and trees.'[41] In *Second Birth* too the universe appears to be at one with the lovers. For Pasternak it was inevitable that he should translate his feelings into metaphors that make nature a witness and support. He consoles his former wife by the proposal that she should 'enter into correspondence with the horizon' [*S gorizontom vstupi v perepisku*] and 'carry on a conversation in the Alpine way' [*Zavedi razgovor po-al'piyski*[42]]. Those who are born anew must become like children, hence no doubt the attraction for him of the thought that is expressed in the refrain of his poem 'Ballad' (1930) – 'as only in early childhood do they sleep' [*Kak tol'ko v rannem detstve spyat*[43]]. Another poem, looking back on the 'union of six hearts' at a holiday house, represents this by the image of families dancing 'in the meadow' of a Brahms intermezzo, 'to a German air as pure as childhood' [*Pod chistyy, kak detstvo, nemetskiy motiv*[44]]. Brahms and Chopin are the musicians invoked in this cycle; it is Chopin who 'alone lays the road of escape from likelihood to simple truth' [*Odin prokladyvaet vykhod/Iz veroyat'ya v pravotu*[45]]. This image leads back to *The Waves*, and the outlet [*vykhod*] to light and the sea that socialism will bring. Through all the unhappiness and disorder attending this second birth of Pasternak's there runs an undercurrent of joy and optimism. He remains what he had been fourteen years before, instinctively drawn to delight even when oppressed with grief, because poetry, music and nature are all in consort.

V

The peculiar stamp of these poems to Zinaida is their greater simplicity and restraint. As yet, though, however dissatisfied he may have begun to feel with his previous manner and the excesses to which it was prone, he cannot achieve the unaffected plainness of Pushkin. Even where the tenor of the lines is wholly natural, they too often give away their self-consciousness by the rhymes. These seldom lack ingenuity, and thereby attract undue attention to themselves. In his work of ten or fifteen years before, the rhymes though often outrageous in their display were yet contained within the total shock-pattern of the poem. The new procedure modifies but does not altogether break with the old – that is to say, he still goes in for paradox, though the paradox is more sober, and while the desire for a classic simplicity is more than once apparent, the realisation of it still mainly eludes him.

One poem in particular reveals indirectly his new concern with a more chastened style:

Любить иных тяжелый крест,
А ты прекрасна без извилин,
И прелести твоей секрет
Разгадке жизни равносилен.

Весною слышен шорох снов
И шелест новостей и истин.
Ты из семьи таких основ.
Твой смысл, как воздух, бескорыстен.

Легко проснуться и прозреть,
Словесный сор из сердца вытрясть
И жить, не засоряясь впредь.
Всё это – не большая хитрость.[46]

[To love some is a heavy cross
But you are beautiful in no roundabout way,
And the secret of your fascination
Adds up to the riddle of life.

In spring is heard the rustle of dreams
And the stirring of news and verities.
You are from the family of such basic things.
Your purport is like the air, disinterested.

It is easy to awake and see the light,
To shake the clutter of words from the heart,
And henceforth to live uncluttered.
That is no very complex business.]

The lyric not only celebrates her beauty and straightforwardness: it claims these qualities as desirable by implication for art. However, a mind that has long been obsessed with subtleties cannot express the ideal of simplicity except through negative terms – 'in no roundabout way', 'no very complex business'. But Pasternak still finds it difficult altogether to refuse difficulty: he loves convolutions [*izviliny*], and at times cannot avoid subtlety [*khitrost'*] for its own sake. In renouncing these habits he yet clings to them. All the same, the best of his poems to Zinaida Neuhaus are remarkably simple and modest in feeling. The ingenuity in these has become unostentatious:

> Красавица моя, вся суть,
> Вся стать твоя, красавица,
> Спирает грудь и тянет в путь
> И тянет петь, и – нравится.[47]

[My lovely, all your essence,
All your form, my lovely,
Constricts the breast and draws to the road
And draws to song and – I like it.]

The play of assonance – *sut'*, *stat'*, *grud'*, *put'*, *pet'* – is as rapid and deft as formerly. The blurting out of 'I like it' is also characteristic: he did this in *My Sister Life*. But there is something in the poem hitherto unheard, or not very often heard, a note almost subdued, of pure contemplation. Pasternak is no longer gesticulating, he no longer demands a hearing as at times in *My Sister Life* or in *Themes and Variations*. The state of his mind is more tranquil, and from that to a full simplicity of expression will not prove a very long or difficult step. The poems record before everything else her presence:

> Ты здесь, мы в воздухе одном.
> Твое присутствие, как город,
> Как тихий Киев за окном. . .[48]

[You are here, we are in one and the same air.
Your presence is like the city,
Like quiet Kiev outside the window. . .]

Or again, he sees her coming into a scene that has already been simplified:

> Никого не будет в доме,
> Кроме сумерек. Один
> Зимний день в сквозном проеме
> Незадернутых гардин.
>
> Только белых мокрых комьев
> Быстрый промельк маховой.
> Только крыши, снег и, кроме
> Крыш и снега, – никого. . .
>
> Но нежданно по портьере
> Пробежит вторженья дрожь.
> Тишину шагами меря,
> Ты, как будущность, войдешь.

Ты появишься у двери
В чём-то белом, без причуд,
В чём-то впрямь из тех материй,
Из которых хлопья шьют.[49]

[No one will be at home
Apart from shadows. Alone
The wintry day in the transparent embrasure
Of undrawn curtains.

Only the white damp flakes'
Rapid flywheel fluttering.
Only the roofs, the snow, and apart
From roofs and snow – no one...

But suddenly through the *portière*
Will run the tremble of an intrusion.
Measuring with steps the silence
You like the future will come in.

You will appear at the door
In something white, unfanciful,
In something straight from the materials
From which snowflakes are sewn.]

The poem itself is not quite 'unfanciful' [*bez prichud*], but in directness of feeling as in the very image of a beloved woman coming to him out of the snow it anticipates one of Zhivago's lyrics written some twenty years later.[50]

VI

If the style is chastened, that may be due to chastened feeling. In the sixth section there are evident notes of self-reproach and uneasiness over his broken marriage. The lyrics inevitably reflect the emotional pattern of *The Waves*, and like that poem they consider both past and future, though it is a future in these lyrics too that will remedy the past. 'The strong', he says in a political poem belonging to the final section, 'the strong have promised the elimination of the last wounds that have overcome us':

А сильными обещано изжитье
Последних язв, одолевавших нас.[51]

The two frankly political effusions in this part are related to the optimism we have already met in *The Waves*. One of them, later to be dropped from the canon, compares the Soviet epoch with that of Peter the Great, and it not only imitates the verse form but also quotes two lines from a poem by Pushkin that drew a parallel between his own age and that of Peter.[52] Such dutiful utterances which steady Pasternak's nerve –

> Итак, вперед, не трепеща
> И утешаясь параллелью[53]
>
> [So then, forward, not trembling
> And taking comfort from the parallel]

– lack the intensity of his more personal writing. But they are not insincere, and certainly they do not indicate bad faith. Pasternak was endowed with a talent for hope, which sets him apart from his peers Mandelstam and Akhmatova. It gave his art a buoyancy which only seems to resemble the optimism of official Soviet verse. *Second Birth* took more on trust than is now conceivable. At Kiev in the summertime, or in Georgia, he could still believe that a benign future would change the condition of humanity. Pasternak never lost his confidence in the goodness of life, or in a liberation to come. It was probably this *naïveté* in worldly matters, and his perpetual unconcern with the dangers around that gave the strength to endure the dark twenty years ahead. He found it impossible to relinquish his inward happiness – the happiness of a man who was made for his art, and who could tell Zinaida

> не как бродяга,
> Родным войду в родной язык.[54]

[Not as a vagrant but as its own I shall enter my native language.]

Pasternak as Translator

I

In the last three decades of his life Pasternak did a very large amount of translation. Indeed, among his contemporaries in the Soviet Union only two other poets can be compared with him as translators: M. L. Lozinsky, famous for his rendering of Dante, and Samuil Marshak.[1] The range of Pasternak's activity is such that it takes in, among the Germans, Goethe, Schiller, Kleist and Rilke; among English poets, Shakespeare, Jonson, Byron, Shelley and Keats; many Georgians, including two predecessors of the generation he knew, A. Tseretelli and Vazha Pshavela; the Polish romantic poet Słowacki; the Ukrainian Shevchenko; the Hungarian Petöfi. The list could be extended; but these are his main interests, and among them the versions of certain plays by Shakespeare (including *Romeo and Juliet* and the four principal tragedies) and of Goethe's *Faust* are the major achievements. When very little of his own poetry could see the light, Pasternak was still able to speak to the Soviet reader through the work of others. There have been times when the most living part of Soviet literature consisted in translations from foreign classics. The general standard is exceptionally high. Poets otherwise liable to the grossest interference from editors and critics have contrived in this way to keep up the tradition of a strict craftsmanship and to maintain attitudes and tones that they could not venture in their own right.

It was fortunate that Pasternak had the opportunity most of the time to translate what appealed to him. Once he complained to Nina Tabidze about slow progress with the second part of *Faust*, calling it 'silly stuff' [*takuyu Vampuku*].[2] Yet the long association with Shakespeare, Goethe and other free spirits must have had many rewards. He never conceived of translation as anything less than a full encounter with the original. Mere correspondence of texts would not do, as he noted in an essay of 1944. The version must grow out of a long familiarity with the primary work of which it should be 'the fruit' and 'historical consequence'.[3] The relation between the two Pasternak conceives as that of a parent stem and grafting slip. He demands from a good translation that it should 'stand on a level with the original and in itself be unrepeatable'.[4] The main thing to transmit is the force of a particular work. Here Pasternak returns to his notion of art in *Safe Conduct* as a force that displaces, or more accurately as the record of what has been effected by this force.[5]

Translation is for Pasternak one more way in which art declares its presence. Here too the outcome is poetry, although not from the same starting-point. It begins like original poetry in an experience, but the experience takes the form of re-creating what has already been created, of trying to repeat the unique and unrepeatable. Somehow the force of art realised in another man's work has to leap across the terminals and to activate a different language. Pasternak will not be content with less than a reconstitution of that force as his ideal. There can be no adequate translation unless the quality of the force is recognised, which involves perceiving its relation to what has already been at work in the literature of the poet who makes the rendering. Thus when first asked to translate some poems by Shelley, Pasternak was reluctant because he thought Shelley 'remote and abstract'. Only by a strict attention to what Shelley was doing did Pasternak and his collaborators on this occasion come to see him as 'the predecessor of that urban mysticism' inspiring the Symbolist poets of a later day. 'Once we had heard in Shelley's invocations to the clouds and wind the future voices of Blok, Verhaeren and Rilke, then he put on flesh for us.' This, he explained, 'relates principally to the "Ode to the West Wind"'.[6]

His first success was with Georgian poetry, on which he began to work in the 1930s.[7] Whereas a decade earlier Blok had reported most unfavourably on his version of Goethe's *Die Geheimnisse* as awkward and esoteric [*kamernyy*],[8] the Georgian poems in Pasternak's translation move freely and have a great air of naturalness. For example, each of seventeen poems by his friend Titsian Tabidze[9] is made very convincing; it is beautifully turned and full of unexpected graces. The effect of restraint cannot easily be matched from his own poetry of the time. Tabidze was astonished that a translator who knew nothing of the Georgian language could perform such miracles. He wrote to a friend:

In Pasternak's translations of contemporary Georgian poets we observe the utmost accuracy of meaning, he has pretty well kept all the images and the placing of words, despite a certain divergence in the metrical character of Georgian and Russian verse, and most important of all one feels in them the melody and not a transposition of images.[10]

Pasternak himself was less satisfied: 'All I related was their images, metaphors and ideas.' He regretted that it was impossible for one ignorant of Georgian and therefore bound to a crib [*podstrochnik*] 'to communicate certain effects of the language, its penumbras, certain strong lights passing over it'.[11]

How then, being at such a disadvantage, did he succeed so brilliantly, as Tabidze and other Georgians claim he did? It is all the more remarkable because Tabidze held the essence of poetry to be its intonation, or 'inner melody' [*vnutrennyaya napevnost'*].[12] When Pasternak came upon this term in the essay by Simon Chikovani which prefaces the anthology of Tabidze's verse in translation, he wrote to him that it must be understood in a special sense: 'Clearly Titsian used this term incorrectly...he understood by it something quite different that had the force of a technical vow upon me at the time of *My Sister Life*.'[13] The 'technical vow' was a commitment to immediacy, to writing down the poem as it came on a flood of emotion. So Pasternak worked in the years 1917 and 1918; and so Tabidze throughout his career felt himself to be the mouthpiece of the spirit, 'untrimmed stalk of a reed/That sings even untouched by lips'.[14] Or to quote the opening of a poem rendered by Pasternak:

Не я пишу стихи. Они, как повесть, пишут
Меня, и жизни ход сопровождает их.
Что стих? Обвал снегов. Дохнет – и с места сдышит,
И заживо схоронит. Вот что стих.[15]

[It is not I who write verses. Like a story they write
Me, and the course of life accompanies them.
What is a verse? An avalanche. It breathes, and
 the breath will bear it away,
And bury you alive. That's what a verse is.]

Tabidze's poetry had in Pasternak's view 'an inexhaustible lyric potential...the presence of untouched spiritual reserves'.[16] There was much in his poetic character that recalls at least the early Pasternak. He had a greater complexity, a more deeply tragic sense than Pasternak at the outset; but the resemblance is to be found above all in his selfless dedication to poetry, and in the devotion he felt for his native landscape. Thus the act of translation became easier because of a strong sympathy between the two men, and it must be remembered too that Tabidze had known Russian poetry, and the poetry that Pasternak himself most admired, from his days at a Georgian high school. Even then he was reading and translating, among others, Blok and Annensky.[17] In a poem of 1936 'From Summer Jottings' ['*Iz letnikh zapisok*'], Pasternak describes him:

> Он плотен, он шатен,
> Он смертен, и, однако,
> Таким, как он, Роден
> Изобразил Бальзака.[18]

[He is thick-set, chestnut-haired,
He is mortal and yet
Such as him Rodin
Portrayed Balzac.]

Tabidze and his fellow poet Paolo Yashvili make their appearance along with Marina Tsvetaeva in the chapter of the *Essay in Autobiography* called 'Three Shades' ['*Tri teni*'].[19] The tragic deaths of all three greatly afflicted Pasternak. It is possible to see from his renderings of Tabidze's verse how this Georgian of whom Pasternak says 'He is severe as a bas relief / And pure as the native ore'[20] was able to elicit such unmistakable sureness in the response of his translator. Because he knew and loved Tabidze so well, Pasternak had no problem in divining his 'inner melody'.

II

With the Georgian translations we have to rely on a sense of their authenticity which cannot be demonstrated. The problem with Pasternak's translations from Shakespeare is the opposite. Our willingness to see them as authentic must overcome certain diffi- culties which hardly exist for the Russian reader, who recognises as we can the vitality of the text in his own language without suffering from our discomfort. The reason for this discomfort is that the Shakespeare of Pasternak has become inevitably the fellow country- man of Pushkin, and while this new Russian *Hamlet* or *Lear* reads like an original play (a more complex play than *Boris Godunov* though with a family resemblance) it has ceased to be Jacobean. Gone is much of the complexity in Shakespeare's metaphorical language, which quite often jarred on Pasternak's sensibilities. For him 'the highest poetry' in Shakespeare alternates with 'undis- guised rhetoric, piling up a dozen empty circumlocutions instead of the one word on the tip of the author's tongue which in his haste he did not find'.[21] This comment on Shakespeare is oddly similar to Shklovsky's on Pasternak: 'He spoke as usual, threw out his words in a dense throng to one side and the other, but the most important thing was not said'.[22] The general effect of Pasternak's translations from Shakespeare is to thin out the original, so that it becomes an autumn wood with fewer leaves and with the outlines showing more clearly. Thus, to take three examples from a single scene in *Othello* (II, i). The First Gentleman's report:

> Nothing at all: it is a high-wrought flood;
> I cannot 'twixt the heaven and the main
> Descry a sail. (2–4)

is reduced to five nervously rapid phrases:

> Нет. Ровно ничего. Сплошные волны.
> Ни паруса. Пустынный горизонт.[23]

The Second Gentleman observes:

> I never did like molestation view
> On the enchafed flood. (16–17)

This again Pasternak cuts down to the essential idea:

> Я равной бури в жизни не видал[24]

– a line that may look prosaic, but catches in its rhythm the tossing of the waves. Finally, Cassio's comment on Othello,

> he hath achiev'd a maid
> That paragons description and wild fame (61–2)

is put aside for the simple statement that he is married *na pisanoy krasavitse* ['to a picture of beauty']. These alterations are in the spirit of Pushkin. The verse Pasternak writes for his Shakespeare translations is taut and lucid; the sense has been winnowed out from the abundance of Shakespeare. Formally too there is a stricter discipline: following, it would seem, the practice of Annensky in his classical verse dramas, Pasternak regularly alternates his lines between masculine and feminine endings.[25] An English reader who knew Russian, coming upon these plays for the first time, could almost be tempted into dismissing them as adaptations of Shakespeare. But they are not that. Pasternak listened very carefully to the tones of each play. Thus in *Hamlet* he heard a music with 'the measured interchange of solemnity and alarm';[26] in *Romeo and*

Juliet the 'wary and broken' speech of the lovers, their voices sub-dued;[27] and in *Lear* he noted that 'people scared to death converse in a whisper', while the language of Shakespeare is that of the Old Testament prophets.[28] And he also attends to personal rhythms, so that the characters are recognisable in Russian speech. Further he is careful to preserve the dynamic relation between all the parts of the play: the structure though more spare is in no way distorted. He followed his own instinct in clarifying Shakespeare, and says that he found particularly in the exchanges of Romeo and Juliet 'a model of the very highest poetry which in its best examples is always nourished by the simplicity and freshness of prose'.[29] That simplicity and freshness became Pasternak's standard throughout the Shake-speare translations.

Of these the first was *Hamlet*, completed in 1940.[30] It has a particular interest because of its significance for *Doctor Zhivago*, which clearly relates to the view expressed by Pasternak in his 'Notes to Translations of Shakespearian Tragedies' [*Zametki k perevodam shekspirovskikh tragediy*] that this is 'not a drama of characterlessness, but a drama of duty and self-denial'.[31] Hamlet was a figure no less important to Pasternak than he was to Blok. A further reason for studying this translation in some detail is that M. L. Lozinsky made an accomplished version of the play, which Pasternak praised highly in a note on translating *Hamlet* of 1942.[32] He called it 'ideal...for its closeness together with the excellent idiom and strict form', and he said that 'more fully than other trans-lations it gives an idea of the outward appearance of the original and its verbal structure, as a faithful representation'.[33] With the greatest skill Lozinsky manages to keep the metaphorical patterning and to a large extent phrase by phrase the movement of Shake-speare's lines. His translation is highly accurate, almost a tracing of the original. Pasternak aimed at something different: 'from the translation of words and metaphors I turned to the translation of thoughts and scenes'. He took 'that deliberate freedom without which there is no coming close to great works'.[34] Like Dryden he prefers paraphrase to metaphrase.

The rhythm that Pasternak heard pre-eminently in *Hamlet* among Shakespeare's plays is that of 'a free individual in history, who has created no idol for himself and therefore is sincere and laconic'.[35] (It is a rhythm that Pasternak regards as a specifically English achieve-ment.) He sees the function of this rhythm in *Hamlet* as threefold. It defines the individual characters; it sustains the 'dominant mood' of the tragedy; also it 'elevates and softens various rough scenes in the drama'. From these hints one can foresee the kind of translation Pasternak will give, depending on his idea of the play. He makes Hamlet inevitably into the artist with a mission to judge his time; the artist whose personal rhythm stands out defining him against the courtiers. Here it seems legitimate to invoke the words of the poem 'Hamlet' attributed to Zhivago: 'everything is swamped in Pharisaism' [*vsyo tonet v fariseystve*];[36] in his notes on *Lear* Pasternak also stresses the 'pharisaic foundation' of all the 'forgeries, cruelties and murders' that dominate the scene.[37] Hamlet, with his great natural gifts, the rapidity of his mind, the way he holds off the servile and treacherous courtiers by the play of a mocking intelligence, is a figure strongly appealing to Pasternak. What impresses him – the spirit of sacrifice in Hamlet – allows for none of the objections that Eliot made about the supposedly pathological disgust of the hero,[38] or Lawrence when he complained that Hamlet was animated by a cold 'self-dislike'.[39] Pasternak sees only the heroism of a born prince and genius who had a destiny to fulfil in the service of times after his own. Pasternak is not happy about the way Hamlet addresses Ophelia in the 'nunnery' scene. He describes it as 'the ruthlessness of a post-Byronic self-loving renegade'.[40] But for him the laceration of this meeting is made bearable by the place it holds, immediately after the 'fresh music' of the monologue 'To be or not to be'. The harshness pervading the play is held inside 'the circle of its harmonies'.

And this gives the clue to Pasternak's purpose. Having listened carefully and caught every individual voice in the play, he devises the 'circle' of his own 'harmonies' in which to place them. The voices are easily recognisable: the self-assurance and natural grace of Horatio; the dejected and valedictory tones of Ophelia when she concludes Hamlet is mad; the academic self-regard of Polonius. The rhythm and weight of the speech are exact for all three:

> (*Horatio*)   Слыхал и я, и тоже частью верю.
> Но вот и утро в розовом плаще
> Росу пригорков топчет на востоке.[41]

> [So have I heard and do in part believe it.
> But, look, the morn in russet mantle clad,
> Walks o'er the dew of yon high eastern hill.]
> (I, i, 165–7)

> (*Ophelia*)   Какого обаянья ум погиб!
> Соединенье знанья, красноречья
> И доблести, наш праздник, цвет надежд,

Законодатель вкусов и приличий,
Их зеркало. . .все вдребезги. Все, все. . .
А я? Кто я, беднейшая из женщин,
С недавним медом клятв его в душе,
Теперь, когда могучий этот разум,
Как колокол надбитый, дребезжит,
А юношеский облик бесподобный
Изборожден безумьем? Боже мой!
Куда все скрылось? Что передо мной?[42]

[O! what a noble mind is here o'erthrown:
The courtier's, soldier's, scholar's, eye, tongue, sword;
The expectancy and rose of the fair state,
The glass of fashion and the mould of form,
The observ'd of all observers, quite, quite down!
And I, of ladies most deject and wretched,
That suck'd the honey of his music vows,
Now see that noble and most sovereign reason,
Like sweet bells jangled, out of tune and harsh;
That unmatch'd form and feature of blown youth
Blasted with ecstasy: O! woe is me,
To have seen what I have seen, see what I see!]

(III, i, 159-70)

(*Polonius*) Всё тут, Лаэрт? В путь, в путь! Стыдился б,
                                                    право!
Уж ветер выгнул плечи парусов,
А сам ты где? Стань под благословенье
И заруби-ка вот что на носу. . .[43]

[Yet here, Laertes! aboard, aboard, for shame!
The wind sits in the shoulder of your sail,
And you are stay'd for. There, my blessing with thee!
And these few precepts in thy memory
Look thou character. . .]

(I, iii, 55-9)

In Ophelia's lament Pasternak has managed to link the two parts by the play on *vdrebezgi*, 'in pieces', and *drebezzhit*, 'jangles', and the cracked bell becomes like that immense one in the Kremlin (*Ivan-kolokol*). Polonius' fourth line achieves an idiomatic prosiness quite in keeping with his nature, while it takes over the Shakespearian image in 'character'. (Literally he says 'notch this on your nose'.) It is more effective than Lozinsky's 'And inscribe my counsels on your memory' [*I v pamyat' zapishi moi zavety*].

Hamlet in Pasternak's version responds to the contemporary world, as any living work must – not, of course, by deliberate adaptation – it is no 'Shakespeare in modern dress' – but by the different angle at which the light falls here and there on the text. Thus in Hamlet's speech to the players (III, ii) 'to show. . .the very age and

154

body of the time his form and pressure' becomes 'to show. . .each age in history its unadorned face' [*pokazyvat'. . .kazhdomu veku istorii – ego neprikrashennyy oblik*] – a task that literature found very hard to perform in the Stalin era; and 'this fell sergeant, death'[44] is translated *tupoy konvoynyy*, the 'obtuse escort' (of political prisoners). In the first version of 1940 Pasternak had apparently rendered Hamlet's lines on 'the whips and scorns of time' (III, i, 70f.) as follows:

> А то кто снес бы ложное величье
> Правителей, невежество вельмож,
> Всеобщее притворство, невозможность
> Излить себя, несчастную любовь
> И призрачность заслуг в глазах ничтожеств. . .[45]

> [For who would bear the whips and scorns of time,
> The oppressor's wrong, the proud man's contumely,
> The pangs of dispriz'd love, the law's delay,
> The insolence of office, and the spurns
> That patient merit of the unworthy takes . . .]
> (III, i, 70–4)

As Vladimir Markov has said, 'these words express accurately Pasternak's own situation in those years'.[46]

In his 'Notes' Pasternak claims that a translator's 'day-by-day progress through the text' puts him in 'the past situations of the author'. Thus he is initiated into 'certain of his secrets'.[47] More than once the 'Notes' refer to Shakespeare's 'realism', a term that crops up in two essays Pasternak wrote during the mid-forties when he was still working on his Shakespeare translations.[48] There are several aspects to this realism. It had always been latent in Pasternak's own poetic language, which is inherently dramatic and open to all the voices of the street. During the 1920s and 1930s Pasternak was compelled like every Soviet writer to study the implications of realism, above all in the prescribed socialist form. A comment of his on *Antony and Cleopatra* makes the point that, whereas throughout Shakespeare's work there is an 'inward realism', only in the Roman plays, with their remoteness from the contemporary scene, was it possible 'to call things by their own names'.[49] Obviously the rendering of Shakespeare's plays allowed Pasternak to achieve that, as the examples from *Hamlet* have shown. He found in Shakespeare what Pushkin had found to be the essence of great dramatic writing, and particularly of Shakespeare's – freedom.[50] For Pushkin Shakespeare had given an example of impartiality. It was not exactly this that Pasternak wanted from him, but the chance to exercise that freedom as Shakespeare had done in the Roman plays, where 'he might say whatever he saw fit in the political or moral or any other respect'.[51] So the realism that Shakespeare revealed to Pasternak was a setting-free of the creative mind to grasp any situation in its moral and political, its fully human, truth. In this way the years of what might be described as a close collaborative work with Shakespeare prepared him for the writing of *Doctor Zhivago*.

A genuine poetic translation is one in which the use of language becomes creative. Everywhere this can be seen in Pasternak's versions of Shakespeare, and not least in his *Lear*. I will confine the examples to certain utterances of Lear himself, not only because the king dominates the play but because with him language is carried to a pitch of intensity not accessible to any one else in the play. The version by Pasternak never fails Lear. His imprecation upon Regan has in the earlier speech ('I prithee, daughter, do not make me mad') the same conscious and majestic restraint as Shakespeare gives it:

> Я стрел не кличу на твое чело,
> Юпитеру не воссылаю жалоб.
> Исправься в меру сил. Я подожду.[52]

[I do not bid the thunder-bearer shoot,
Nor tell tales of thee to high-judging Jove.
Mend when thou canst, be better at thy leisure.]
(II, iv, 223–5)

Later on the heath his voice rises to the same thick frenzy as in the original:

> Вой, вихрь, во-всю! Жги, молния! Лей,
> ливень!
> Вихрь, гром и ливень, вы не дочки мне,
> Я вас не упрекаю в бессердечье.[53]

[Rumble thy bellyful! Spit, fire! Spout, rain!
Not rain, wind, thunder, fire are my daughters,
I tax not you, you elements, with unkindness.]
(III, ii, 14–16)

When he asserts his regal dignity, the flash of arrogance is the same:

> Король, и до конца ногтей – король.
> Взгляну в упор, и подданный трепещет.[54]

[Ay, every inch a king.
When I do stare see how the subject quakes.]
(IV, vi, 107–8)

Pasternak also catches the exact intonations of Lear's humility at the meeting with Cordelia:

> Не смейся надо мной. Я – старый дурень
> Восьмидесяти с лишним лет. Боюсь,
> Я не совсем в своем уме. Признаться,
> Я начинаю что-то понимать,
> И, кажется, я знаю, кто вы оба,
> И ты и он, но я не убежден,
> По той причине, что не знаю, где я.
> Своей одежды я не узнаю,
> Где я сегодня ночевал, не помню.
> Пожалуйста, не смейтесь надо мной![55]

> [Pray do not mock me.
> I am a very foolish fond old man,
> Four score and upward, not an hour more or less,
> And, to deal plainly,
> I fear I am not in my perfect mind.
> Methinks I should know you, and know this man;
> Yet I am doubtful; for I am mainly ignorant
> What place this is; and all the skill I have
> Remembers not these garments; nor I know not
> Where I did lodge last night. Do not laugh at me.]
> (IV, vii, 59–68)

And the same broken simplicity is there in the last scene when he holds the dead Cordelia in his arms:

> Мою
> Бедняжку удавили! Нет, не дышит!
> Коню, собаке, крысе можно жить,
> Но не тебе. Тебя навек не стало,
> Навек, навек, навек, навек, навек! –
> Мне больно. Пуговицу расстегните. . .
> Благодарю вас. Посмотрите, сэр!
> Вы видите? На губы посмотрите!
> Вы видите? Взгляните на нее![56]

> [And my poor fool is hanged! No, no, no life,
> Why should a dog, a horse, a rat have life,
> And thou no breath at all? Thou'lt come no more:
> Never, never, never, never, never.
> Pray you undo this button. Thank you, sir.
> Do you see this? Look on her.]
> (V, iii, 303–8)

Pasternak catches the note of agony in his opening phrase – *Moyu / Bednyazhku udavili* – where the repeated *u* sound, particularly at the second and third occurrence, seems to express a naked grief. He reproduces the impatient listing of 'a dog, a horse, a rat' in Shakespeare's second line (though the Russian words compel him to adopt

157

an order of size, from horse down to rat). It was not possible in his metrical system to adopt the falling rhythm of 'Never, never, never, never, never', but his solution of *Navek, navek, navek, navek, navek* is equally effective, though it may suggest finality rather more than futility. 'Pray you undo this button' in his rendering follows the statement *Mne bol'no* – 'I suffer.' Explicitness is a feature belonging to Pasternak's translations from Shakespeare in general no less than to Schlegel-Tieck. His orderliness, clarity, and precision derive conceivably from their example, but more certainly from that of Pushkin, which anyone writing blank-verse drama in the Russian language cannot avoid. These qualities also suit Pasternak's philosophical mind. Where Shakespeare is most direct and luminous, Pasternak can meet him, with a purity of expression that seems almost the perfect equivalent.

III

His knowledge of German was very complete. It astonished Renate Schweitzer, who noted the skill with which he was able to realise the effects of Goethe's language in *Faust*. (He worked on this translation from 1949 until 1952.)[57] When Frau Schweitzer finally met him, she found that 'he spoke such good German one could forget he was a Russian'.[58]

The version of *Faust* is, as I have said earlier, a capital work, and it probably had some effect on the writing of *Doctor Zhivago*. Goethe's poem is one to encourage philosophic breadth, it has many symbolic episodes, and it takes an intellectual for its hero. Yet one may suspect that the German romantic poets of the earlier nineteenth century (Lenau for instance) and Rilke in his own time stirred Pasternak's imagination more deeply, and for that reason I shall not consider it here. The German work that clearly did interest him very much was Schiller's romantic drama *Maria Stuart* of which his translation was published in 1958. One of his best poems in *When the Weather Clears*, 'Bacchanalia' ['*Vakkhanaliya*'], recalls the wintry first night of his *Maria Stuart* in Moscow, and the spectacle of the young actress wearing her white striped dress with her hair in a plait, presumably a few moments before the execution scene (V, vi).[59] The passage in 'Bacchanalia' describing her is similar to the 'Hamlet' poem in *Zhivago*. Here too the actor is wholly identified with his part:

То же бешенство риска
Та же радость и боль
Слили роль и артистку,
И артистку и роль.[60]

[The same wild daring,
The same joy and pain
Have fused the role and the artist,
The artist and her role.]

It happens that almost at the same time a translation of *Maria Stuart* was made by Stephen Spender for Peter Wood's production at the Old Vic.[61] In his Preface Wood notes that *Maria Stuart* 'is a nineteenth-century melodrama requiring a style of presentation which we do not accept in this country outside the opera house'.[62] Spender decided that it would be necessary 'to free Schiller from the poetic fashion of his time, and release his ideas within a sparer, more modern, idiom'. He takes very large liberties, often cancelling or transposing the lines, and allowing himself to 'pare, compress, touch up, vary, elucidate'.[63] The result was a gain in dramatic power and a wholesale shedding of Schiller's rhetoric. Pasternak was less embarrassed by the rhetoric, which through judicious trimming he makes if not Shakespearian (though it stands up to his translations from Shakespeare) at least in the line of Pushkin's 'Little Tragedies'. He has not altered the form; he observes the proportions of the various speeches; he even accepts the passages in rhyme, without making them sound artificial. He writes an extremely practised and lucid verse; lighter, more rapid than Schiller's; the lines broken into shorter units. Here and there it has been impossible to escape the accents of melodrama: *Bezumets, proch'!* ['Madman, hence!'].[64] But he manages to bring great dramatic liveliness into the speeches, and something of the personal rhythms he had noticed in Shakespeare, so far as it can be deduced from Schiller's play. Sometimes he develops his own music, as in Mary's speech to her grieving servants.[65] Here Pasternak repeats his translation of the opening phrase, 'Was klagt ihr?' ['What are you lamenting?'], three times so that the question, *Chto plachete vy?* ['Why do you weep?'] introduces each of the three long sentences of her exhortation. When Mary leaves for the block, the hurried few words from her improve upon those of the original in dramatic force:

Что, Анна? Верно, мне пора идти?
Пора на казнь идти? Пора прощаться?
Вон и судья с жезлом. Иду. Иду.
Прощайте все.[66]

[What, Hanna? Is it really time to go?
Time to go to execution? Time to say goodbye?
Here is the judge[67] with his wand. I go. I go.
Goodbye all.]

Traditionally *Maria Stuart* had been a protest play on the Russian stage. Before the revolution Mary's part was taken memorably by the actress Mariya Ermolova. None of these political overtones were lost on the author of *Doctor Zhivago*. His poem 'Bacchanalia' recognises the appeal of Schiller's heroine as a symbol:

> Всё в ней жизнь, всё свобода
> И в груди колотье,
> И тюремные своды
> Не сломили ее.[68]

> [She is all life and freedom
> And pain at her breast,
> And the prison vaults
> Have not broken her.]

In one place he has made Leicester's words applicable not only to the England of Elizabeth I:

> Наши нравы
> Известны вам? Как всем зажаты рты.
> Как все трусливы в этом женском царстве!
> Героев нет, и обескрылел дух,
> И вся страна под башмаком у бабы.[69]

> [Are our ways
> Known to you? How the mouths of all are stopped,
> How all are cowardly in this woman's realm!
> There are no heroes, and the spirit has lost its wings,
> And the whole country is under a wench's thumb.]

'How the mouths of all are stopped' does not feature in Schiller's text; 'How all are cowardly' is more explicit than 'Sucht nach dem Heldengeist' ['Seek out the heroic spirit']. These reverberations are not to be found in the passage as Spender has given it. An English translator, unless he happens to be a Catholic, does not readily see Elizabeth as a tyrant. So Leicester merely laments that

> this woman ties us
> All to her apron strings[70]

– which is the voice of any court official under a strong-minded female monarch.

IV

Had Pasternak published only his translations, he would still hold a position in Russian literature comparable to that of Zhukovsky. The bulk of his production in this field is formidable, the standard extremely high. It was, of course, the accident of living at this particular time that made him a translator, but like everything else in life he welcomed the experience. And with his wide culture and linguistic abilities he could not have been better suited to interpret great foreign works for the benefit of the Soviet public. There were times when it irked him not to be able to get on with the writing of his own poetry. He told Aleksandr Gladkov in March 1942: 'I have been translating for six years. I ought at last to write something.'[71] But Gladkov also notes that once he had committed himself to a translation he 'made himself become really absorbed' in it.[72] And Gladkov describes the single-mindedness of his work on *Romeo and Juliet* when evacuated to Chistopol. They met in the communal dining-room during the winter months of 1941–2:

The premises were not heated. And there coming into this dining-room where the temperature was the same as on the street and where nobody removed clothing, Pasternak felt obliged to take off his overcoat and hang up his hat on a peg. Not only that, but he brought his work with him into the dining-room: an English–Russian dictionary, a miniature volume of Shakespeare and the current page of his translation. I remember too some long sheets on to which he copied difficult passages. While waiting for his portion of watery cabbage soup. . .he worked on.[73]

Translation could never fully replace his own writing. But if he gave much to it he received something in return. He found in Shakespeare, for example, 'an inner freedom inconceivable' to those of his own time.[74] Translating great works from the past not only provided a spiritual refuge, it kept him in touch with a living tradition, it fortified and enlarged his mind. One recalls Blake in his solitude engraving scenes from Chaucer and Dante. The discipline of translation prepared Pasternak for the final stage of his vocation. It took him further away from modernism and impelled him to examine again the problems of communication in poetry. This was the benefit he gained from what must have seemed at times a servitude, an enforced distraction of his talent from its right aims.

A Fresh Start in Poetry: 'On Early Trains'

I

At the Minsk Writers' Conference in 1936 Pasternak made a strikingly independent speech on the theme of 'Modesty and Boldness'.[1] The title formulates a poetic programme: it calls for renovation under the guidance of these two principles neither of which had much to recommend it in official eyes. He explained his position thus: 'For some time to come I shall write badly, from my previous point of view, until the moment when I grow used to the novelty of the themes and situations I want to touch on.' He would write badly on account of difficulties both artistic and ideological – artistic because he would be moving into a field of 'topical journalism [*publitsistika*] and abstraction', ideological because 'on these themes that are common to us all I shall not speak in the common language; I am not going to repeat you, comrades, I am going to dispute with you.' He asks them to accept the inevitable, as he does himself: 'for some time I am going to write like a cobbler, forgive me'.[2]

As examples of this cobbler's work he mentioned two hastily drafted poems which had appeared in *Izvestia* during January. They are very unlike one another. The earlier of these, written in praise of unremitting labour and the national leaders, is scarcely more than a jingle.[3] (It has an unusual rhyme for Stalin, associating him with *smekh u zavalin*, 'laughter on the mounds' – these form a kind of bench for old people that skirts a peasant hut.) The other poem, 'The Artist' ['*Khudozhnik*'], is one in which he takes up the dispute with his comrades. It consists of four lyrics in sequence, and was inspired by his friendship with the Georgian poet G. N. Leonidze.[4] In the tradition of Pushkin's well known sonnet 'To the Poet' ['*Poetu*'][5] the first lyric asserts that all the struggles of an artist are with himself.[6] The poem finds deeply congenial his 'obstinate self-will' [*stroptivyy norov*]. There is also in it an echo of Blok's speech

162

'On the Poet's Function' [*O naznachenii poeta*'] made shortly before his death in 1921.[7] The artist in Pasternak's poem longs for 'peace' [*pokoy*] and 'freedom' [*volya*] – keywords in the demand of Blok on that occasion.[8] The third lyric describes the artist's readiness to throw everything on to the fire of his imagination – not only the furniture, but 'friendship, reason, conscience, daily life' [*Druzhbu, razum, sovest', byt*]. These values are transcended rather than discarded, since they have been fused into the poem. Its last lines make this clear when the exhalation from the poet's rhymes in the crucible blesses the sleeping children.[9] They look forward to the scene in *Doctor Zhivago* where Yury at Varykino writes his poems while Lara and Katya are already sleeping.[10] Here too Pasternak opposes the artist's dedication and his home life to a ruling philosophy which called for quite other allegiances. As he had proclaimed at Minsk, 'Art without risk and spiritual self-sacrifice is unthinkable.'

II

The four lyrics comprising 'The Artist' were placed by him at the front of his volume *On Early Trains* [*Na rannikh poezdakh*]; this contained poems of the years 1936 to 1944. (His war poems, later to be included under this title, originally came out out in a separate volume of 1945, *Earth's Vastness* [*Zemnoy prostor*].)

With this collection Pasternak inaugurated a new phase in his poetry which many of his admirers have found disappointing, while others, notably Wladimir Weidlé, have greeted it as a liberation from false procedures.[11]

The latter view was evidently Pasternak's own. His *Essay in Autobiography* speaks harshly of the 'flourishes' [*vykrutasy*] that had often been ruinous to his ear, and of the 'trinkets' [*pobryakushki*] that he hung upon words to the neglect of their meaning.[12] In this charge there is a little truth, but Pasternak has succumbed to the temptation of dismissing all that was good in the earlier works for the sake of what had succeeded it. A poet who develops, as he must to save himself from repetition, will often be irked by the conservatism of his readers. When Pasternak gave up the innovatory brilliance which had won him such acclaim, for a manner of writing far more restrained and simplified, he found it natural to turn upon the vices, real or imaginary, of his former style. But the paradox here is that the new style does not call for a renewed effort of concentration. It appears, though deceptively so, that Pasternak has submitted to the canons that make Soviet poetry in general so unadventurous. Before, a lyric by Pasternak was startlingly unlike the birds of dull plumage in the forest of Soviet song. Now, it would be not only his war poems that looked more conventional. The verse of his last two decades might seem to have cultivated modesty rather than boldness.

Weidlé has pointed out that two poems written by Pasternak for children in 1924, 'The Menagerie' ['*Zverinets*'] and 'The Merry-go-round' ['*Karusel'*'], already achieve that straightforwardness and accessibility which was ultimately to be his ideal in verse.[13] Children's poetry requires a particular awareness of its audience. There is no doubt that Pasternak in the last two decades of his life became more sensitive to the difficulties confronting the reader. When preparing his poems for the abortive 1957 edition, he found much in the earlier work to alter. It had too many shortcomings: 'These places, their hazy obscurity destroy the whole of which they constitute a part. So as to save the poems spoiled by them I have allowed myself to renovate them slightly or to rewrite separate stanzas of them over again'.[14] The aim now is to make his poetry simple and direct – but none the less powerful. In the *Essay in Autobiography* he discusses the originality that can transform a tradition from within – as when Chopin gave a new life to the idiom of Mozart and Field. What matters to him now is the 'note of startling naturalness' which 'in art is wholly decisive'.[15]

His speech at Minsk called for a revival of 'the saving tradition' which Tolstoy began with his 'tempests of exposure and brusqueness' [*bestseremonnostey*].[16] Two years before at another congress of writers he had defined poetry as being 'prose in action...the language of organic fact'.[17] There seems little doubt that his experience of writing prose had encouraged the search for a greater simplicity in verse. Weidlé sees anticipations of his later style not only in the two poems already mentioned but also in 'certain pages of prose', and here he names *The Last Summer* as the place to look for them.[18]

It is not Tolstoy alone among the classical writers but also Pushkin and Tyutchev who are invoked in Pasternak's speech at Minsk. One way of accounting for his later style of poetry would be to say he has put the last traces of modernism behind him in favour of these three nineteenth-century masters. By drawing nearer to Pushkin, to Tyutchev and to Fet than ever before he was letting himself be borne on the tide of socialist realism which, in his own interpretation of it, he appeared to accept at Minsk. It is ironical, of course, that in the years following he should not have been able to write any poems, with the exception of his 'Travel Notes' ['*Putevye zapiski*'] on the Georgian experience, dating from the summer of 1936 – a verse cycle which he regarded with little satisfaction.[19] His projected novel in prose and the translating of Shakespeare occupied him at this time to the exclusion of his own poetry. When this returned, in the earlier part of 1941 a few months before Hitler invaded the Soviet Union, with the series 'Peredelkino', he had totally reformed himself as a poet. The dozen lyrics under that name cannot be called cobbler's work. They have achieved an effortless clarity, a contemplative calm, which signify some profound change in Pasternak. Before he had been immersed in the sea of experience. Now he is at once in it and with his mind's eye looking on from the farther shore. In that sense the poems are classical: their detachment is emphasised by the continuity they show with the Russian lyric of the previous century. Innovation here goes on quietly within an established mode.

Pasternak observes in the *Essay in Autobiography* that he had never felt sympathetic towards the experiments of Andrey Bely and Khlebnikov in their quest for a new language: 'I have never understood these pursuits. In my view the most astonishing discoveries have been made when the content so overfilled the artist's mind that it allowed him no time to consider, and he hurried on to utter his new statement in the old language, without examining whether it was old or new.'[20] The signs of hurry, of immediate expression, are less obvious in these poems than the indications they give of ease, naturalness and order. It is particularly the last feature that Sinyavsky has stressed. He quotes from Pasternak's poem 'The Old Park ['*Staryy park*'], which belongs to the war cycle, a quatrain about a wounded soldier thinking of the play he will write:

Там он жизни небывалой
Невообразимый ход
Языком провинциала
В строй и ясность приведет.[21]

['There he will bring the unimaginable course of a fantastic life through the language of a provincial into order and clarity.']

Sinyavsky comments: ' "The language of a provincial" is the everyday living discourse free from literariness which had been Pasternak's old ideal. But a concern with "order and clarity" is something new in his understanding of the problems of art.'[22]

Order and clarity are seen by Sinyavsky as possible for Pasternak once he could escape in his poetry from the domination of metaphor. The act of perception is no longer 'dissolved in the plenitude' of things but 'retains its independence'. He now selects more carefully his impressions; and he thinks more than hitherto.[23] That is to say, he allows himself to formulate his ideas more in the manner of Tyutchev who combines impressions of nature with philosophical statement and aphorism.

Equally important, I think, is the phrase 'the language of a provincial'. Undoubtedly it had been Pasternak's aim from the first, as Sinyavsky says, to write in a language 'free from literariness'. His poetry had often disconcerted by an indifference to the propriety of a word in the particular context: it cared not in the least for decorum which, unlike the Symbolists but following Futurist practice, Pasternak overrides as may suit him. For that reason Mandelstam could speak of his achievement, no less than Khlebnikov's, in at last thoroughly secularising the Russian language.[24] But here it seems possible that Pasternak's insistence on the provincial aspect may mean something which Sinyavsky could not disclose when he wrote his introductory essay for the Soviet edition of 1965. Zhivago's uncle Nikolay, considering the significance of Christ in history, went on to describe him as 'emphatically human, deliberately provincial, Galilean'.[25] The novelty of Christian writing, as Auerbach has shown,[26] was that it united sublimity of theme with humility of language. When Pasternak made his soldier choose 'the language of a provincial', it is not a consciously proletarian idiom that he seems to have in mind. The connotation of homeliness and perhaps of bygone tradition is probably there; but one may suspect that Christian humility is indicated too.

The question of Pasternak's turning to Christian images and all that this entails must be left to the following two chapters, which deal with *Doctor Zhivago*. At this point the need is to establish the main features of his later poetry. A new interest in Christian tradition may certainly have much to do with the change that took place in his writing, though its effect is by no means as far-reaching as for example in the later poetry of Eliot from *Ash Wednesday* on. None of Pasternak's lyrics can be termed devotional, nor are they meditative in the manner of some sections in *Four Quartets*. The subjects of his poems (outside a moderately large group of those attributed to Zhivago) remain pretty much what they were. Their novelty lies in the treatment, which is a matter of a different control. As Sinyavsky explains, 'the early Pasternak had been too consistent in his impressionability to be clear'.[27] A kind of pedantry, one may suppose, if that word is appropriate to a mind so eagerly receptive and mobile, kept him to the logic of his associations (rather as Joyce was kept to the unconscionable logic of word-play). Now Pasternak has mastered his sensations: there has been no loss of spontaneity, but the pressure comes not from a welter of sense-perceptions and the emotions that flood in with them, but from the intelligence striving for order and clarity. The balance has changed. Even when, as Pasternak puts it in *Doctor Zhivago*, 'the relation-ship of forces in the creative act is turned upside down'; when the 'primacy' passes from the poet's will seeking means of expression to the language itself:[28] even at that time the intelligence is an equal partner with the language. Pasternak's later poetry admits no confu-sion.

III

A good example is 'First Frost' ['*Zazimki*'], dated 1941 by Struve and Filippov, but 1944 by Ozerov in the Soviet edition.[29] An earlier version of this poem was entitled 'Winter Holidays' ['*Zimnie prazd-niki*']; four stanzas from it were afterwards dropped.[30] The final text has achieved a stillness and a purity of outline in accordance with the scene it describes:

Открыли дверь, и в кухню паром
Вкатился воздух со двора,
И всё мгновенно стало старым,
Как в детстве в те же вечера.

Сухая, тихая погода.
На улице, шагах в пяти,
Стоит, стыдясь, зима у входа
И не решается войти.

Зима, и всё опять впервые.
В седые дали ноября
Уходят ветлы, как слепые
Без палки и поводыря.

Во льду река и мерзлый тальник,
А поперек, на голый лед,
Как зеркало на подзеркальник,
Поставлен черный небосвод.

Пред ним стоит на перекрестке,
Который полузанесло,
Береза со звездой в прическе
И смотрится в его стекло.

Она подозревает втайне,
Что чудесами в решете
Полна зима на даче крайней,
Как у нее на высоте.

[They opened the door, and into the kitchen like steam
Rolled in air from the yard,
And all instantly became old
As in childhood on evenings like this.

Dry, still weather.
On the street at five paces
Stands, ashamed, winter at the entry
And cannot resolve to go in.

Winter, and all's again as at first.
Into the hoary distances of November
Off go the willows, like blind men
Without staff and guide.

Ice-bound are river and frozen osier,
And over there on the bare ice,
Like a looking-glass on a dressing table,
Is set the black firmament.

Before it stands at the cross-roads
Which are half under drifts,
A birch with a star worn in the hair
And gazes at herself in its glass.

She secretly suspects
That with wonders most strange
Winter abounds at the last *dacha*
As for her it does on the height.]

Weidlé chooses this poem to illustrate the new style of hard-won simplicity at its best.[31] One striking difference from most of Pasternak's work hitherto appears at the very start: 'They opened the door' (or 'the door was opened'). The poet himself is withdrawn from the scene; and when the willows wander away like blind men they are not muttering about him, as they would have been at the time of *My Sister Life*. The door opens on to a world that, as always with Pasternak, continues its own life, and only the birch-tree retains the old habit of speculating about human affairs in the last *dacha*.

However, the vision here has not changed essentially from that of his earlier poems. 'Winter, and all's again as at first' [*vsyo opyat' vpervye*], and the final adverb, which was used by Pasternak in his second autobiography to describe the quality of Tolstoy's creative contemplation,[32] transmutes the world into something seen with the

same immediacy. The moment the door opened 'all. . .became old/
As in childhood' on evenings like this. The notion is continued in
the 'hoary distances of November'.

Each stanza brings a new perception. In the first, a shift back to
childhood; in the second, winter's shame and hesitation; the willows
like blind men lost in the third; the dark sky above the ice like a
looking-glass on a dressing-table in the fourth; then, in the fifth, the
birch-tree with a star in its hair gazing into the glass; and lastly the
tree's sense of a marvel taking place not only where it stands, but
in the *dacha* too at the farthest edge. Only in childhood can such
conceits come naturally: they show the mind unchecked by conventional thought as it tries to make sense of appearances. This leads
to the supposition of 'wonders most strange' – *chudesa v reshete*,
literally 'in a sieve'; the phrase could hold something of irony, and
it keeps the poem in touch with an adult world.

So Pasternak has found a genuine simplicity, whether in the syntax, which runs with ease and despatch, or in the vocabulary, which
is plain and informal, or in the rhymes, modest but neat. He now
stands much nearer to Pushkin, although his imagination still turns
far more consistently to metaphor than Pushkin's would have done.
This is because for Pasternak until the day of his death poetry meant
the disclosure of hidden relations between things: hypothesis made
actual in the concurrence of word and image. But I have already
quoted Sinyavsky to the effect that Pasternak's imagination was no
longer captive to metaphor. In these poems there is not the same
assault upon the poet's mind from all that confronts him. He is able
to dispose images and events with a greater calm, and no longer
shocks the reader into attention by rapid elliptical movement. The
poet wishes to be understood on a first perusal, even when his meanings are not altogether simple. The danger of such an aim is that it
may bring a reduction of poetic energy.

IV

The Peredelkino sequence is domestic and rural. It takes for its subjects a timeless moment of rest under pine-trees, the advent of winter
with transfiguring frost, a Christmas tree, the song of thrushes by a
railway halt in the wilderness. One poem, 'The City' ['*Gorod*']
interprets winter in terms of a possible wider implication – *ne
vremya goda,/A gibel' i konets vremyon*[33] ['not a season of the year,
but disaster and the end of seasons']. However, the circle is drawn

close: the pine forest allows the poet to share its holiday, a noontide stillness has fallen upon the 'shady haunt of the thrushes' [*priton drozdov tenistyy*] whose way of life is to be an example for artists, and all the talk is about the Christmas tree: *o yolke tolki odni*. . .[34] Pasternak seems very far from his civic preoccupations of the 1920s. Already the image has formed that was later to become so familiar, in photograph and reminiscence, of the poet digging his garden at Peredelkino:

> Я за работой земляной
> С себя рубашку скину,
> И в спину мне ударит зной
> И обожжет, как глину.
>
> Я стану, где сильней припек,
> И там, глаза зажмуря,
> Покроюсь с головы до ног
> Горшечною глазурью.[35]

> [I at work on the soil
> Shall throw off my shirt,
> And on my back will strike the heat
> And scorch it like clay.
>
> And I'll stand where it's hottest
> And there, screwing my eyes,
> I shall be covered head to foot
> In a pottery glaze.]

But in the lyric after which his volume was called, 'On Early Trains', he describes himself making trips into Moscow, and the journey brings a different awareness:

> Сквозь прошлого перипетии
> И годы войн и нищеты
> Я молча узнавал России
> Неповторимые черты.
>
> Превозмогая обожанье,
> Я наблюдал, боготворя.
> Здесь были бабы, слобожане,
> Учащиеся, слесаря.
>
> В них не было следов холопства,
> Которые кладет нужда,
> И новости и неудобства
> Они несли, как господа. . .[36]

> [Through the tragic reversals of the past
> And the years of wars and poverty
> Silently I recognised Russia's
> Unique lineaments.

Overcoming admiration
I watched, worshipping.
Here were peasant women, people from suburbs,
Students, locksmiths.

In them were no traces of the servility
That want will impose,
And innovations and discomforts
They bore like masters. . .]

This poem was dated March, 1941, three months before the German invasion.[37] The experience of the next four years had a profound effect upon Pasternak as on all Soviet citizens and on all Russians abroad. From Peredelkino he went to firewatching on Moscow rooftops; he was evacuated for a while with other writers to the little town of Chistopol, east of Moscow on the Kama, and finally in 1943 he was allowed to visit the front at Orel. This 'Excursion to the Army' ['*Poezdka v armiyu*'] he recorded in a prose article;[38] but already in the autumn of 1941 he was writing poems about the war. In all, there were to be fourteen of these.

The common dangers, the privations and sorrows of that time gave him, and many others, a sense of belonging to the people. Nadezhda Mandelstam may have been right in contrasting Pasternak's middle-class love of the *dacha* and its comforts with the almost Franciscan choice of poverty made by her husband;[39] but when Pasternak was called upon to face hardships, he took them cheerfully. Aleksandr Gladkov writes of the first winter in Chistopol:

In the discomforts and difficulties of existence he looked for the good side. 'After all here we are closer to the basic conditions of life', he would often say. 'In this time of war everyone ought to live like this, especially artists. . .'
I have seldom met anyone as patient, steadfast and unspoilt as Pasternak. A simple and modest life seems to have been a necessity for him.[40]

Pasternak had often shown a respect for the ordinary Russian people. The tribute in the poem 'On Early Trains' to 'peasant women, people from suburbs,/Students, locksmiths' was nothing unprecedented in his work. But the war revealed to him what reflection on the war of 1812 revealed to Tolstoy – the Russian people as an independent moral force in the conflict. 'The whole people had conquered from top to bottom, from Marshal Stalin to ordinary workers and plain soldiers', he wrote in his article of 1943.[41] It is put differently in the 'Epilogue' to *Doctor Zhivago* by Dudorov to Gordon:

When the war flared up its real horrors, the real danger and the menace of real death were a blessing in comparison with the inhuman domination of pretence and they brought relief since they limited the bewitching power of the dead letter.

People not only in your position, in penal servitude, but positively everyone at home and at the front breathed more freely, filling their lungs, and in rapture, with a sense of genuine happiness, hurled themselves into the furnace of the grim struggle to death and to salvation.[42]

The poems in which Pasternak responds to the war are almost without exception disappointing. One already mentioned, 'The Old Park', describes how a young wounded soldier finds that the hospital in which he lies at Peredelkino is the home of his ancestors; and since Pasternak had known before his Marburg days Dmitry Samarin who lived there,[43] some personal feeling enters the poem. There is a note of profound shock in the first poem, 'A Terrible Tale' ['*Strashnaya skazka*'], when it speaks of the children's terror and their mutilations as things never to be forgotten or forgiven.[44] And the final poem of thanksgiving, 'Spring' ['*Vesna*'], is at once intimate and expressive of a general mood:

Всё нынешней весной особое.
Живее воробьев шумиха.
Я даже выразить не пробую,
Как на душе светло и тихо.

Иначе думается, пишется,
И громкою октавой в хоре
Земной могучий голос слышится
Освобожденных территорий. . .

[All in this spring is special.
Livelier the stir of the sparrows.
I do not even try to express
The light and stillness in my spirit.

One thinks, one writes differently.
And, a loud octave in chorus,
The deep earth-voice is heard
Of the liberated territories. . .]

The final verse reflects the importance to him of Moscow, with a feeling not unlike that in the final sentences of *Doctor Zhivago*:

Мечтателю и полуночнику
Москва милей всего на свете:
Он дома, у первоисточника
Всего, чем будет цвесть столетье.[45]

[To the dreamer and nocturnal man
Moscow is dearer than all on earth:
He is at home in the primary source
Of all with which the century will blossom.]

But the other poems are mainly gestures of solidarity such as any poet will be tempted to make in a great national crisis. Anna Akhmatova had the surer instinct when in the desperate February of 1942 she wrote the lyric 'Courage' ['*Muzhestvo*'].[46] The subject of her concern is the Russian language which the generation at war must pass on 'free and pure' [*svobodnym i chistym*] to their grandchildren. From the urgency of her writing it might appear that only then had she realised fully what the language meant to her. War poems like any others ought to make a discovery.

V

The Michigan editors have added to the first cycle of war poems, which are grouped under their original heading 'Months of War (The End of 1941)' ['*Voennye mesyatsy (konets 1941 g.)*'], two lyrics he wrote 'In Memory of Marina Tsvetaeva' ['*Pamyati Mariny Tsvetaevoy*'].[47] Further variants of these poems are given in the Moscow edition of 1965.[48] Tsvetaeva took her own life at Yelabuga (also on the Kama east of Chistopol) on 31 August 1941. She had consulted Pasternak in 1935 about returning from France to the Soviet Union,[49] and finally came back in 1939. Her suicide distressed him, and he was not free from a sense of having failed to help in time. 'In the silence of your going', the second lyric says, 'there is an unspoken reproach' [*B molchan'i tvoego ukhoda/Upryok nevyskazannyy est'*].[50] These two lyrics, deeply felt, and a few pages of the chapter 'Three Shades' in his second autobiography close the record of what at one time had been an intimate friendship, though it was maintained for many years solely through correspondence.

Tsvetaeva in a letter of 1928 to Leonid Pasternak claimed that she and his son were made akin by their 'common German roots, somewhere deep in childhood, "*O Tannenbaum, O Tannenbaum*", and all that grew thence.'[51] The poet's sister Josephine has enlarged upon these affinities in home background between Tsvetaeva and Boris Pasternak.[52] Important in her view is what they both shared with Rilke – an absolute devotion to art linking them 'more indissolubly than if they had been members of one family'.[53] Marina Tsvetaeva saw Pasternak as her 'brother in the fifth season of the year, the sixth sense, and the fourth dimension',[54] and it was in this region of the impossible that she encountered the one poet whom she thought her equal 'in strength. . .in power. . .in being' [*ravnosilen, ravnomoshchen, ravnosushch*], as a poem of 1924 put it.[55]

173

Pasternak began their correspondence two years before this. They had met in the past, but it was only with the appearance of *My Sister Life* and at almost the same time of Tsvetaeva's *Vyorsty* [*Versts*, 1921–2] that they recognised one another's gifts. For a while the correspondence ran high until it finally abated. Tsvetaeva addressed many poems to Pasternak, many letters straining with breathless intimacy, and she published in an émigré journal her famous panegyric, the essay of 1923 'A Downpour of Light' ['*Svetovoy liven'*].[56] Pasternak, as she explained early on in their correspondence, underlining the phrase, signified for her '*a natural phenomenon*'.[57] On his part he admired her as 'a woman with the active spirit of a man, decisive, militant, indomitable'.[58] He thought in retrospect that only two poets when he first came to know her work, she and Aseev, 'expressed themselves as human beings and wrote in classical language and style'.[59]

The similarities between Tsvetaeva, daughter of a Moscow art historian, and Pasternak – their extraordinary devotion to poetry, their veneration for Rilke, and their failure to see politics in political terms – inevitably brought them together. Pasternak writes of 'common influences', and says that their 'points of departure, aims and preferences' were the same.[60] An alliance (or so Tsvetaeva regarded it) was formed between them which begins to approach that between Mandelstam and Akhmatova, but only begins. Tsvetaeva was even more strongly Muscovite than Pasternak in her allegiances.[61] She accepted Rilke it may be even more fervently; and yet, perhaps because of this, Rilke had more to give Pasternak. However, her support in the 1920s, when Pasternak was treated by his Soviet contemporaries with a respectful suspicion, must have meant a good deal to him. Not all the advice she offered was good: 'You know, Pasternak', Tsvetaeva urged in 1923, 'you ought to write something large.'[62] Thirty years later this would make sense: at the time it was too close to the demands of Soviet literary mentors for a work on the epic pattern. He found in Tsvetaeva a sincerity to match his own, and a comparable lack of worldliness. Once Mayakovsky had ceased to command his sympathy, she probably stood closer to him than any poet in the Soviet Union did.

The suicide of Marina Tsvetaeva, eleven years after that of Mayakovsky, followed so many disasters that it could not make on him an impression of the like intensity. The shock, all the same, was permanent. He places her shade in his final memoirs with those of the two Georgian poets dear to him, Titsian Tabidze and Paolo Yashvili.

Marina touched on the most real affinity of all when she wrote to his father: 'J'appartiens aux temps passés par toutes mes racines. Et ce n'est que le passé qui fait l'avenir.'[63] That was to be the burden of *Doctor Zhivago*.

12

'Doctor Zhivago'

I

Henry James wrote of Hawthorne's *The Scarlet Letter* that 'the subject had probably lain a long time in his mind'.[1] A dozen or fifteen years before the novel itself Hawthorne can be seen sketching out some of its themes in short stories. The same is true of *Doctor Zhivago*, no less capital in its importance for Pasternak than *The Scarlet Letter* was for Hawthorne; only, if the Michigan editors are right, the subject and the ambition to develop it in a novel occupied him for an even longer period. They suggest that the lost fictional work of which *The Childhood of Luvers* formed a part may have been a 'prototype of *Zhivago*', and in a fragment published towards the end of 1918, *Lovelessness* [*Bezlyub'e*], they see the germ of the subsequent novel that was to include Yury Zhivago and his opposite Pavel Antipov, who is lightly foreshadowed there.[2] This they have printed as the fourth of five short narratives, all of which have a bearing on the novel, at the end of their second volume. The other four were published, and presumably written, in the second half of the 1930s. These are 'The Proud Beggar' ['*Nadmennyy nishchiy*', 1939]; 'Aunt Olya' ['*Tyotya Olya*', 1939]; 'From a New Novel about 1905' ['*Iz novogo romana o 1905 g.*', 1937]; and 'A District in the Rear' ['*Uezd v tylu*', 1938].

The first three are set in the period of the 1905 revolution and in Moscow; both 'Lovelessness' and 'A District in the Rear' take another scene – the Urals – and another time – the First World War: the latter is dated precisely August 1916. 'Lovelessness' belongs to such a different stage of the novel, if this was in any real sense the same novel, that it may be discounted here. The other four pieces are written in a much more economical style, free from any affectation; and the narrator speaks in the first person. (From 'The Proud Beggar' we learn that his name is Patrikiy.[3]) It is not difficult to place them in the frame of the book that finally appeared. Thus, 'Uncle' Fedya, 'the proud beggar', is that 'disorderly old man and windbag Ostromyslensky' who had charge of Yury before he went to the Gromekos.[4] The whole story here became two sentences in the final version. Anna's wardrobe which brought about her death[5] makes its appearance in the chapter 'From a New Novel about 1905'. Both this and 'Aunt Olya' – she is a half-sister of Alexander Gromeko – describe Moscow during the civil disorders of 1905. Olya takes the floor at workers' meetings and visits the railway repair shops; in the other story first a detachment of armed workers and then a Cossack patrol in pursuit of them, led by an overbearing young officer, demand entry to the Gromekos' house. Alexander's sympathies are with the workers. These chapters would have supplemented in an interesting way the account of Moscow during 1905 – a mere glimpse, however memorable – towards the end of the second chapter in *Doctor Zhivago*. But the balance of the eventual book must have demanded their exclusion, like that of the story about Uncle Fedya.

When George Reavey came upon 'A District in the Rear' at the end of the 1950s, he suggested a number of correspondences between this tale, together with *The Childhood of Luvers* and *The Last Summer*, and *Doctor Zhivago*.[6] These extend not only to common names and incidents, but also to basic conceptions of character. Thus Lara's foreign parentage is anticipated by that of Arild in *The Last Summer* and of Evgeniya Istomina in 'A District'. The last-named resembles Lara in having married a schoolmaster who taught in the Yuryatin *gymnasium*, went to the war, and was reported missing. She has a little daughter named Katya, and at the end of the second excerpt is clearly about to become involved with the narrator, whose wife is named Tonya, with a son Shura. The maiden name of Istomina was Luvers, so that she appears to be Zhenya from Perm grown up. Mr Reavey compares two descriptions, one of Lara's beauty, one of Istomina's; these are very similar. Mr Reavey notes further that the narrator of this story feels the same dissatisfaction with his family life that Pasha felt during the war,[7] and is tempted likewise to join up. He complains to his wife that 'The source of independent life has been lost.'[8] His diagnosis of the evils that have come upon Russia is different from Zhivago's and Lara's after the civil war; but his sensibility and judgment, so far as we encounter them, put him very close to Zhivago.

And the writing, already in 1938, shows all the restraint and delicacy that mark so many descriptive passages of *Doctor Zhivago:*

Tonya and Shura were still asleep when I tiptoed away from them into the light of the night now at an end. Round about, knee-deep in the grass and the wailing of gnats, stood the birch-trees, gazing somewhere at one point from which autumn was approaching. I went in that direction.[9]

It is plain that Pasternak's novel must have been maturing fast by the end of the thirties. We know from witnesses like Afinogenov the playwright and Nadezhda Mandelstam that his mind was full of it at that time.[10] There appear to have been two changes that were necessary before he could complete the work. The first is technical. As I have remarked, the four fragments of the thirties are all written as first-person narrative. The child in 'The Proud Beggar' is easily recognisable as Yura. Later in the story, Uncle Fedya says he has already heard about the boy's 'trials of the pen'. He also refers to him as having a horse's mug' ['*morda loshadinaya*'][11] which suggests too ready an identification with Pasternak himself (Akhmatova's poem of 1936 says he 'likened himself to a horse's eye'[12]). The novel would inevitably have become less rich if Pasternak had retained the first-person narrator. And his decision was sound not to leave it as an *apologia* for his life by Yury. It is Lara and his friends who must testify to the man he was.

The second change was one of circumstances. Nadezhda Mandelstam, speculating on the feasibility of writing a full-scale novel in her country at that time, points out that Pasternak could have made little headway until the war had given 'a momentarily restored sense of community'. At the height of the purges, that sense did not exist in Russia; but without it the novelist has no wind in his sails.

Pasternak told Aleksandr Gladkov that he came back to work on his novel after the war when it was obvious that the hopes he and others entertained at that time would not be fulfilled: 'The novel was for me a most necessary private outlet. Impossible to sit with arms folded. You had to answer for your own life and for what had been given to you.'[13]

II

What is said of the youthful Yury Zhivago would seem to represent Pasternak's own ideas, though obviously somewhat later in life:

Already in his schooldays he had dreamed of prose, a book of biographies, where in the form of a secret cache of explosives he could put all that was most astounding in what he had managed to see and think over. But for such a book he was still too young, and he made do instead with the writing of poems, as a painter all through life might paint studies for a great work he had planned.[14]

'He made do instead with the writing of poems...' Eugene Kayden, the American translator of Pasternak's verse, received a letter from Pasternak which echoes these reflections:

You say I am 'first and last a poet, a lyric poet.' Is it really so? And should I feel proud of being just that? And do you realize the meaning of my being no more than that, whereas it hurts me to feel that I have not had the ability to express in greater fullness the whole of poetry and life in their complete unity? But what am I without the novel, and what have you to write about me without drawing upon that work, its terms and revelations?[15]

Nicola Chiaromonte quotes a letter on the same lines to a South American editor at the time *Doctor Zhivago* appeared: 'Fragmentary, personal poems are hardly suited to meditating on such obscure, new and solemn events. Only prose and philosophy can attempt to deal with them.'[16]

'Prose and philosophy' meant the example of the Russian novelists in the nineteenth century; and *Doctor Zhivago* upsets our expectations by not conforming to that example. Those who feel disappointment with Pasternak's novel are for the most part readers who make demands upon the book which it refuses to meet – refuses with seeming *naïveté* or arrogance. He has written what purports to be a history of his own time, containing scenes in the street or on the battlefield that must inevitably risk comparison with *War and Peace*. There are episodes like the murder of Ginz the commissar which are based on fact lightly disguised;[17] references to the first decrees of the Bolshevik government and the New Economic Policy; descriptions of the workers' rising in Moscow at the end of 1905, of the fighting in the Carpathians during the second autumn of the First World War, and of charred villages and untended fields after the civil war had passed over them. All these passages are vivid and exact; they convince like the moments of history caught in *Nineteen Five* and *Lieutenant Schmidt* (from which their treatment may be derived). Yet we must not look for the minute and dense documentation of Solzhenitsyn's *August 1914*. Pasternak is deliberately careless of chronology. No satisfactory time-table can be devised for the civil war chapters; and the episode in which Gordon and Dudorov speak of their experiences in prison fits better with the 1930s than the actual date assigned to it of 1929. At one point in the novel Pasternak offers an excuse. 'Perhaps it was so', he writes in the chapter that describes Moscow on Zhivago's return a few months before the October Revolution, 'or perhaps the doctor's impressions at the time were overlaid by the experience of later years.'[18] There has been a conscious foreshortening in the novel, the main action of which, as Pasternak explained when he first published some of Zhivago's poems, occurs between 1903 and 1929.[19] The delineation, colouring and sequence of facts in the novel are not necessarily at fault, merely the intervals between them have closed up.

So with coincidence, which crowds in after the appearance of Pasha Antipov, and Lara's attempt upon Komarovsky. What had begun as a series of unperplexing scenes that recall Tolstoy in *Childhood* or Chekhov in *The Steppe* suddenly turns into a maze of correspondences and symbolic hints. Zamyatin had said categorically that no other procedure was open to fiction seeking to represent the post-revolutionary age than 'a synthesis of the fantastic and common life [*byt*]',[20] such as is found in his own fable *We* or in Bulgakov's *The Master and Margarita*. But these authors have either chosen a setting distant in time, or, as Bulgakov does, they underline what is purely fantastic with obvious irony. However, Samdevyatov, the bizarre patron of Zhivago's family at Yuryatin, and Evgraf, the elusive half-brother of Yury, are presented in the same apparent good faith as Liberius or the old Swiss governess, Mlle Fleury. The procedure that Pasternak is following once his book gets under way makes him appear in a very dubious relation to Tolstoy, or even to Dostoevsky whose work does admit symbolic patterning and coincidence, though not with the boldness of *Zhivago*.

Was Pasternak, as Aleksandr Gladkov for one has maintained,[21] unwise in choosing the novel form for his principal work? Nadezhda Mandelstam has described all the pressures that drove writers in the Soviet Union during the 1920s to attempt 'major forms'; and something was said above on Pasternak's ambition to go beyond the lyric.[22] He had already shown himself to be highly skilled in the writing of shorter prose fiction. Every poet with the ambition to work on a large scale must be aware of the challenge to his art presented by the great nineteenth-century novelists. Pasternak would no doubt have answered Lawrence's question, 'Why the Novel Matters', in the way that Lawrence himself did: 'in the novel you can see, plainly, where the man goes dead, the woman goes inert. You can develop an instinct for life, if you will, instead of a theory of right and wrong, good and bad.'[23] His poems had shown, and were always to show, an 'instinct for life'; and the very title *Doctor Zhivago* (connected with *zhivoy*, 'living') indicates that this would be the governing theme of his novel. By adopting this form as it had come to him from Tolstoy, always so important in Pasternak's thinking about art and its relation to life, and from Dostoevsky whom he also admired very much at one time, he would be able to deepen his explorations, and to pursue what Tolstoy had called 'the endless labyrinth of linkings'.[24]

At first sight the linkings in *Doctor Zhivago* may appear forced to the point even of absurdity: 'The mutilated man who had died was private of the reserve Gimazetdin, the officer who shouted in the wood, his son, Second Lieutenant Galiullin, the nurse was Lara, Gordon and Zhivago the witnesses, they were all together, all close by, and some did not recognise, others had never known, one another.'[25] More instances can be picked out even on a cursory reading. They show little of the novelist's prime ability, so marked in Tolstoy or George Eliot, to connect the lives of individuals by threads only made visible when they tauten. Pasternak does not aim at such a complication of social causes. History for Zhivago bears a strict affinity to 'the life of the vegetable kingdom'. It answers to profound seasonal changes, which prepare themselves invisibly; to seek an explanation in the terms used by economists or political thinkers would be wholly inadequate.[26] When Pasternak reveals the pattern of coincidence with which his novel is heavily overlaid, he intends no illumination of human affairs that could be called a science. These 'crossings of destiny' (*sud'by skreshchen'ya* as they are termed in Zhivago's fifteenth poem, 'Winter Night' ['*Zimnyaya noch'*']) attest an inscrutable providence that directs the course alike of nature and man's life. In this scheme Evgraf has an intelligible place, however contrived his appearance may look in a novel.

The inter-relatedness that Pasternak pursues throughout *Doctor Zhivago* is of another kind from that usual with novelists. Yury says of the revolution in its first stage: 'It isn't only people who talk. Stars and trees have come together and converse, night flowers philosophise and stone edifices hold meetings.'[27] The affirmation of Lara at Yury's funeral expresses the same intimacy between man and the universe: she reflects that 'They had loved one another because all things around had wished it so: the land beneath them, the sky over their heads, the clouds and trees.'[28] This apprehension belongs not to the novelist, but the lyric poet. The narrative of *Doctor Zhivago* provides what linkage it can between such moments of lyrical surmise. Pasternak's imagination works in a contrary direction to the novelist's. When he wrote *Doctor Zhivago* it was actually more as a successor to Blok and the Symbolist poets than to Tolstoy and the great Russian novelists that he approached his task.[29]

III

The singularity of *Doctor Zhivago* lies above all in its form. Of its seventeen 'parts' or chapters the last comprises the poems by Zhivago which his friends have preserved. Dimitri Obolensky is right in finding fault with the English translation when it places these poems as a supplement to the novel – a supplement which many of the book's English-speaking readers most probably skip. The novel has a tripartite structure: first the fifteen chapters of the main narrative, beginning with the funeral of Yury's mother, and ending with his own; then the Epilogue, set in 1943 with a final scene 'five or ten years' later; and to conclude, 'The Poems of Yury Zhivago', numbered like the sections of the preceding chapters, and constituting a second and parallel narrative, which moves from spring through summer, autumn and winter to spring again.[30] It seems important to note that Pasternak could not in shaping his work dispense with 'fragmentary, personal poems'. There was precedent enough for setting the journal of Yury within the narrative,[31] although this does not greatly concern the action, as it does in Lermontov's *Hero of Our Own Time* [*Geroy nashego vremeni*, 1841]. But no Russian novelist had found it necessary to follow up the prose narrative with poetry. Probably the nearest counterpart to Yury Zhivago in the classical Russian novel is that suggested by Max Hayward – Prince Myshkin of Dostoevsky's *The Idiot*.[32] Myshkin resembles Zhivago in not sharing the assumptions of other characters in the story; and again like Zhivago he proves incapable of taking his place in the society to which he belongs. However, it is also true that, no less than his inverted double the murderer Rogozhin, he can be fully revealed through his relations, unsatisfactory though these are, with that society. But Zhivago's life is disastrously incomplete without his poetry, and his perceptions are more important than anything he does – except in so far as he refrains from action in order to preserve his freedom as a poet.[33] To explore the nature and predicament of the artist has become an imperative need for many novelists in this century. None except Pasternak has felt obliged to reflect back on the story of the artist's life the art he creates to the extent of showing that art entire. Thomas Mann in *Doctor Faustus* describes the effect of Leverkühn's *Faust* cantata; but that is a different thing – the cantata itself, like the novel *The Middle Years* in Henry James' story of that name, has to be taken on trust.[34]

Doctor Zhivago is a work that contains many oppositions: its structure even in detail relies on antithesis. Socially and politically the novel contrasts the old and the new orders in Russia: the old, unjust certainly and repressive, but depicted here as making possible some civilised, even humane, conduct; and the new, allowing generous impulses to sanction intolerance and savagery. The domestic virtues of Tonya are set against the lawless fascination exerted by Lara. The first 'innocent' stages of a revolution, as seen in 1905 and in the early summer of 1917, when people act out surprising parts and a miller and a deaf mute form their own village republic,[35] stand against the ruthless lack of respect for persons shown by the Bolshevik professionals. The main opposition is that between Yury himself and those who have capitulated to the ethos of the new system – Pasha Antipov, Liberius the partisan leader, and the 're-educated' Dudorov and Gordon (though later they become the disciples of Zhivago after his death, when a premonition of freedom following the war is abroad). However this opposition between Zhivago, who makes for life, and the others who in their censure of his attitudes make for death, is complicated by a further one which Yury suffers himself, as moral being and moral agent. In the latter capacity he fails, avoiding any decision but that of surrender or withdrawal so as not to impose his will upon others. (Zhivago waits upon events like Kutuzov in *War and Peace*, but the outcome of his battle is paradoxical: 'I am defeated by them all', as a poem of his puts it, 'and only in that consists my victory'.[36]) Yet as a moral being he is very significant, though the novel alone cannot demonstrate this. Yury's rare virtue of inspiring freedom and unconcern [*veyanie svobody i bezzabotnosti*][37] exists at its purest in the poetry, which complements the idea of him that the prose narrative has intimated, and rounds off what had been inconclusive. It is the combined achievement of the prose and verse to establish a state of grace in Yury which has no relation to works but depends on the response of a truly disinterested imagination.

Pasternak's novel follows the tradition of Pushkin in *Eugene*

Onegin, of Turgenev in *Rudin*, of Goncharov in *Oblomov*, by taking its title from the hero's name. The three works mentioned above centre upon a representative man, a private not a public figure, and show the modification of his life by social pressures. An understanding of the hero leads to an understanding of his time (this is true also of *Anna Karenina* which provides a significant and fairly complete picture of Russia in the 1870s). The hero's weaknesses are symptomatic, they reveal a social malaise; his virtues (which the time may thwart or deform) hint at a scheme of values in opposition to those upheld by society. These solitary heroes, at odds with their surroundings, are given an historical dimension. On no side are they isolated from the influences of their age, even when like Oblomov they deliberately withdraw from it. The Russian novelist in the nineteenth century had learned to give attention to detail while entertaining a large vision; he generalised from the evidence of particulars firmly grasped; and so achieved a classical authority, being at once comprehensive and exact.

Judged by these standards *Doctor Zhivago* must be imperfect. Pasternak offers a far less elaborate survey of the historical events than Tolstoy in *War and Peace* (though his metaphysical view is a large one, especially when opened out by the poems). The private lives of Yury, Lara, Pasha, the Gromekos, make contact with history: in December 1905, for instance, Lara and her mother witness the rising of Moscow workers, and again in October 1917 Yury and his family are surrounded by the street fighting which led to Bolshevik power in Moscow as in Petrograd. There is also a keen impressionistic sense of a country in crisis – the 'thin, decently dressed old women and old men' in Moscow trying to sell artificial flowers, coffee-heaters, evening gowns, obsolete uniforms;[38] the typhus-stricken crowds encamped at a Moscow railway station;[39] and, following the civil war, unharvested fields overrun with mice, and dogs turned wild roaming the burned-out villages.[40] The battle for Yuryatin, with the 'Giant Kinema' in flames;[41] the sight some years later of people reading the proclamations posted by the Reds, on a cold evening towards spring;[42] or the description of Moscow at the beginning of NEP in 1922[43] – all these are glimpses into the historical past which might have come from a very observant book of memoirs. Yet it is noteworthy how seldom Yury and the people nearest to him ever happen to be present on those occasions that one imagines Tolstoy would have wanted to depict. That is to say, history is enacted in this novel exclusively through its effects on private lives.

No historical figures are presented, apart from one fleeting encounter with Tsar Nicholas II, an awkward and unsure man inspecting his troops on the Galician front in 1916.[44] It is only fictional leaders (Strelnikov, Liberius, Galiullin) who cross the scene. And in this Pasternak works closer to Tolstoy's notion of the historical process than Tolstoy himself. The real makers of history, so *War and Peace* insists, are not the sovereigns, their generals and ministers, but the multitude of small people whose unsystematic and limited actions obscurely meet the demands of the historical moment. Yury Zhivago agrees with this. 'Those who make revolutions are active men, one-sided fanatics, geniuses of self-limitation.'[45] But such organisers constitute merely the yeast that ferments a natural process, like the invisible growth of grass. And Zhivago does not participate in history, even to the extent of Pierre Bezukhov; he simply learns to read it aright.

Some of Pasternak's detail has been challenged. Would Pasha, the son of a railway worker whom the regime had exiled, and Lara (though there was indeed the connection with Komarovsky in her case) so easily have gained admission to Moscow University? How many White generals in the civil war had origins similar to those of Galiullin, son of a Tatar house-porter? Pasternak did not reject verisimilitude, even though he strains it at points like these. As he explained to Stephen Spender, his aim was 'to show the liberty of being, its verisimilitude touching, adjoining improbability'.[46] In this way he defended 'the frank arbitrariness of the "coincidences"' throughout the book, beginning with that conglomeration of destinies linked surprisingly together by the five o'clock express in the first chapter. 'Improbability' time and again had been made actual in his poetry; the coincidences are in line with the juxtapositions so frequent there; he is seeking the truth not as Pushkin, Tolstoy or Chekhov – all three, incidentally, admired by Zhivago – would have conceived it, in particulars that accord with common experience, and therefore seem to be verifiable. Rather he proceeds in the manner of Dostoevsky, or of Shakespeare in the romances. (Stuart Hampshire's recognition of a debt to Shakespeare very much pleased Pasternak.[47]) Both these predecessors can be arbitrary in the interests of a moral and metaphysical design. For Pasternak, the whole of life properly seen is a revelation. Ultimately the scope of *Doctor Zhivago* extends very far. Where Pasternak pushes verisimilitude over the confines to improbability his excuse must be that which he gave for Rembrandt, Michelangelo and Titian (he was defending the speed and complexity of Shakespeare's metaphors): 'With their insatiable desire to paint the whole of the universe that threw them into turmoil they had no time to paint otherwise.'[48]

IV

'The liberty of being' exemplified with such readiness for sacrifice by Zhivago derives from a Christian philosophy of life which his uncle Nikolay expounds early in the book.[49] Between Nikolay Niko-laevich and Zhivago there exists an eager sympathy, since they are both creative, but very soon in the revolutionary summer of 1917 Nikolay Nikolaevich begins to enjoy the role of 'political phrase-monger'.[50] Though his ideas continue to inspire Yury, the man him-self is unequal to them. It is Zhivago alone who can help others fully by his example 'to break through to freedom, to the fresh air', as Lara says in her lament for him[51] (and the manner of his own death, struggling to let air into a crowded tram, becomes a symbolic enact-ment of this, as many critics have recognised[52]). A preoccupation with true freedom runs through the novel. The little Jewish boy Misha Gordon feels excluded by his origins from 'the sense of a supreme and crucial unconcern' [*chuvstvo vysshey i kraeugol'noy bezzabot-nosti*] which all other people seem to share.[53] It is denied to Pasha who lacks 'the gift of the unexpected', and whose heart is not unprincipled enough;[54] Gordon and Dudorov in the later 1920s wil-lingly turn their backs upon it;[55] and it is taken away from Lara by Komarovsky, whose 'prisoner for life' she acknowledges herself to be even as a girl.[56] Pasternak does not hesitate to associate the pos-sibilities of this freedom with a particular class in a social order since gone: Gromeko claims that his family 'parted with the rage of acquisitiveness already a generation back'.[57] A focus for kindly and spontaneous feeling is provided in the Christmas party given by the Sventitskys in 1911. This connects the traditional warmth of a Russian Christmas with the hospitable ways of an educated family who seem in their own fashion heirs to the Rostovs in *War and Peace*, and also with the art, so much admired by Zhivago, of Blok, foremost among Russian poets at that time.[58] The natural haunt of freedom would appear to be a drawing-room hung with Christmas decorations, where intelligent people no longer troubled by 'the rage of acquisitiveness' could celebrate the season of good will toward men.

The mourners were singing 'Eternal Memory' as the novel

opened, and it often laments the passing of old courtesy and consideration. Three incidents on the rail journey to the Urals reveal what has been lost. There is the notice in a ruined station begging passengers not to disquiet themselves because the first-aid box has been temporarily sealed up;[59] there is the strange mutedness of the people at another station which makes Zhivago think that they are concerned not to disturb those sleeping in the train, as once would have been the case (actually a waterfall nearby has deadened the customary din);[60] and there is the solicitude of the country stationmaster on their arrival: 'The newcomers were struck by the quietness at the station, the absence of people, the neatness. It seemed to them unusual that there was no shoving or swearing all round. Life in these backwoods here lagged after history, it was left behind. It had still to attain the savagery of the capital.'[61] What Pasternak wants most to recapture in this part of his novel is the sense of community, and this involves a deep interest in tradition, a piety towards the past. He sets over against the drastic measures of those who take it upon themselves to mould life as if it were an inert substance,[62] the self-renovation of life itself: 'A Russian song is like water in a mill-pond. Seemingly it has been halted and does not move. But in the depths it flows out unceasingly with the spring floods [iz veshnyakov] and the stillness on its surface is illusory.'[63] The old woman Kubarikha recites her spell over a sick cow, and in its garbled phrasing Yury can discern traces of some ancient chronicle from the dark ages. He is puzzled by the manner in which 'the tyranny of tradition has so seized him'.[64] But apparent nonsense hides a real meaning; and he is able to understand Lara's significance for him in terms of the folk imagery used by Kubarikha. When Yury escapes to her from the partisans, she has become symbolised by the rowan-tree, the actual one standing outside the camp, and the other in Kubarikha's song; and he addresses his absent love in the language of popular poetry: 'I shall see you, my perfect beauty, my rowan-princess, drop of my very blood.' (The Russian words begin to dance, with the play of diminutives and internal rhymes.)[65]

On the last pages of the novel it seems to Zhivago's friends that Moscow has been 'the principal heroine of the long tale' (just as St Petersburg had been that of Blok's autobiography in his lyrics[66]), and in their minds it becomes 'this holy city'.[67] Lara, 'the girl from another circle', daughter of a Belgian engineer and a russified Frenchwoman, clearly stands in the novel at times for Russia itself; she answers to Zhivago's 'youthful prototype', the female image he

has formed for himself early in childhood that he can identify with
'all his own life, all God's world, all the sunlit expanse stretching
before him' one bright autumn day when he is with the partisans.[68]
But Lara is eventually lost; she returns to Moscow after a long
absence under the protection of Komarovsky; and whereas Zhivago
dies 'at home in history', as his uncle would say,[69] because he is duly
commemorated by his friends and lives on in his poetry, Lara
vanishes into oblivion: 'she died or disappeared no one knows
where, forgotten under some anonymous number on lists subsequently mislaid, in one of the countless mixed or female concentration camps of the north'.[70] Yury, who stayed in Moscow once he
had gone back there, has nothing to reproach himself with so far as
his vocation is concerned. Not to desert Moscow, the heart of Pasternak's Russia, is to keep faith with home and tradition – as one of
Yury's poems says: 'so that beyond the city boundary the earth
should not grieve alone' [Chtoby za gorodskoyu gran'yu/Zemle ne
toskovat' odnoy].[71] Pasternak does not imply that Lara's fate was
deserved, and yet he has not allowed the all-capable Evgraf to inter-
cede for her.

The phrase 'this holy city' cannot fail to suggest the long-
established idea of Moscow as the 'third Rome', successor to Byzan-
tium when it too fell as Rome had done. ('Legendary features of the
third Rome' could still be discerned in Moscow of the 1890s.[72])
Pasternak shows a respect for Orthodox doctrines (as expounded by
Sima, who leans heavily on the interpretations of Nikolay Nikolaevich[73]), and it is obvious from the poems in Part XVII that he accepts
gratefully the time-honoured rituals and commemorations of the
Church. He is no iconoclast like Tolstoy; and at the same time not
an impassioned seeker for a code of moral conduct as Tolstoy was.
The reference to Moscow as a 'holy city' follows from his conviction
that to live in history is to live in the awareness of grace, of a divine
purpose in things. In the spring of 1917 Yury had the sense of living
'as in the time of the apostles'.[74] When Moscow has achieved the
promised freedom, it will live once more in history.

V

Doctor Zhivago is often explicit – and sometimes excessively so –
as in the conversations of Sima above mentioned, of Nikolay Nikolaevich at the beginning, and of Yury and Lara in Yuryatin on his
return,[75] and Yury and Pasha at Varykino.[76] But also in the tradi-

tion of Shakespeare and the great novelists, it often resorts to implication by contrast. One example is the opening of the chapter 'On the High Road'. Yury has been captured by the partisans in the woods and conscripted for service. The narrative breaks off at this point, and the new chapter begins: 'There were towns, villages, settlements. The town of Krestovozdvizhensk, the station Omelchino...' and so through a list of a dozen place-names, understandably omitted from the English translation. Yet it is a pity they went, because their catalogue belongs with the statement that follows: 'A highroad passed through them, very, very old, the oldest in Siberia, the ancient post road.'[77] Along this road in distant times had gone troikas with the mail, waggons with their various loads, convicts chained and on foot. 'And the forests murmured all round, dark, impenetrable.' Here is the Russia of legend and recent memory; like the forests, dark and perhaps impenetrable, yet 'the road lived as one family'. Over the town of Krestovozdvizhensk stands the Monastery of the Exaltation of the Cross after which it was named. Winter is ending: Holy Week has succeeded Lent.

At the seventh hour by church reckoning, but by ordinary calculation at one in the morning, from the weightiest, hardly stirring bell of the Exaltation there broke off and floated away, mingling with the dark and damp of the rain, a wave of still, dark and melodious humming. It thrust off from the bell as there breaks away from the bank, and sinks, and dissolves in the river a flood-cleansed earthen clod.[78]

The whole passage, which moves into the reflections of the shopkeeper's wife Galuzina, evokes a scene recalling the intricate descriptions of a bygone Russia by Leskov.[79] Although Galuzina is the merest *meshchanka* or small trader's wife, who clings to the memories of past comfort – her velvet dress and her wineglasses of the same violet-to-lilac hue – the 'richness and order' she mourns are precisely what the partisans set out to destroy. Veneration for the icon in her bedroom consorts with anti-semitism and other dark prejudices; the Russia her husband is exhorting young men to defend is scarcely more than a figure of turgid rhetoric. All the same, Pasternak finds something to regret in this world, called by the nineteenth-century critic Dobrolyubov ·'the kingdom of darkness' [*tyomnoe tsarstvo*]. There is a famous poem of Blok's written at the beginning of the First World War, which depicts the mixture of greed and superstition in the church-going and money-grubbing class of the *meshchane*. It ends with the sudden avowal: 'Yet even so, my Russia, you are dearer to me than any place' [*Da, i*

189

takoy, moya Rossiya,/Ty vsekh krayov dorozhe mne].[80] Pasternak in the high road chapter seems to share this attitude, though he responds to the Christian tradition that Blok shows to have been debased with a more conscious sympathy.

The editorial board of *Novy Mir* to whom Pasternak somewhat naively submitted his novel took strong exception to the political bias they noted. Yury in the field with a partisan unit befriends a White cadet. During the skirmish this boy was wounded:

> The doctor lay unarmed in the grass and observed the course of the battle. All his sympathy was on the side of the heroically falling children. From his heart he wished them success. These were the scions of families probably close to him in spirit, of his education, his moral complexion, his ideas.[81]

When the battle grows fiercer he is compelled to take up a rifle and cannot help hitting several of the cadets despite his avoiding action. The boy whom he saves and protects does not conceal from Yury and the medical assistant that when released on recovery he will serve again with the Whites.[82]

It would be easy to infer from this episode that Pasternak has made his membership of the 'internal emigration' no longer passive. Lara had spoken at Varykino of the complexity that surrounds all political issues: 'It is, you see, only in bad little books that the living are divided into two camps and never come into contact.'[83] The writer as witness to his time cannot simplify in the manner of Liberius, whose inexorable harangues provide the context here for Yury's refusal to see the White cadets as his enemies. Just before Lara uttered that protest she had told Zhivago about the atrocities committed by the Whites. There was abundant bestiality in either camp, as the book reveals. Pasternak's aim is to bring the whole age to judgment, and the verdict comes from Lara. She blames the World War for having destroyed the authority of individual conscience: 'It was then that falsehood came to the Russian land. The chief disaster, root of the future evil, was loss of faith in the value of one's own opinion... There began to grow the dominion of the phrase, at first monarchical, then revolutionary.'[84]

The tragedy of Russia is that the lie invaded domestic no less than public life: 'How could a man so sensitive and exacting towards himself as Pasha, who so infallibly distinguished reality from appearance, pass over this insinuating falsehood and not notice it?'[85] Nadezhda Mandelstam in her first book speaks of a woman who asked her 'why all those students who thirst after truth and righteousness are always so keen on poetry'. She concludes it is because poetry forms 'the golden treasury in which our values are preserved'.[86] If the evil in Zhivago's age arose from mendacious rhetoric, then the importance of poetry becomes clear. In his Varykino journal Yury had opposed to 'the spirit, dominant in our time, of the high-flown phrase' another style, practised by Pushkin and Chekhov, which deliberately avoids every kind of pretension.[87] Such is the style he had always sought for his poetry, one that should be 'imperceptible' and not 'drawing anyone's attention' upon itself;[88] his Moscow pamphlets are written so as to be accessible to all, 'in colloquial form', but very far from popularisation;[89] and Lara in her lament for Yury uses 'the simple everyday words of sturdy unceremonious talk'.[90] The political idiom, on the other hand, is 'bombastic precisely because it lacks talent'.[91]

VI

The possession of talent, so liberating for those who care to learn from him, makes Yury the central figure in Pasternak's scheme. As a doctor he excels by his powers of diagnosis. When Yury's son is born, he happens at the same time to receive congratulations from his colleagues on recognising *echinococcus*.[92] The two achievements are clearly to be contrasted: in his son's birth he can take little pride – it has all been Tonya's risk and Tonya's triumph. Yury, a father who abandons all his children (there is that accusatory nightmare in which Shurochka, the son just mentioned, remains shut out with the menacing flood-water[93]), lives his full life in another relationship, a communion with the natural world transfigured by the artist's impassioned awareness. Pasternak says in a note on *Romeo and Juliet* that 'love is equivalent to creation... The most sublime thing art can dream of is to overhear [love's] proper voice, its always new and unprecedented language.'[94] Yury's intuitions about medicine and science stem from the poetical faculty just as did those of Goethe; they are a function of that impressionability which made him so original in his thought as a young man.[95] He tells Tonya's mother (having just rightly diagnosed her illness) that 'talent in the highest and broadest sense is the gift of life'.[96] It reveals itself above all in a readiness for the unexpected.[97] In the spring of 1917 the entire Russian people gave itself up to the unexpected; all were seemingly reborn, capable of realising their true selves in freedom.[98]

Komarovsky, the evil genius of Lara, warns Zhivago that communism has its style, and 'nobody so manifestly offends against this

manner of living and thinking' as he does.[99] Yury can accept no
'social demand'; he sets his poetry before the practice of medicine; he speaks slightingly of Marxism to Samdevyatov, denying its
claim to be considered a science;[100] and he would like to inform his
friends, who have been 're-educated' in a prison camp, that 'the
single living and bright thing' about them is to have been his contemporaries and to have known him.[101] Thus the novel carries on an
active polemic against all that is summed up in the self-blinding
tirades of Liberius which assume that 'the interests of the revolution
and the existence of the solar system' are 'one and the same
thing'.[102] Liberius, in his confidence that the future can easily be
moulded to design, represents the dead opposite of talent; but
Pasha, in spite of possessing 'to a rare degree...the gift of moral
purity and justice',[103] has been ruined by the same inability to find
his true self. Pasha's talent, as Yury diagnoses on meeting him, is
one merely for imitation.[104]

VII

In Zhivago's final encounter with Strelnikov there is a moment when
the latter recalls vividly how Lara would shake a carpet.[105] Zhivago
has just told him that Lara would have given anything to regain her
domestic life with Pasha which 'the social delusion'[106] had
destroyed. At the time of saying this, she had been 'putting the
room in order'; and Pasha, with a delicate insistence, gets Zhivago
to describe all the details of this scene. Thus, on the eve of Pasha's
suicide, Yury helps to revive in him the memory of a private world
which he had long excluded from his thoughts. Blok, as we have
already noted, in the poem *Retribution* [*Vozmezdie*] had spoken of
the twentieth century as bringing an 'even more homeless [*eshcho
bezdomney*] darkness' into life than the 'iron and truly harsh' nineteenth had.[107] In the role of Strelnikov Pasha had done his share to
render the age homeless beyond any conception Blok could have
formed when he wrote the lines: once every man feels 'a secret male-
factor, a still unmasked deceiver', driven by bad conscience to tra-
duce himself,[108] this is the ultimate homelessness. Lara's actual
words were:

If Strelnikov had again become Pasha Antipov. If he had given up his
madness and rebellion. If time had turned back. If somewhere far away, at
the edge of the world, by a miracle the window of our home had been lit
up with the lamp and books on Pasha's writing-table, I think I would have
crawled there on my knees.[109]

That miracle cannnot be; the course is irreversible for Pasha, and
for Lara herself who must eventually submit to her past embodied
in Komarovsky. We cannot deny the truth of Tonya's complaint
(which goes with a genuine admiration for her) that Lara was born
'to complicate life' and 'lead astray'.[110] Nonetheless, Lara is
allowed to reproduce, briefly and precariously, the miracle for which
she longs, at Varykino with Yury. 'Our days are numbered now',
he has said,[111] as he had seen them to be numbered even before the
October Revolution on his return from the front to Moscow.[112] At
the edge of the world, in Mikulitsyn's abandoned home, Katya
builds a house for her doll out of the playthings that had once
belonged to Liberius. Lara is struck by the little girl's 'instinct for
housekeeping [*domovitost'*], the indestructible urge for the nest and
for order'. 'Children', she says, 'are not ashamed of the truth, while
we in our fear of seeming to lag behind are ready to betray what is
most dear'.[113] The whole episode of Varykino revisited becomes a
celebration of 'what is most dear'. Together, they restore a full
household routine by day, while Yury sits under the lamp to write
down his poems at night. But it cannot last. The wolves are waiting
outside in the moonlight; Komarovsky will soon appear to take Lara
away; and Yury will soon be wandering through a devastated
country that cries out for the tending of human hands.

VIII

In Zhivago's imagination the wolves 'come to represent the hostile
force' seeking to destroy Lara and himself or at the least to drive
them out of Varykino. He begins to think of a fabulous dragon in
the ravine as symbol for that force, and this leads to his poem about
Saint George who rescues the maiden from a monster.[114] Now Yury
is one Russian form of the name George; and it must be intentional
that the town where so much happens in Zhivago's life should bear
the name Yuryatin. Once you look into the pattern of possible
symbolic allusion in Pasternak's novel, as Edmund Wilson first
showed the way, comparing it with *Finnegans Wake* and the cab-
balistic writings of the Hebrews,[115] every name and every incident
seems to invite a gloss. The Rowlands in their book provide a commentary 'designed to interpret for the general reader the deeper
levels of meaning which lie hidden under the surface story'.[116] This
goes far beyond the researches and guesses of Wilson (some of
which, like the attempt to relate Vechinkin in the sign 'Moreau and

Vechinkin' with Hamlet, are purely fantastic). The difficulty of accepting the novel as Wilson and the Rowlands see it lies in the notion of 'deeper levels of meaning' which stay hidden until the keys are applied. This is not to deny that some further meanings of real importance will emerge from a study of Yury's poems. Pasternak always contended that art was 'symbolic in essence', as he told Eugene Kayden,[117] or as he argued in *Safe Conduct*.[118] Grant that a significant life must be lived 'in history',[119] and it follows that analogues will reveal themselves, because history in Pasternak's view answers to a design. The poems help to elicit that design: they show the analogy between art and resurrection, and thus between Zhivago (as Hamlet initially) and Christ, and between the fallen Lara with her devotion to the life-giving Yury and Mary Magdalene. But the metaphor of 'deeper levels of meaning' is unsatisfactory. The action and its import, the character and his role, must reveal themselves primarily in the light of other actions and characters within the novel. A symbolic meaning that has been 'hidden under the surface' is sterile like the talent hidden in the earth: it never properly comes into circulation until too late.

Certain symbols that recur in the novel – the candle, rowan-berries, mice or rats – are prominent and require no special elucidation. Of these the candle is most important. Pasternak emphasises this when the sight of a candle behind Pasha's window inspires Yury with the opening lines of a poem which, completed years later, will celebrate the love of a man and a woman.[120] Yury himself will one day lie dead in that room. There is little need to trace the appearances of this symbol: its meaning presents no problem. The rowan-berry, from Kubarikha's song, refers to Lara; and when the blood on the snow from Pasha's left temple is compared with 'berries of the frozen rowan' that seems to signify what he has lost in Lara.[121] The mice running in the neglected fields when Yury makes his way home to Moscow have been preceded by mention of the rats swarming on the stone gutter of Lara's final lodging before marriage,[122] and again of the rats in her room at Yuryatin opposite the House with the Caryatids.[123] Here perhaps we are reminded that ruin awaits Lara, as it did Russia after the civil war; but that is not an invitation to identify her in season and out with Russia. Sometimes these connections may be highly elusive, not perhaps even fully present to the author's mind.

Finnegans Wake merely distracts in a consideration of *Doctor Zhivago*, because the two works never meet. Pasternak describes a scene that is always palpable and very distinct: even when Yury dreams, the outlines of things remain firm, though other meanings may lurk behind, as one would expect in a dream. Nor has Pasternak fallen into the whirlpool of verbal associations. *Doctor Zhivago* must be taken as a novel about the actual experience of a generation in a particular phase of Russian history. Pasternak does indeed aim to give a new dimension to the term 'history'; but he begins with the known events and the common conditions. He protested to Olga Carlisle that 'the novel must not be judged along theological lines' and he added: 'Nothing is further removed from my understanding of the world.'[124] This would seem to confirm that meanings must be sought, as in any true novel, on the surface to begin with; and the symbolic hints that gather as the story develops must all find their warrant in the action before the reader's eyes. Too much 'theological interpretation' results in an overweighting of this or that detail, a preoccupation with 'themes' at the expense of the novel's proper life, and perhaps a disregard of the simple and obvious.

The choice of personal names in a fiction is seldom fortuitous, as the example of Dickens, or Dostoevsky, or for that matter Henry James can show. Zhivago was the name of a well known Moscow merchant family;[125] and a scientist called Zhivago is to be found in *The Great Soviet Encyclopaedia*. But, as Wilson suggested, Pasternak chose it for his hero because of the Biblical phrase 'Why seek ye the living among the dead?'[126] where in Church Slavonic 'the living' would be rendered *zhivago*. The name Lara may have some allusion to St Larisa, more probably to Larisa Reisner, the revolutionary heroine whom Pasternak invited in a poem of 1926 to 'saunter into the depth of legend' [*Bredi zhe v glub' predan'ya, geroinya*].[127] Evgraf, who in Zhivago's delirium brought on by typhus seems to be the symbol of his death, but also helps to write his poem,[128] must be explained primarily as derived from the Greek adjective *eugraphes*, 'writing well'; and when Yury asks himself how there can be profit from death, he has forgotten his own thoughts at the time of Anna's funeral: art, he concluded then, 'persistently reflects upon death and persistently thereby creates life'.[129] Samdevyatov's name, as he tells Yury, derives from San Donato, which has become distorted on Russian lips. He belongs apparently to the princely house of the Demidovs.[130] The expression *sam-devyat'* means 'a ninefold harvest'; and perhaps there is a hint in his name of the mythical '*tri-devyatoe tsarstvo*',[131] the 'thrice-nine kingdom' of folk-tale. These allusions seem enough to establish the role of Samdevyatov in

195

Yury's and Lara's lives, which is beneficent and mysterious; it is also, as Lara says, meddlesome, and in some ways to be compared with that of Komarovsky.[132]

Pasternak has depicted him as a party member, trusted though oddly eclectic in his ideas. The Rowlands have noted that Samdevyatov belongs to the time he characterises in conversation with Yury: 'a transitional period, when theory does not yet march with practice'.[133] They elicit more hints from his first name and patronymic, Anfim Efimovich, arguing that since *San* has become *Sam* in his surname, Anfim must be derived from Greek *amphi* 'on both sides'; while Efim is the Russian equivalent of Joachim, and Pasternak has chosen for Samdevyatov's 'prototype' 'the twelfth-century Italian mystic, theologian and abbot, Joachim of Floris, whose prophecies of the Three Ages, according to Berdyaev, were congenial to the Russian mind'.[134] They proceed to point out a parallel between Joachim's historical triad and 'certain Marxist dogmas'. But this method of interpretation tends to assume that spotting the 'prototype' is decisive. So Pasternak's novel insensibly yields place to a tight-knit and ingenious system of occult meanings (Evgraf's mother was a Princess Stolbunova, *stolb* means a pillar, which is 'a common Asiatic metonym for the supreme Heaven-god thought to dwell above the world-pillar supporting the sky at the North Star' – and finally Evgraf's mother becomes Mnemosyne, daughter of Uranus, living in a house with five windows that symbolise the five senses[135]). Undoubtedly there are aspects of *Doctor Zhivago* which bear some relation to myth; but the degree to which account should be taken of this will depend upon our sense of the novel's coherence as a record of relations between men and women. The symbolic meanings, where they exist, are regulated finally by the poems.

IX

Doctor Zhivago is not altogether satisfactory as a novel because, in the words Pasternak used when explaining his book to Stephen Spender, he wanted above all to convey an 'atmosphere of being'. Whereas the nineteenth-century novelists gave a deterministic world ruled by 'the law of sequels and retribution', Pasternak had before his eyes 'a sort of painted canvas roof or curtain in the air' which was 'pulled and blown and flapped by...an immaterial unknown and unknowable wind'.[136] *Doctor Zhivago* tries to account for more than a novel should. Evgraf is indispensable to Pasternak's metaphysical design, but he never gains credence as a character in the novel. Yet Pasternak shows no sign of embarrassment over Evgraf, because Yury is able to accept the comings and goings of his half-brother as revealing the 'participation of a secret unknown power' in his life.[137] It can be objected that Lara too exists more fully for Yury than for the reader, at any rate once her girlhood is past. Sometimes the exchanges between Yury and her sound like the colloquy of a mind with itself, as when he tells her: 'Go on. I know what you will say next. How you make sense of everything! What a joy it is to listen to you!'[138] As Nadezhda Mandelstam says, such dialogues are 'simply variations on Pasternak's own words'.[139] The reality of other people in the novel is dependent very much on their significance for Zhivago. Tonya, for example, becomes vividly present to the reader when Yury takes her handkerchief at the Sventitskys' dance: 'The handkerchief gave out a mingled odour of tangerine skin and of Tonya's palm... This was something new in Yury's life, never experienced and keenly penetrating him through and through.'[140] She exists briefly as the mother of his child, and as the injured wife who writes him a letter of farewell. But her significance is that she too, like Dudorov and Gordon, was alive in Zhivago's day and knew him.

Though Pasternak would have liked it to be otherwise, he was 'first and last a poet, a lyric poet'. Dramatically, his novel lacks power; it is not everywhere realised with the same adequacy; and objection has been raised to the artificial idiom spoken by Markel the porter and Galuzina the shopkeeper's wife.[141] Yet given that the book at its core is lyrical, and brought alive by the presence of Yury, what an extraordinary keenness and fertility of perception he turns upon the surrounding world! *Doctor Zhivago* is a poet's novel, with an intensity in its writing at many points which recalls the Pasternak of *My Sister Life*.

That intensity is focused finally in the poems proper that form the last section of the book, and for which the novel has provided an elaborate context.

13

The Poems of Yury Zhivago

I

The twenty-five lyrics credited to Zhivago are in no sense an appendix of the novel. Formally they constitute its last chapter; and there will be occasion later to discuss what they add to the significance of Zhivago's life-story. A point we should consider first is that Pasternak has taken pains to describe the genesis of certain poems. Like Coleridge he seems to have found 'What is poetry? is so nearly the same question with, what is a poet? that the answer to the one is involved in the solution of the other'.[1] Yury's poems are there as the evidence of his creative power, but the activity that produces them, and the nature of the power itself, greatly interested Pasternak. The paragraphs in his chapter on the second visit to Varykino which describe Yury the poet at work are not unprecedented in Pasternak's own writing. He had already shown the process of creation in *The Last Summer*.[2] Nor is it surprising that other Russian poets should have taken a similar interest in the condition of their minds when the imagination sets to work – this power which, to quote Coleridge once more, is 'first put in action by the will and understanding, and retained under their irremissive, though gentle and unnoticed, controul'.[3] Pushkin in a fragment of 1833, 'Autumn' ['*Osen'*'], anticipates the Varykino passage when he tells how poetry awakens in him as he sits by the stove in a silent room.[4] The mind, after groping 'as if in sleep', suddenly receives images together with the necessary rhymes. He represents the imagination as 'a ship motionless in moveless water' [*nedvizhim korabl' v nedvizhnoy vlage*] which the breeze catches and propels on its way. Anna Akhmatova offers a much closer analysis in her little poem 'Creation' ['*Tvorchestvo*', 1936].[5] She, like Pushkin, attends to the process itself – a preliminary languor, then the emergence of one dominant sound among many that are stirring in the consciousness, the stillness of concentration, and at last utterance, immediate and sure.

Pasternak gives a more detailed account than either.[6] He tells very precisely how Zhivago 'experienced the coming on of what is called inspiration'. This happens at the moment when 'the relation of the forces that control creation is as it were turned on its head'. Now the language takes over: 'language, the native place and repository of beauty and sense [*rodina i vmestilishche krasoty i smysla*], itself begins to think and speak for the man'. In this juncture the poet feels that his work is being directed by 'the condition of world thought and poetry', so that the poem he writes has become the next inevitable step in its development.

The language 'by the power of its own laws' will create the necessary forms for the poetry. It appears that the mind has been cast in a passive role as the river of sound flows through it. The 'will and understanding', to recall Coleridge's sentence, are now in abeyance. Control comes from the operation of language itself, and – a more difficult concept – from the necessities of poetry which determine what should be written next.

Zhivago is highly sensitive to questions of language, and his views on this matter accord closely with Pasternak's. We have noted already[7] his concern with 'an imperceptible style, not drawing anyone's attention', which must be 'restrained and unpretentious', and hides its originality 'under the cloak of a customary form in general use'.[8] The notes made by Yury shortly before his death refuse 'pastoral simplicity' (which might have been expected in his poem 'The Christmas Star') as untrue to the age. It is only the language of a great modern city that he considers to be truly alive.[9] Pastoral simplicity (or what aspires to it) does not derive from the village – though Pasternak had been prepared to accept this was so in the case of Esenin[10] – but from academic bookshelves. Yury does not write here as a Futurist, and there is no trace of the Futurist manner anywhere in his poetry. Rather he should be seen as a true contemporary poet who has woken up to the character of his time. 'The new urban actuality' surrounds him as it did Verlaine, who was able to give his language 'that boundless freedom which...is encountered only in the masters of prose dialogue in the novel and drama'.[11]

The poet who fully responds to his age in the manner of Verlaine will possess like him an 'historical tact', a 'sense of mundane appropriateness inseparable from genius'. These will guide him towards his proper subject – the urban life of his own day, with the disquiet and perplexities brought by it – and towards the right language.[12] So the poet who recognises his task can find the place assigned to him in historical development.

Was Zhivago really a poet of that kind?

II

It would appear that no work corresponding to these specifications was found among Yury's papers. He had wanted to present the modern city with all its turmoil as 'an immeasurably vast overture to the life of each one of us'.[13] Although the novel suggests that 'Hamlet', the opening poem, bears some relation to this ideal, nowhere is there more than a sketch of 'the city ceaselessly and without a break stirring and rumbling out of doors'.[14] However, a poem in Pasternak's later work – 'Bacchanalia' ['*Vakkhanaliya*', 1957][15] – does answer to the description Zhivago gave of Pushkin's poetry once it had learned to accommodate 'objects': 'Into the verse as through the window into a room there rushed from the street light and air, the noise of life, things, actualities.'[16] Some half-dozen of Zhivago's poems have a recognisably urban setting, but an equal number belong to the country, taking their scenes from farm, *dacha* and forest. The impression of an urban poetry is further weakened by the many poems towards the close that depict episodes from the life of Christ in fairly traditional terms. Their world is rural, with villages and small cities (Bethany, Jerusalem), and although it stands in Zhivago's poems side by side with Moscow (and in one of them St Petersburg), the effect is to bring out the still semi-rural character of the Russian city as Zhivago sees it. There are nightingales in his poem about St Petersburg ('White Night' ['*Belaya noch'*']), garden fences, apples and cherry-trees.[17] 'Summer in the Town' ['*Leto v gorode*'] closes with image of 'secular, scented, still flowering limes' [*Vekovye, pakhuchie/Neotstvetshie lipy*],[18] which connect in the reader's mind with those other limes in the countess's secular and overgrown garden at Melyuzeevo.[19] And 'Earth' ['*Zemlya*'] which proclaims its Moscow setting in the first line is crowded with flower-pots in wooden mezzanines, the spring sunsets freeze along the fences [*po zaboram stynut zori*], and there are

transparent twigs of the same willows, swellings of the same white buds on the window, at the cross-roads, on the street and in the studio:

> И тех же верб сквозные прутья,
> И тех же белых почек вздутья
> И на окне, и на распутье,
> На улице и в мастерской.[20]

The city that Zhivago evokes is Moscow of the 1920s, still retaining many links with what it had been in Pasternak's childhood, when 'Moscow yet preserved its ancient aspect of somewhere out of the way, fantastically picturesque'.[21] (The book by Vladimir Gilyarovsky, *Moscow and Muscovites*, confirms that impression.[22])

The language that accords with this scene has to be flexible, but it shows no conspicuous traces of Soviet urban speech. There are two extremes to be accommodated in Zhivago's poetry. One is that of popular life, as in 'Wedding' ['*Svad'ba*', No. 11] where George Katkov has noted the rhythm is that of the *chastushka* or (mainly ribald) factory jingle,[23] and there are popular words to be found, such as *gulyanka* for the party, and three names for the accordion, *bayan, tal'yanka, akordeon* – the last two definitely from colloquial usage. The other extreme is that of the legendary, as in 'Fable' ['*Skazka*', No. 13] which begins with an archaic equivalent of 'once in times of yore' [*Vstar', vo vremya ono*] and has many expressions from folk poetry (e.g. *retivoe*, 'the ardent thing' for heart'). Similar are the poems with a Biblical theme. 'The Garden of Gethsemane' ['*Gefsimanskiy sad*', No. 25] paraphrases the words of Jesus, with a touch of archaism for instance in *Vas Gospod' spodobil/Zhit' v dni moi* ['The Lord *deemed you worthy* to live in my days'], or in *Dusha skorbit smertel'no* ['My soul is sorrowful unto death']. Both these examples come at the same time very near to the colloquial; ordinary speech is being elevated, given the associations of scriptural idiom.[24] Zhivago is capable of a genuine grandeur in the farewell stanzas of 'August' ['*Avgust*', No. 14], or the concluding speech of 'Gethsemane'. His poems prove capable of holding ancient and modern together, just as that on the Nativity ('Christmas Star') can shift from the shepherds, the cave, the ox and the camels, to 'all the future of galleries and museums', and 'all the Christmas trees in the world'.

III

Zhivago's poems on the departure of Lara, we learn, gradually moved away from their 'true prototype' with each revision.[25] This statement ought to discourage any looking for too-definite connections between a given poem and an incident in the novel. There is little point in speculating about the girl from Kursk in 'White Night' whose mother was the not-too-prosperous owner of an estate in the steppes. Nor does it seem necessary to seek an explanation for the third poem, 'In Holy Week' ['*Na Strastnoy*']. A source for it, Donald Davie says, can be found in the first five sections of Chapter 10, 'On the High Road'. The events in that chapter were reflected in the mind of Galuzina, the shopkeeper's wife – an unusual procedure, since apart from Gordon and Dudorov in their boyhood it is mainly Zhivago and sometimes Lara who perform this function of the observing intelligence – but, Davie argues, 'we are given no reason to think that Zhivago was ever in Krestovozdvizhensk'. He asks: 'How can Zhivago know a time and a place of which he has no experience, and know them moreover through the mind of a woman he never met?'[26] The answer – that subsequently Zhivago comes across Galuzina's sister,[27] who could have told him about it – is ingenious but surely misconceived. While certain poems – 'Parting' for instance ['*Razluka*', No. 16] – can be related immediately to the text[28] (though even this was apparently written about the arrest of Ivinskaya in 1948[29]), why should it be necessary to lodge every poem somewhere in the novel, finding here a reference to Komarovsky, here one to Marina, and taking altogether too literally the ascription of the poems to Yury Zhivago? They are not there for the decoding, nor would they gain a whit more significance even if it could be proved which ones Zhivago wrote at, or with reference to, particular moments described in the novel. Pasternak has commented on Verlaine's 'assigning in his personal confessions the chief role to historical time and circumstance'[30] and he says of Chopin that 'like the rest of the great realists he looked upon his own life as a means of knowing every life in the world'.[31] Also it is observed of Zhivago that 'beyond his lament for Lara he also lamented that far off summer in Melyuzeevo' when the revolution was like a god come down to earth.[32] All this goes to suggest that, while the poems must seem plausibly the work of Zhivago, the character in the novel, it is their testimony to his time that matters, and not the depth of their roots in his personal experiences as described in the novel. Their scope is not exclusively determined by the prose narrative. Yury need never have been in Krestovozdvizhensk, nor have heard about the place from Galuzina's sister. But the poem 'In Holy Week' is entirely characteristic of him, and what it has to say could not have found a place in the novel itself, except as a far less effective addition to his journal.

What the poems do is to impart a 'broad serenity' [*umirotvoryonnaya shirota*] in which 'the particular case' is raised to 'the generality of what is known to all'.[33] Zhivago's troubled and unsatisfactory life is freed from contingency, and the key moments in his experience – all that was most alive to the imagination – now form a paradigm for the artist in this age. Instead of Yury, the spokesman to introduce the series is Hamlet; and the concluding words of the last poem are given to Christ. The twenty-five lyrics are brought together into a significant order, like those of *My Sister Life* and *Second Birth*. They do, in fact, constitute all the verse that appears to have been written by Pasternak between 1946 and 1953, the years when he was most actively engaged on the novel. Those that did not arise from the process of writing the novel itself – and there appear to be one or two – still easily find a place in the sequence – 'Parting' for example and 'Meeting' [*Svidanie*', No. 17]. Of the rest it may be said that their origins lie not so much in particular passages of the novel, but in the length and breadth of the imaginative experience that went into its making. It would seem that no significant part of the novel has failed to achieve resurrection in the poems.

IV

About the religious aspect of the series both Dimitri Obolensky[34] and George Katkov[35] have written authoritatively. The closing sequence from 'The Miracle' ['*Chudo*', No. 20] on – though 'Earth' [*Zemlya*', No. 21] is an interpolation – takes its rise from the Orthodox liturgy for Holy Week.[36] The first specifically religious poem 'In Holy Week' comes third in the whole series, thus – like 'Hamlet' at the onset – preparing for the conclusion. Nine poems follow that are secular in theme, and appear to spring from the personal life of Zhivago. However, one of these 'The Wedding' ['*Svad'ba*', No. 11] could be taken as celebrating a sacrament of the church. 'A Tale', the thirteenth poem, is related by Katkov to the oral tradition of Russian religious poems [*dukhovnye stikhi*]; it leads on to 'August' which describes the poet's funeral and ends with his speech of farewell to life and art. Next come three poems about lovers' meetings, a parting, and the vision of a meeting again. The eighteenth poem, 'Christmas Star', fulfils Yury's aim in 1911 of writing 'a Russian adoration of the Magi, in the Dutch style, with frost, wolves and a dark fir forest'.[37] The following poem 'Dawn' ['*Rassvet*', No. 19], addressed to Christ,[38] preludes the scenes from Holy Week.

It will be evident that the secular poems are interpenetrated by the religious, so that, as the boy Misha Gordon comes to see, 'all that takes place is accomplished not only on earth, in which they bury the dead, but further in something else which one group names the kingdom of God, a second, history, and a third differently again'.[39] So the poem 'Earth' – which has an unmistakable allusion in its final stanza to the Last Supper[40] – is admitted to the Holy Week cycle because spring and resurrection cannot be separated, and already in the third poem we have found the earth waiting for the Easter events. Broadly it may be said that the poems differ from the novel in presenting a world that at every point seems to open on to the supernatural. In 'The Garden of Gethsemane' the Milky Way begins where the grass-plot breaks off, and the olive-trees attempt to walk in the air as Christ walked on the water.[41] Miracle is the element in which the poems of Yury Zhivago move naturally.

V

'Hamlet' as the overture to the series at once establishes what will be its dominant tone by the end. The hum of voices dies down; and the actor whose play is life itself steps on to the boards. He prays that this cup may pass from him, but there can be no changing the script. Alone and among Pharisees he must live out his tragic destiny, which is to obey the will of his father. Pasternak's understanding of Hamlet, as one who has been 'chosen by the will of chance to be the judge of his own time and the servant of one more remote',[42] expresses the predicament known to himself and other poets of the time; and already these lines stress the bond between his conception of art as sacrifice and the story of Christ's Passion. 'Hamlet' resembles Blok's famous poem 'The Steps of the Commendatore' ['*Shagi komandora*', 1910–12][43] in treating its subject as a myth that can be worked anew. The Hamlet who under the binoculars of a theatre audience can pronounce Christ's words in Gethsemane has become what Mary Magdalene and Christ are in these poems, a necessary image for the poet's contemplation – something that is given, but rediscovered in the light of his own experience. We must not say too literally, Yury's experience: that provided a focus for Pasternak's thought in the series, but Yury can scarcely be described as a *persona* whom he had adopted for writing these poems.

Hamlet is alone, as Christ will be alone in Gethsemane. 'The order of the acts has been set' [*produman rasporyadok deystviy*], and therefore we may expect the following poems each to reveal its appointed place in the drama. And a drama, perhaps on a Faustian scale, is what follows. The connection of its scenes may not be always apparent, but it develops through the seasons from March and a celebration of Holy Week round to another spring among Moscow houses, and returns to the story of Holy Week until the moment of Christ's being betrayed in Gethsemane. 'March', the second poem, celebrates the renewal of nature: 'These nights, these days and nights' [*Eti nochi, eti dni i nochi!*] when 'the hands of spring are full' [*Delo u vesny kipit v rukakh*]. But the next poem, 'In Holy Week', comes back to a bare and darkened earth: it is still in March, which 'scatters the snow [like alms] at the church porch to a throng of cripples' [*razbrasyvaet sneg/Na paperti tolpe kalek*], but the theme now is not spring but resurrection. This poem demonstrates that the season cannot be separated from the religious festival. The fir-trees look like worshippers; trees in town are like a destitute crowd staring through the church gratings. The air mingles the scent of communion wafers with the headiness of spring [*I vozdukh s privkusom prosfor/I veshnego ugara*]. The effect is one of gathering up the previous poem and sweeping on with the sense of dedication imparted in 'Hamlet'.

In the next poem, 'White Night', spring has advanced – apple-trees and cherry-trees are in bloom, and the nightingale rouses both 'rapture and confusion' [*vostorg i sumyatitsu*]. The speaker and the young girl from Kursk share a 'timid loyalty' to their secret with the wide panorama of St Petersburg below them. All the surroundings appear to eavesdrop on their conversation: if it is love the speaker hints at in his low voice, then the non-human world wishes to participate. The poem that follows, 'Flooded Roads in Spring' ['*Vesennyaya rasputitsa*', No. 5], has a close counterpart in Section 16 of Chapter 9, with the horseman out late and mention of the partisan pickets. Here, however, the contrast lies with 'White Night'; and the sound of the nightingale whistling is like Nightingale the robber [*Solovey-razboynik*] on his seven oaks in the legend. Katkov comments that this reference brings out the 'violent and even criminal side' of love in contrast to its 'poetic and sublime character'.[44] If 'White Night' is a song of innocence, this will be one of experience, with voices laughing and weeping in the floods, and the sunset like a conflagration [*pozharishche zakata*]. The notes of the nightingale are the expression of 'madness, pain, happiness, torments' [*Bezum'ya, boli, schast'ya, muk*].

The conflagration of sunset [*pozhar zakata*] continues into the sixth poem, 'Explanation' ['*Ob"yasnenie*']. It is a careworn city-piece, where women in cheap print-frocks wear down their shoes and are crucified nightly in the attics; and in its second part it speaks of 'reopening the dried scab of spring fever' [*Razberedish' prisokhshiy strup/Vesenney likhoradki*]; love is a dangerous current that crosses at a touch; the poet is helpless before the appeal of female beauty; held by night in 'a ring of misery' [*kol'tsom tosklivym*] he responds above all to the 'passion for breaking away' [*strast' k razryvam*]. The seventh poem 'Summer in the Town' evokes a sultry evening, and submits like its predecessor to a mood of uneasiness and fatigue.

'Wind' ['*Veter*'] and 'Hops' ['*Khmel'*'], Nos. 8 and 9, can be described as brief notations of feeling: unhappiness in the first – the wind is mournfully shaping a cradle song for the woman – intoxication (the other meaning of *khmel'*) in the second. They close the sequence of six poems which have followed spring into summer, under the domination of a love that cannot be resisted. There has been no memory of the Passion which overshadowed the third poem, or of Hamlet's destiny. These poems are closer to the experience of Magdalene from which she longs to free herself at the end of the series.

'Indian Summer' ['*Bab'e leto*'] brings not only a change of season – and autumn is a rag-and-bone woman sweeping away refuse – but the entry into a world of household activity, shredding, pickling, peppering, with 'hubbub and laughter' [*gomon i smekh*] which are carried over into the poem that follows, 'Wedding' ['*Svad'ba*', No. 11]. This is a noisy accordion-filled celebration, suddenly turning to a moral insight which will become cardinal for the poems – that life is 'only a dissolution of ourselves in all others as if a present to them':

> Только растворенье
> Нас самих во всех других
> Как бы им в даренье.[45]

The twelfth poem, 'Autumn' ['*Osen'*'], seems to look across to the fifteenth, 'Winter Night' ['*Zimnyaya noch'*'] since both proclaim the glory and the abandonment of a sexual passion as reckless as Antony's for Cleopatra. The lovers will 'perish without deceit' [*gibnut' otkrovenno*]; and the same note is to be heard in 'Winter Night':

Мело, мело по всей земле
Во все пределы.
Свеча горела на столе,
Свеча горела.

Как летом роем мошкара
Летит на пламя,
Слетались хлопья со двора
К оконной раме.

Метель лепила на стекле
Кружки и стрелы.
Свеча горела на столе,
Свеча горела.

На озаренный потолок
Ложились тени,
Скрещенья рук, скрещенья ног,
Судьбы скрещенья.

И падали два башмачка
Со стуком на пол.
И воск слезами с ночника
На платье капал.

И всё терялось в снежной мгле
Седой и белой.
Свеча горела на столе,
Свеча горела.

На свечку дуло из угла,
И жар соблазна
Вздымал, как ангел, два крыла
Крестообразно.

Мело весь месяц в феврале,
И то и дело
Свеча горела на столе,
Свеча горела.[46]

[The snow was sweeping, sweeping over all the earth
To all the limits.
A candle was burning on the table,
A candle burning.

As in summer swarming the midges
Fly to the flame,
There flew together flakes from the yard
To the window frame.

The blizzard moulded on the glass
Circles and arrows.
A candle was burning on the table,
A candle burning.

207

On the lit up ceiling
Lay shadows,
Crossing of hands, crossing of feet,
Destiny's crossings.

And there fell two shoes
Knocking on the floor.
And the wax with tears from the night-light
Dripped on to a dress.

And all was lost in the snowy gloom
Hoary and white.
A candle was burning on the table,
A candle burning.

The candle was blown on from the corner,
And the heat of temptation
Lifted like an angel two wings
Cross-wise.

The storm was sweeping all the month in February
And ever and again
A candle was burning on the table,
A candle burning.]

This poem is firmly attached in its origins to the moment when Yury sees the candle burning in Pasha's window, as he drives to the Sventitskys' party with Tonya.[47] Lara reflects when Yury lies dead in the same room that 'from this flame seen from outside...there came into his life its predestination'.[48] But these connections are virtually shed by the poem as it stands in sequence. This is the record of a love already described in 'Autumn' – the 'blessedness of a fatal step' [*blago gibel'nogo shaga*].[49] The storm that rages up to the limits of the world (threatening to bury them?); the midges drawn to the destructive flame; the circles and arrows on the window (circles from which there can be no breaking out, arrows against which there is no defence?); the shadows on the ceiling; the falling of the shoes; the weeping of the wax; the recognition that all has been lost in the snowy gloom; the heat of temptation that becomes an angel who raises the symbol of the cross: all these indications work together to heighten the sense of doom and helplessness. The poem is preparing us for the confessions of Mary Magdalene at the end of the sequence.

However, between 'Autumn' and 'Winter Night' two very different poems from these have been placed. The first, 'Fable', according to the novel, was written by Zhivago to link up his other attempts in verse.[50] It recounts the legend of Saint George and the

Dragon, and its language is terse and archaic. At the close both the knight and the maiden are struggling to come round [*silyatsya ochnut'sya*] – the nightingale in Yury's Varykino diary seemed to be calling out *Ochnis'*! with a 'plea or admonition' that the listener should come back to his senses.[51] Davie reads into the poem 'an allegory of sexual encounter'[52] and given its context in the series this cannot be ruled out. However, the time scale, emphasised at the beginning and end of the last section ('Years and centuries' [*Gody i veka*]) seems to transcend individual lives, though their pattern may also be found there. The poem is about the struggle for freedom, and what freedom signifies will have become plain by the close of the sequence in 'The Garden of Gethsemane'. The freedom of an individual or of Russia itself depends upon the same attitude.

'August' imagines the poet's death. It was probably assigned this position because Zhivago does die in August. Standing here, it recalls the poet's mission, and evokes the supernatural 'light without flame' which on the day of the Transfiguration shines forth from Mount Tabor. The voice that speaks his farewell is the 'former prophetic voice' [*prezhniy golos. . .providcheskiy*] – Hamlet had shown that power of prevision, catching in the far-away echo what would happen in his time [*v dalyokom otgoloske/Chto sluchitsya na moyom veku*].[53] Here heaven is 'solemnly neighbouring' [*Sosedstvovalo nebo vazhno*]; art is allied to miracle-working in the last line [*I tvorchestvo, i chudotvorstvo*]. This poem includes in its farewell the woman who has defied an 'abyss of humiliations' [*bezdne unizheniy*], and so connects with 'Autumn'; but the main effect is to recover the note of 'Hamlet' and to anticipate the final religious poems.

After 'Winter Night' come the last two wholly secular poems in the series – 'Parting' and 'Meeting', Nos. 16 and 17. Both are dated 1953 in the Soviet 1966 edition[54] and they form a pair: the sudden vision of the lost woman concluding the first poem leads on to her appearance before the poet when he opens his door in the second. The sea metaphor in the first, so variously turned, relates to Lara;[55] but the poem is generalised: 'From the threshold the man looks' [*S poroga smotrit chelovek*]. These are two poems in which 'grief of the spirit has heightened the sensibility'[56] – the needle left in a piece of sewing brings the image of the whole woman to mind; or, in the second, he sees her in her autumn coat without hat or goloshes, and chewing the wet snow in her agitation:

Одна в пальто осеннем,
Без шляпы, без калош,
Ты борешься с волненьем
И мокрый снег жуешь.[57]

They demand their place in the sequence because the 'havoc'
[*razgrom*] of which the first one speaks was a common disaster in
Zhivago's life-time, as the unforeseen arrests multiplied; and the
extreme desolation at the end of the second poem which sees the
lovers vanishing from the earth and nothing but gossip left, prepares all the more effectively for the sudden hope of the Nativity
in the poem that follows.

'Christmas Star', No. 18, is the longest piece in the series, the
next longest being 'The Garden of Gethsemane'. 'Miracle', the third
of these poems that relate incidents from the life of Christ, adopts
the same metrical form as the bulk of 'Christmas Star'. All three are
circumstantial narratives from Scripture, realised with an elaborate
care, and unmistakably bearing the stamp of the poet who composed the rest of the series. 'Christmas Star' is seen partly as a
children's crib – the word *vertep*, 'cave', in its third line also means
a marionette Christmas play, and the donkeys, each smaller than
the other, with their 'little steps' [*shazhkami*] seem to belong to the
world of the child's imagination, together with the Christmas trees,
apples and golden bells. The poet has avoided that false 'pastoral
simplicity' which he censured in the papers found after his death.[58]
The 'drovers and the sheep-breeders' [*pogonshchiki i ovtsevody*],
the swearing crowd, the sheepdogs [*ovcharki*] particularly useful
against wolves, all perhaps belong to the Urals. Certainly the *dokha*
– a coat made from the skin of the *saiga* or steppe antelope –
shaken out by the shepherds derives from that district, according to
Dahl. It is not merely a play world that Pasternak describes: the
star is compared with 'the reflected glare of arson, like a farm on
fire and the burning of a threshing-floor' [*Kak otblesk podzhoga,/
Kak khutor v ogne i pozhar na gumne*]. These were the signs of
1917, and Davie is right, I believe, in suggesting that the poem connects 'the convulsion of the Revolution with the convulsion which
began at Bethlehem and ended at Calvary'.[59] Zhivago had wanted
to write a poem like this as a tribute to Blok. Davie makes allusion
to two of Blok's *Italian Verses* [*Ital'yanskie stikhi*, 1909] on the
Annunciation and the Assumption. Both were inspired by frescoes,
in Perugia and Spoleto,[60] and are thus little more than pictorial.
Much more relevant here seems to be *The Twelve* ['*Dvenadtsat'*',

210

1918]. Both poems begin with the wind, which does not disappear from 'Christmas Star' – in the middle of describing candles, chains, tinsel he interpolates: 'Ever more cruelly and savagely blew the wind from the steppe' [*Vsyo zley i svirepey dul veter iz stepi*]. But the coldness of the infant is dispelled by the warm breath of the animals. By implication this poem counters in the same way the violence and homelessness of 'The Twelve'. Blok's poem unites the ideas of revolution and Christianity by the sudden vision of Christ at the end. In Pasternak's poem it is the Christmas star that comes forward at the close, to look on the child; and the affirmation brings no surprise, no paradox.

A Western reader is bound to seek some comparison with Eliot's 'Journey of the Magi' – the work of another poet whose roots (or lack of them) were urban. Eliot wrote a more private poem than Pasternak; it is another step towards establishing his faith, and he leans on Bishop Lancelot Andrewes for support in the opening lines. There is nothing in 'Christmas Star' to match the 'hard and bitter agony' felt by the Magi. Pasternak's poem is joyful and perhaps naive. Eliot may seem to give even more 'Dutch' (or Flemish) detail –

> Then the camel men cursing and grumbling
> And running away, and wanting their liquor and women. . .

He had read Browning's *Karshish*; and these aspects of the poem seem more literary than anything in Pasternak's. We know from Eliot's admission in *The Use of Poetry and the Use of Criticism* that many of the images in the second paragraph are personal – that 'they represent the depths of feeling into which we cannot peer'.[61] The images and comparisons used by Pasternak carry none of this burden, or if they do, give no sign of it. When he compares the radiant child asleep with 'the light of the moon in the hollow of a tree-trunk' [*Kak mesyatsa luch v uglublen'e dupla*], the image is simply an aid to seeing, and it further conforms with the spirit of intimacy that pervades the whole poem: all is related, mutual, in its appropriate place. And when he dwells on what lay in the snowy fields – 'fences, gravestones, shafts in the snow-drift' [*Ogrady, nadgrob'ya,/Ogloblya v sugrobe*] – the significance comes from the intermingling of these objects – reflected in the sound – as they seem to be held together in watchfulness. 'The frosty night resembled a fable' [*Moroznaya noch' pokhodila na skazku*]. As Yury noted in his journal of such a night, 'earth, air, moon, stars are bound together, riveted by the frost'.[62]

Religious illumination in this series begins appropriately with 'Dawn' ['*Rassvet*', No. 19] which tells of Christ's recovered significance for the poet after many years of neglect.[63] It is a city poem, and it takes up at its conclusion the idea expressed in 'Wedding' – that life must be a dissolution of ourselves in others. Now 'people without names, trees, children, homekeepers' are with the poet. He is overcome by them all, and that is his sole victory.

> Со мною люди без имен,
> Деревья, дети, домоседы.
> Я ими всеми побежден,
> И только в том моя победа.[64]

'Miracle' ['*Chudo*', No. 20] recounts the withering by Jesus of the fig-tree which bore no fruit.[65] The version in Matthew ends with a statement on the power of faith. This poem gives a barren scene by the Dead Sea, and Christ's bitterness [*gorech'*] matches that of the salty waters that lie so still in view. It is about the joylessness of that which is unfree and so totally without talent. The miracle – here one of destruction – always comes when nobody is prepared for it.

The last four poems, like 'Miracle', record incidents which are commemorated by the Orthodox Church in the liturgy for Holy Week. But they are preceded by 'Earth', the twenty-first poem, in which spring breaks into the Moscow streets which fraternise with window-sills [*ulitsa za panibrata/S okonnitsey*]. But the underlying sense is of anxiety – the 'mingling of fire and terror' [*smes' ognya i zhuti*], of sorrow in the distances, and the need for human suffering in a secret stream to warm the chill of existence [*Chtob taynaya struya stradan'ya/Sogrela kholod bytiya*]. It leads on naturally to 'Evil Days' ['*Durnye dni*', No. 22] on the first four days of Holy Week,[66] which ends with the resurrection of Lazarus. The modern connotations of this poem, with its reference to the 'dark powers of the temple' that give Christ over to be judged by the rabble (*I tyomnymi silami khrama/On otdan podonkam na sud*), are perfectly clear, and the anguish of the previous poem, with the apathy denounced in its predecessor, 'Miracle', binds these three lyrics into a single group.

That leaves the two poems spoken by Mary Magdalene, who has her place in the Orthodox Liturgy of Holy Week. The analogues with Lara's life cannot be missed; but the poems are made too narrow in their meaning if Lara's relation to Komarovsky, or Lara's funeral lament over Zhivago, rather than the confessions and grief of Magdalene herself, come into the foreground. When she breaks her life before him like an alabaster vessel [*Ya zhizn' svoyu ...*/ *Kak alebastrovyy sosud,/Pered toboyu razbivayu*] it is the doctrine of freedom through sacrifice that returns – as expounded by Nikolay Nikolaevich.[67] Only in this way can Magdalene escape from her past. The final poem, 'The Garden of Gethsemane', keeps very close to Matthew's account of the agony and betrayal in the garden,[68] with Christ's sayings paraphrased as simply as possible. It is a story that had not been told in Soviet literature for forty years,[69] and Pasternak would seem to be discovering it anew for himself. He concludes with the image of the centuries coming out of the darkness like a convoy of barges floated down for Christ's judgment. Hamlet, the artist, had also been chosen as the judge of his times.

VI

It will have been obvious that Zhivago's poems, while not at variance with the spirit of his book, give a different emphasis. Little in them, for example, corresponds with the pentecostal days of the opening revolution at Melyuzeevo; and public events, as in *My Sister Life*, are hinted at rather than treated directly. He will content himself with saying 'Then came war, devastation' [*Potom prishla voyna, razrukha*], but for what that devastation meant we have to consult the novel. (Necessarily there can be no reference by Zhivago to the devastation of the Second World War, recorded in the Epilogue.) But the poems do succeed in making the history of Zhivago's time bear a moral interpretation, the one given by Nikolay Nikolaevich; and what in the uncle's words was abstract assertion now takes on body and symbolic power. Zhivago's testament, the poems, really could have inspired his friends after the poet's death. Their confidence and peace of mind in that final paragraph are warranted by what they have read. As a poetic statement the twenty-five lyrics have a completeness and a coherence that are deeply satisfying.

14

The Final Stage: 'An Essay in Autobiography'; 'When the Weather Clears'; 'The Blind Beauty'

I

The closing decade of Pasternak's life was dominated by *Doctor Zhivago* – first the writing of it in those disheartening post-war years, when also the internment of Olga Ivinskaya drove him to seek relief in this personal testament and witness to his time;[1] and then its reception. As early as June 1952 he reported to the Georgian poet Simon Chikovani and his wife that friends on the whole did not care for it and considered it a failure.[2] The sense of isolation was already growing on him. By March 1947, as Gladkov records, his good standing in Soviet literary circles, much enhanced during the war, was beginning to totter; Fadeev, then secretary of the Writer's Union, from which Akhmatova and Zoshchenko had been expelled in the previous year, made a sharp attack on him.[3] Ivinskaya, to whom he was deeply devoted and whose fate threatened to become that of Lara – to perish anonymously in one of the concentration camps in the north – was never during these last years of Pasternak's life safe for long from the K.G.B. And he understood well enough what would be the consequences of publishing his novel. In August 1957, three months before Feltrinelli released the Italian translation, he told Gladkov a cloud hung over him: 'They want to make me a second Zoshchenko.'[4]

It was the award of the Nobel Prize for Literature in October 1958 that let loose the storm. This recognition did not ostensibly follow upon the appearance of *Doctor Zhivago*, yet most people in his own country and abroad assumed a connection. As one American critic puts it, 'Even in the years to come, it will remain impossible to read *Doctor Zhivago* with completely undivided attention' because

214

'we can never wash the finger marks of politics' from this as from any other work issuing from the Soviet Union.[5] Pasternak had never sought fame: *Byt' znamenitym – nekrasivo* – 'To be celebrated is an ugly thing', he wrote in a poem of 1956.[6] Now suddenly the full horror of fame descended upon him – fame outside the Soviet Union, and at home notoriety and execration. The journal *Literaturnaya Gazeta* printed a long letter from the editorial board of *Novy Mir* which explains why they had not been willing to publish *Doctor Zhivago* when it was offered to them. He was expelled from the Writers' Union, and his own Moscow branch recommended that he should forfeit Soviet citizenship. Pasternak then declined the prize, and wrote to Khrushchev pleading that he might not be separated from his native land:

For me that is impossible. I am bound to Russia by my birth, my life, my work.
I cannot conceive my fate apart from and outside her.[7]

Khrushchev relented; and Pasternak lived on for another year and a half, now publicly accounted a member of the 'internal emigration'. Overnight he had become a world figure like Tolstoy – similarly mistrusted by the authorities, no more the master of his own time, overwhelmed by correspondence, at once elated by the success of his novel and troubled that this might have come for the wrong reasons.

In the first agony of rejection he wrote a poem entitled 'The Nobel Prize' ['*Nobelevskaya premiya*'] comparing himself to a hunted animal:

Я пропал, как зверь в загоне.
Где-то люди, воля, свет,
А за мною шум погони,
Мне наружу ходу нет.

Темный лес и берег пруда,
Ели сваленной бревно.
Путь отрезан отовсюду.
Будь что будет, всё равно.

Что же сделал я за пакость,
Я убийца и злодей?
Я весь мир заставил плакать
Над красой земли моей.

Но и так, почти у гроба
Верю я, придет пора –
Силу подлости и злобы
Одолеет дух добра.

215

Всё тесней кольцо облавы
И другому я виной:
Нет руки со мною правой,
Друга сердца нет со мной!

А с такой петлей у горла
Я б хотел еще пока,
Чтобы слезы мне утерла
Правая моя рука.[8]

[I am finished like a beast at the kill.
Somewhere are people, freedom, light,
But after me the din of pursuit,
For me there is no way out.

Dark forest and edge of pond,
Timber of a fallen spruce.
The path is cut off on every side.
Come what may, it is all the same.

What vile thing have I done,
Am I a murderer and scoundrel?
I have made the whole world weep
Over the beauty of my land.

But even so, nearly in my grave
I believe the time is coming –
The power of baseness and spite
Will be mastered by the spirit of good.

Ever more close is the ring of the battue.
And I am to blame for another thing:
I have not with me my right hand,
The friend of my heart is not with me!

With a noose like this at my throat
I could still want it
That my tears should be wiped away
By my right hand.]

There was a sense in which Pasternak had always felt himself to be irremovably at home in the world, even though – as when his close friend Meyerhold was arrested in 1939 – he had at times faced extreme peril.[9] Akhmatova wrote some lines after his death that called him 'a converser with the woods' [*sobesednik roshch*[10]]. The tribute is characteristically precise: she saw that Pasternak's intimacy with the natural scene was unique and profound. Yet in this poem he feels for the first and only time estranged from it. The tree has fallen and turned to dead timber; the dark forest makes no response and the pond seems an alien element. Strong in the poem – despite the hope of its fourth stanza – is the conviction that his enemies have found their opportunity to destroy him.

This did not happen. Pasternak was now supported by a presence that proved no less effective than Evgraf had been to Zhivago – the sympathy and admiration of foreign writers and artists, and of countless anonymous readers who sent him their messages. Whatever the imperfections of *Doctor Zhivago*, it spoke ,powerfully for the free human spirit; this book was the thaw that set rolling the torrents of spring. Pasternak's example has counted immensely in the effort to keep Russian literature alive, and with it the moral strength of the Russian people.

II

For the collected edition of his poems which was to appear in 1957 Pasternak had written the memoir known to English readers as *An Essay in Autobiography*. It has been quoted freely above, and at this point calls for consideration as a final statement in certain ways parallel to *Doctor Zhivago*. Less fully than the novel, but in the same spirit, the memoir conveys a sense of the age in which Pasternak had survived. It enabled him to survey once again the territory of *Safe Conduct* and to speak in valedictory terms of the writers and artists who had given him most.

Safe Conduct had been both a progress report and an act of discovery. The *Essay in Autobiography* when it returns to the same episodes does so with the greater detachment of one who has seen the outcome of his own life (or so it appeared in 1956 when he was writing the work).[11] Such memories as it takes up for the first time are controlled by a similar distancing. The personal disasters of poets whom he had known continue to move him deeply; but they can be contemplated from a more hopeful time, in which the whirlpool was stilled. The death of Mayakovsky had come upon him during the actual composition of *Safe Conduct* and he was grief-stricken and shocked to the core. *An Essay in Autobiography* is meditative and final in a way that was impossible for *Safe Conduct*.

He felt dissatisfaction with the earlier work – it had been 'spoilt by unnecessary mannerism, the general fault of those years'.[12] But the new memoirs are not intended to overlay it, or to recite the same story in plainer language. They form a supplement and at times a corrective; the emphasis falls differently, and new figures appear such as Blok or the 'three shades' of Tsvetaeva, Yashvili and Tabidze, while others are given more prominence, like Tolstoy and Rilke. He comments on the faults of his writing until the last

217

period, and also on the work and the fate of others in relation to his own ideals and achievement. When contemplating the suicides of Mayakovsky, Esenin, Tsvetaeva, Yashvili and his accuser ten years before, Fadeev, he recognises in their final state a feeling of absence and emptiness he had never himself experienced. 'They were all tormented unspeakably, tormented to the pitch where a feeling of anguish already constitutes a spiritual sickness. And besides their talent and bright memory let us also bow compassionately before their suffering.'[13] Father Zosima in *The Brothers Karamazov* bowed before the suffering that was to befall Mitya.[14] He felt compassion out of his own strong belief, as a Christian who could understand the place of suffering in human experience. Pasternak's language is that of Christian tradition. But for him suicide has a particular meaning which would occur to a poet whose aim was to leave, like Verlaine, 'the vivid record of what he had felt and seen'.[15] By the act of suicide people 'give themselves up for lost, turn away from the past, they declare themselves bankrupt and their memories unreal'.[16] By contrast a man in the hands of his executioners has not given up his memories: 'if he wishes he can make use of them, before death they can help him'.

The *Essay in Autobiography* was not written *in extremis*. However, it examines once more the pattern given to his life by remembered meetings and choices made in the light of these. Pasternak could accept his past, despite the imperfections he noted in his performance as a writer. Both *Doctor Zhivago* and certain poems that followed it make clear his sympathy for the Christian faith. But this could scarcely be deduced from the *Essay*, nor indeed was there a place for it in a preface to pass the censors of the State Publishing House. He could speak openly of acknowledged evil – the time from the late 1920s when 'literature came to an end'.[17] To convey the realities of life since the revolution he could prescribe a manner of writing that would 'make the heart stop beating and the hair stand on end'.[18] But it was not possible for him to hint at any profession of Christian belief. The *Essay* is, like *Safe Conduct*, preoccupied with his art. During the last two decades of Pasternak's life he was indubitably led to interpret his ideals for art in a way that accords with a Christian outlook. More doubtful is whether Christianity can be said to have underpinned his art. It may well have made clear to him the ideas he came to hold about personal freedom and self-sacrifice. But the essence of Pasternak's art had always been a religious trust in its own powers.

III

Pasternak's last collection of verse, *When the Weather Clears* [*Kogda razgulyactsya*] spans the period from 1956 until 1959. These poems, together with an unfinished play, *The Blind Beauty* [*Slepaya krasavitsa*], form an epilogue to his work which had reached its climax in the prose and poetry of *Doctor Zhivago*. For this book, not published in his lifetime, he had chosen an epigraph from Proust:[19] '*Un livre est un grand cimetière où sur la plupart des tombes on ne peut plus lire les noms effacés.*' Elsewhere Pasternak says that there are virtues in oblivion, which is helpful to the artist: 'To lose things in life is more necessary than to acquire them. The grain yields no shoot if it does not die. One should live without pause, look forward and nourish oneself on the living supplies which together with memory produce oblivion.'[20] There he was referring to lost manuscripts. The peculiar creative oblivion he fostered can be understood from a poem 'The Soul' ['*Dusha*'], which appears undated in the Michigan edition. It belongs to an unusual mode for Pasternak, the elegy with a theme of civic indignation, accompanied by a 'sobbing lyre':

Душа моя, печальница
О всех в кругу моем,
Ты стала усыпальницей
Замученных живьем.

Тела их бальзамируя,
Им посвящая стих,
Рыдающею лирою
Оплакивая их,

Ты в наше время шкурное
За совесть и за страх
Стоишь могильной урною,
Покоящей их прах.

Их муки совокупные
Тебя склонили ниц.
Ты пахнешь пылью трупною
Мертвецких и гробниц.

Душа моя, скудельница,
Всё, виденное здесь,
Перемолов, как мельница,
Ты превратила в смесь.

И дальше перемалывай
Всё бывшее со мной,
Как сорок лет без малого,
В погостный перегной.[21]

[My soul, sympathiser
For all in my circle,
You have become the burial-vault
Of men tormented alive.

Embalming their bodies,
Dedicating to them verse,
With a sobbing lyre
Lamenting them,

You in our self-seeking age
For conscience and dread
Stand like a funeral urn,
Cherishing their dust.

Their torments combined
Have bowed you to the ground.
You reek of decaying corpses
In morgues and sepulchres.

My soul, a vessel,
Everything seen here
Grinding down as a mill does
You have mingled together.

You must grind down farther
All that has happened to me,
For almost forty years,
Into graveyard humus.]

'The Soul' stands third in this volume. It speaks more directly of
suffering at the hands of history than any poem outside the *Zhivago*
cycle, and it offers a new definition of poetry, the process which
makes 'graveyard humus' out of sorrow and disaster. In his novel
Pasternak had observed that 'the kingdom of plants' is 'a very near
neighbour to the kingdom of death'.[22] 'The grain yields no shoot
if it does not die.' Thus personal loss is made bearable in the 'broad
serenity' that art achieves by its transformations;[23] many of the
names are effaced, but the pity remains.

This is a singular poem for Pasternak to have written, blending as it does the style of eighteenth-century formal ode [*Ryda-
yushcheyu liroyu/Oplakivaya ikh...Stoish' mogil'noy urnoyu/
Pokoyashchey ikh prakh...*] with the cadences and images of
something much older and deeply traditional [*Dusha moya,
pechal'nitsa/O vsekh v krugu moyom...Ikh muki sovokupnye/
Tebya sklonili nits...*] The feeling of the poem and the consolation
it provides bring it within range of Zhivago's last poem, 'The
Garden of Gethsemane'.

The two lyrics that precede it are both declarations of artistic principle. The first of them, making in its course yet another tribute to Chopin, ends with a brief formulation that describes this poem itself no less than the aim of poetry in general:

> Достигнутого торжества
> Игра и мука –
> Натянутая тетива
> Тугого лука.[24]

> [Of an achieved triumph
> the play and the torment –
> The tight stretched string
> Of a taut bow.]

The second, 'To be celebrated is an ugly thing' [*Byt' znamenitym-nekrasivo'*] proclaims the principles that had always governed Pasternak's writing:

> Цель творчества – самоотдача,
> А не шумиха, не успех. . .

> [The end of creating is to yield oneself up,
> And not making a stir, not success. . .]

> Но быть живым, живым и только,
> Живым и только доконца.[25]

> [To be alive, simply alive,
> Simply alive to the end.]

The former statement is contrasted by Nadezhda Mandelstam with his earlier 'Definition of Poetry' in *My Sister Life.*[26] 'To my ear,' she remarks, 'it sounds a little like something from an official report', and she finds the word *tvorchestvo*, 'creation', too grand, while *samootdacha*, 'yielding oneself up', seems in her opinion to betray 'a secret desire to assert and promote oneself'.[27] The comment is acute, as always with her, but too harsh. The moral stand taken by Pasternak is not, I maintain, suspect. Yielding himself up to his art had never in any way been difficult for him. But those who value more highly his earlier poetry than his later, as Nadezhda Mandelstam does, are bound to have noticed, and responded perhaps a little uneasily, to one feature. This final volume accentuates the liking for aphorism which had already shown here and there, for instance, in *Spektorsky*. The effect can be lapidary, as when in the poem 'Change' ['*Peremena'*] explaining a shift in his attitude to what he had regarded as the special virtues of the poor and of working people, he declares:

Я человека потерял,
С тех пор, как всеми он потерян.[28]

[I have lost the human being
Ever since he has been lost by all.]

The poem 'Night' ['*Noch'*'] ends with an exhortation to himself:

Не спи, не спи, художник,
Не предавайся сну, –
Ты – вечности заложник
У времени в плену![29]

[You must not sleep, artist,
Nor yield to slumber:
You are eternity's hostage
By time held prisoner.]

– the last couplet, as we have already seen, chiming with the philosophy of Rilke.[30] Again, 'After the Storm' ['*Posle grozy*'], leads up to another moral for the artist in particular:

Не потрясенья и перевороты
Для новой жизни очищают путь,
А откровенья, бури и щедроты
Души воспламененной чьей-нибудь.[31]

[It is not commotions and upheavals
That clear a way to the new life,
But the discoveries, storms and bounties
Of some man's spirit on fire.]

Statements like the last have their place in poetry, but one can detect in them a hint of something like 'an official report'. They correspond to some of the didactic passages in *Zhivago* when the voice of Uncle Nikolay can directly or indirectly be heard.

However, the characteristic poems in *When the Weather Clears* succeed not by their neat moral conclusions (which now seem more of a return visit than a discovery) but by their fidelity to a scene observed, or a mood caught and externalised.

V

His achievement is summed up best in the poem that closes the group, 'Unequalled Days' ['*Edinstvennye dni*']:

На протяженьи многих зим
Я помню дни солнцеворота,
И каждый был неповторим
И повторялся вновь без счету.

И целая их череда
Составилась мало-помалу –
Тех дней единственных, когда
Казалось нам, что время стало.

Я помню их наперечет:
Зима подходит к середине,
Дороги мокнут, с крыш течет,
И солнце греется на льдине.

И любящие, как во сне,
Друг к другу тянутся поспешней,
И на деревьях в вышине
Потеют от тепла скворешни,

И полусонным стрелкам лень
Ворочаться на циферблате,
И дольше века длится день,
И не кончается объятье.[32]

[In the course of many winters
I remember the days of the solstice,
And every one was unrepeatable
And repeated itself anew beyond counting.

And their whole sequence
Took form little by little –
One of days unequalled, when
It seemed to us time stood still.

I remember them every one:
Winter comes to its mid point,
Roads are wet, roofs dripping,
And the sun basks on the ice-block.

And lovers, as in a dream,
Draw together in more haste,
And in the trees on high
Starling-boxes sweat with the heat.

And the dozing hands are unwilling
To turn on the clock-face,
And more than a century lasts the day,
And there is no end to the embrace.]

This might be a description of 'midwinter spring. . .its own season'
like the passage in *Little Gidding*. Both Eliot and Pasternak are
concerned with an experience out of time; and the ending of this
poem might appear no less symbolical than the privileged moments of *Four Quartets*. Yet there is no philosophy, no religious
doctrine lying under the surface here. The meaning of the poem is
restricted to the notation which records not only particulars (the
sun basking on the ice, the thaw that shows like sweat on the

starling boxes) but also the relations between them established by
the advance of the poem, as it also 'takes form little by little'. The
result is completely satisfying, a surely held instant which the very
movement of the verse shows to be continually building up anew
to the final seemingly endless embrace. What Pasternak says about
the winter solstice defines the quality of his perceptions as found
in so many late poems: they are unrepeatable because unique,
but for the same reason, since this poet lives by and through the
unique, the series repeats itself 'beyond counting'.

In general these poems are about transformation: *Chto stalos' s
mestnost'yu vsegdashney?* ['What has become of the everyday
scene?'] one of them asks;[33] and the question is implicit in all the
rest. Their usual key, no longer as at the beginning of Pasternak's
career raised to an ecstatic pitch, has become deliberately muted.
These are so many visits to listening-posts:

> Как музыкальную шкатулку,
> Ее подслушивает лес,
> Подхватывает голос гулко
> И долго ждет, чтоб звук исчез.[34]

> [Like a musical box
> The forest overhears it [a bird's twittering],
> Takes up the voice resonantly
> And waits long for the sound to vanish.]

> Петух свой окрик прогорланит,
> И вот он вновь надолго смолк,
> Как будто он раздумьем занят,
> Какой в запевке этой толк.

> Но где-то в дальнем закоулке
> Прокукарекает сосед;
> Как часовой из караулки
> Петух откликнется в ответ.[35]

> [A cock gives his throaty cry,
> And then he is again long silent,
> As though taken with the reflection
> What this striking up could mean.

> But somewhere in a distant nook
> Away crows a neighbour;
> Like a sentry from the guardpost
> The cock calls in reply.]

> В лесу молчанье, тишина,
> Как будто жизнь в глухой лощине
> Не солнцем заворожена,
> А по совсем другой причине.[36]

[In the forest there is silence, stillness,
As though life in the remote hollow
Was not bewitched by the sun,
But there was quite another reason.]

The poem from which the last quotation comes actually has the name 'Stillness' ['*Tishina*'], and it is stillness that characterises the late poetry of Pasternak quite as much as the simplicity of style does. Indeed, the two are inseparable. The restrained metres, the unobtrusive originality of the rhymes, the almost casual concatenation of sound effects – *Otchayannye kholoda/Zaderzhivayut tayan'e*[37] ['Desperate cold spells/Hold back the thaw'] – and the mildness of the conceits – *Osen'. Skazochnyy chertog/Vsem otkrytyy dlya obzora*[38] ['Autumn. A fabulous palace/Open for everyone to inspect'] – all testify to an inner peace. It is a very rare thing for poetry in this age continually to celebrate happiness and to express gratitude for life wholly unbidden. Such an attitude scarcely seems believable in a serious artist. Yet in Pasternak it is habitual, and with the years this habit intensified:

«О, Господи, как совершенны
Дела Твои, – думал больной, –
Постели, и люди, и стены,
Ночь смерти и город ночной.»[39]

['O Lord, how perfect are
Thy works', the sick man thought,
'The beds, and the people, the walls,
The night of death and the city by night.']

Those lines are spoken by a man who supposes himself to be dying. The poem from which they are taken bears the title 'In Hospital' ['*V bol'nitse*'] and it is based on Pasternak's experience of a heart-attack in 1953. The entire work reads as follows:

Стояли как перед витриной,
Почти запрудив тротуар.
Носилки втолкнули в машину,
В кабину вскочил санитар.

И скорая помощь, минуя
Панели, подъезды, зевак,
Сумятицу улиц ночную
Нырнула огнями во мрак.

Милиция, улицы, лица
Мелькали в свету фонаря.
Покачивалась фельдшерица
Со склянкою нашатыря.

PASTERNAK

Шел дождь, и в приемном покое
Уныло шумел водосток,
Меж тем как строка за строкою
Марали опросный листок.

Его положили у входа.
Всё в корпусе было полно.
Разило парами иода,
И с улицы дуло в окно.

Окно обнимало квадратом
Часть сада и неба клочок.
К палатам, полам и халатам
Присматривался новичок.

Как вдруг из расспросов сиделки,
Покачивавшей головой,
Он понял, что из переделки
Едва ли он выйдет живой.

Тогда он взглянул благодарно
В окно, за которым стена
Была точно искрой пожарной
Из города озарена.

Там в зареве рдела застава
И, в отсвете города, клен
Отвешивал веткой корявой
Больному прощальный поклон.

«О, Господи, как совершенны
Дела Твои, – думал больной, –
Постели, и люди, и стены,
Ночь смерти и город ночной.

Я принял снотворного дозу
И плачу, платок теребя.
О, Боже, волнения слезы
Мешают мне видеть Тебя.

Мне сладко при свете неярком,
Чуть падающем на кровать,
Себя и свой жребий подарком
Бесценным Твоим сознавать.

Кончаясь в больничной постели,
Я чувствую рук Твоих жар.
Ты держишь меня, как изделье,
И прячешь, как перстень в футляр».[40]

[They stood as before a shop-window,
Almost damming up the pavement.
The stretchers were thrust into the car,
Into the cab leaped the orderly.

226

THE FINAL STAGE

And the ambulance, passing by
Footwalks, doorways, idlers,
The night confusion of the streets,
Dived with its lights into the gloom.

Policemen, streets, faces
Flickered by in the lamplight.
The attendant swayed
With her ammonia phial.

Rain fell, and in the casualty ward
Forlornly sounded the gutter,
As line after line
They scribbled the questionnaire.

He was put in the entry.
The block had no room at all.
There was a reek of iodine fumes,
And in at the window blew the street.

The window held in its square
Part of the garden and a scrap of sky.
At wards, floors and dressing gowns
The newcomer looked closely.

When suddenly from the nurse's questions
As she shook her head
He saw that out of this business
He would hardly come alive.

Then he glanced in gratitude
At the window, behind which the wall
Seemed, as by a spark of fire
From the city, lit up.

In the glare glowed the gate
And, illuminated from the city, a maple
Made with its gnarled branch
A farewell bow to the sick man.

'O Lord, how perfect are
Thy works', the sick man thought,
'The beds, and the people, the walls,
The night of death and the city by night.

I have taken my sleeping draught
And I weep, tugging at a handkerchief.
O God, tears of emotion
Hinder my sight of Thee.

It is sweet to me by the dim light
That scarcely falls on the bed
To acknowledge myself and my fate
As Thy gift beyond value.

Now at my end in a hospital bed
I feel the burning of Thy hands.
Thou holdest me as Thy handiwork
And dost hide me as a ring in its case.']

227

The core of this poem is to be found in a letter that he wrote to Nina Tabidze on 17 January 1953 at the time of his illness:

When it happened, and they took me away, and for five hours that evening I lay first in the casualty ward, and then for the night in the corridor of the usual vast and overcrowded city hospital, during the intervals between loss of consciousness and the onsets of nausea and vomiting I was possessed by such calm and bliss!... And nearby everything followed such a familiar course, objects grouped themselves so distinctly, shadows fell so sharply! The long corridor, a whole verst, with the bodies of sleepers, sunk in twilight and silence, finished at a window on to the garden, with the inky murk of a rainy night and the reflection of the glare from a city, the glare of Moscow, beyond the tops of the trees. And this corridor, and the green glow of the lampshade on the duty sister's table by the window, and the silence, and the shadows of the nurses, and the proximity of death beyond the window and at my back – all this in its concentration was such a fathomless and super-human poem!

In the minute that seemed the last of my life, more than ever before I wanted to talk with God, to glorify what I saw, to catch and imprint it. 'Lord', I whispered, 'I thank Thee for having laid the colours so thickly and for making life and death such that Thy language is majesty and music, that Thou hast made me an artist, that creation is Thy school, that all my life Thou hast prepared me for this night.' *And I rejoiced and wept* from happiness.[41]

The Michigan editors give the date 'Summer 1956' for Pasternak's poem. This makes it more than three years after the experience. Akhmatova too had been told by him all he had undergone that night, so that, as Nadezha Mandelstam relating this observes, he was able to use 'an already existing account'. There seems therefore good reason to believe that the poem grew out of Pasternak's letter to Nina Tabidze, which must have 'caught and imprinted' the details of that time in their final clarity. Mrs Mandelstam does not care for a poem with origins like these: 'I can always very closely distinguish between verse that wells by itself up from the depths of the mind and that which sets forth a preconceived idea.'[42] For her it had 'too programmatic a ring', although Akhmatova had singled out this particular poem from the body of Pasternak's later verse.[43]

The criticism does not seem entirely fair. Pasternak's letter to Nina Tabidze speaks of every element in the scene having been concentrated so as to form 'a fathomless and superhuman poem'. The window looking on the garden, the glare of Moscow outside, the rain, the tree (now identified as a maple) have been preserved in the poem that eventually records that night. However, the realisation in Pasternak's stanzas is more complete than in his letter. For one thing, we are made to sense the city that surrounds the hospital as inseparable from the scene within: even as he lies there, a gust of air comes in from the street. Now, apart from the nurse who explains the seriousness of his condition, the patient is left alone to confront the climax of a happy life. Gone are the sleepers, the shadows of the nurses; the green glow of the sister's lampshade no longer holds his attention. All that matters is the last sight of the city, its reflection upon the night sky as the maple gives a farewell bow, and his outpouring of gratitude to God. It may not be fanciful to see, in the statement that because the building was full they put him in the entry, an inverted image of the Nativity. Just as the child in Zhivago's poem was greeted by the Christmas star,[44] so here the maple in the hospital garden bids the dying man goodbye. In his death he is cradled like Jesus at the beginning of life. I do not think that Pasternak is here arrogating more to himself than he would regard as the privilege of any believer – to be counted as a precious thing in the sight of his God.

The poem 'In the Hospital' departs very little from the language and even the word-order of prose. Its narrative form is absolutely straightforward. And yet, while submitting so readily to these restraints, Pasternak has not for one moment slipped into banality as Wordsworth did in some of the *Lyrical Ballads,* or as many Soviet poets, including Yevtushenko, have done. This is partly because his diction never falters: it remains altogether natural, and can place a sleeping draught [*snotvornogo dozu*] in the context of language that is rising to the scriptural, because nowhere earlier has it sought to be consciously poetic. The transformation that makes this so unlike the prose account in its final effect comes about from the poet's parleying with language which even here, despite the scrupulous plainness, exerts a steady pressure to impose another design. Thus three things seen on the journey – policemen, streets, faces – are linked together as a single experience by affinities of sound: *Militsiya, ulitsy, litsa.* So are the sights that the sick man attends to in hospital – *K palatam, polam i khalatam* – wards, floors and dressing-gowns. The ninth stanza (about the maple) shows an intricacy of sound that recalls Pasternak's earlier style:

> Tam v zareve rdela zastava
> I, v otsvete goroda, klyon
> Otveshival vetkoy koryavoy
> Bol'nomy proshchal'nyy poklon.

This poem's simplicity is that of an ornate manner unwound, the legacy of which can be traced for example in the pleasing interest of

229

many rhymes, and the alterations of pace governing the rhythm. The language retains the freedom asserted in Pasternak's earlier poetry to slide at will into extreme informality – *Chast' sada i neba klochok; On ponyal, chto iz peredelki/Edva li on vyydet zhivoy.* The co-presence of these terms with a more elevated range is well illustrated in the final stanza, which opens with the most prosaic account of the poet's situation – *Konchayas' v bol'nichnoy posteli* – and then glorifies it, as his feeling demands, with the eloquence that follows. This quatrain indeed can be seen to demonstrate the whole process of Pasternak's later poetry which turns the commonplace into revelation.[45]

Pasternak in this last phase of his poetry is still writing out of the inspiration that first came into full tide forty years earlier. There are no love poems here apart from 'Nameless' [*'Bez nazvaniya'*[46]] which is playful and detached; but the apprehension of the natural world, though calmer, remains what it had been; all is familiar to the reader who has found Pasternak to be essentially one of the most consistent poets in Russian literature, whatever the differences of tone and manner. A stanza of 'Music [*'Muzyka'*], written in the summer of 1956, recalls – but these things had never been lost for Pasternak – the sights, sounds and preoccupations of that revelatory summer in 1917:

> Раскат импровизаций нес
> Ночь, пламя, гром пожарных бочек,
> Бульвар под ливнем, стук колес,
> Жизнь улиц, участь одиночек.[47]

> [The roll of improvisations carried
> Night, flame, thunder of fire tenders.
> The avenue under a downpour, the clatter of wheels,
> Street life, the fate of men by themselves.]

VI

Pasternak's last major project, *The Blind Beauty*, was left unfinished at his death in May 1960. There had been many distractions – translating, a visit to Georgia, the calls of a world-wide correspondence – but to the end he was eager to push on with this drama which would complement his novel. For the latter he had gained experience in many tales and draft chapters; *The Blind Beauty* however, could draw on no original dramatic work of his own, though he had translated plays by Shakespeare, Schiller and Kleist, and during his later years was much interested in Chekhov. Some of his lyrics had shown a dramatic talent, or at least the capacity to write an arresting monologue. But he knew far less about the stage than did Blok, nor had he the theatrical impulse, the natural gravitation towards a stage, of Mayakovsky. The likelihood of his being able to put together a convincing play was therefore not strong.

Only four scenes were written, but they are enough to make possible a judgment and to predict the outcome. The first two belong to the Prologue, set in the years 1835 and 1850; the action then shifts to 1860, one year before the Emancipation of the Serfs. Pasternak told Olga Andreyev Carlisle, who visited him in the last months of his life, that the conclusion would take place in 1880.[48] From her account it would seem that he was planning a trilogy, but the scenes we have suggest that the plot would have been fully developed in a Prologue and two acts of a single play, covering the span of some fifty years.[49] It would have been rather long, though the intrigue is scarcely more complicated than, for example, that of a play by Chekhov.

The blind beauty from whom the work derives its name is a young serf woman, cast for a heavily symbolic role. The spendthrift count in a struggle with his valet who is also the countess's lover fires amiss and shatters a plaster bust. The flying fragments deprive her of sight, though she can discern dimly the flame of a candle. Later there is some talk of a cure. This beautiful victim, as Pasternak explained to Mrs Carlisle, stands for Russia itself; and when Lusha would recover her vision, in the unwritten third part, this was to symbolise the reawakening of Russia towards the end of the nineteenth century. The periwigged bust which the count had broken also carried symbolic meaning in so far as it had been a talisman for the prosperity of his house. Beyond this the play bears no obvious symbolism, though all the action and the characters have been conceived in representative terms: this was meant as a panorama of Russian history in the years that cradled the revolution. Lusha brought up the countess's son whose father had been the valet, and this boy became an artist, the outstanding actor in the troupe maintained by the count's heir. It would come about through his agency that a foreign doctor would cure Lusha's blindness.

Had Pasternak written a short verse play on this subject, it might have been comparable with Yeats' *The Countess Cathleen* which its author described as not 'more than a piece of tapestry',[50] but which could move an audience preoccupied with their national destiny. However, Pasternak's fable had to be realised in drama of a different sort[51] – drama that for all its 1omantic colouring could not forget the social specification of plays by Ostrovsky, Turgenev and Tolstoy. Alexandre Dumas the elder, who actually did visit Russia at that time, appears in the fourth scene,[52] and the story of a valet in love with the count his master's wife, later to revisit her as Lieutenant Rimmars of the Swedish army, might seem to call for the introduction of this romancer. But Dumas in fact comes as an observer taking notes of Russian society, and Sasha the new count's tutor comments for his benefit on the strange Russian types that are paraded before him. He tells Dumas: 'Russia is ruled not by tsars but by huntsmen, village constables, N.C.O.s who have risen to be police inspectors, officials of the lowest grade.'[53] (Sasha has particularly in mind the local police chief, Straton, whom the countess had so much resented, foreseeing he might eventually be appointed governor.[54]) The exhibits shown to Dumas at the posting-station – he is snow-bound on his way to the count's theatre in the country – include a Fourierist ready to strike his servant (whom he has not emancipated) for failing to trust the promises of the gentry; an ensign who has embezzled public funds; a landowner who has drunk away his estate and is supported by two old retainers, now mendicants for his sake; a grand duke who believes in the glorious future of the Russian people; and – a pledge for the grand duke of this future – Prokhor, once the Count's butler, flogged and exiled for the death of his master which had really been a bandit's work, and now flourishing as innkeeper and 'hero of local legend'.[55] This Prokhor in the unwritten last act would become a merchant and patron of the arts, like Sergey Shchukin 'who collected all those beautiful French paintings in Moscow at the turn of the century'; while the tutor would end up as a terrorist.[56] It is the latter who observes of the Russians that 'with us the civic sense of sober daily life and personal dignity has died or weakened', while the Messianic theme and that of the 'mutuality of all mankind' has grown to a unique degree.[57]

In the first scene Pasternak had shown the condition of rural Russia under serfdom in the 1830s. The count's estate is going to ruin through his extravagance; the peasants are cowed and resentful; the gentry keep out of the way while recruits are being taken for twenty-five years' service; there are bandits patrolling the neighbourhood; and revolt is in the air of a hot, cholera-laden summer. The memory of the count's insanely cruel forebear, Domna the Murderess, evoked by her domino costume in the opening scene, still haunts Pyatibratskoe. Domna was suggested by a noblewoman of Catherine's time, Saltykova,[58] just as the theatre company of serfs maintained by the younger count had its prototypes in Russian history.[59] This scene recalls the setting of Pushkin's prose tale *Dubrovsky*, just as the final scene depends for its notation on the novelists of two or three decades later, especially Turgenev and Tolstoy.

In much of the first scene we hear the conversation of peasants – Prokhor the butler, Lusha the 'blind beauty' and Glasha, the other married servant, Pakhom the father of Lusha who steals some of the countess's jewels, and many more. The third scene in which, twenty-five years later, Pakhom is dying with a bad conscience, has only peasants participating, and bears a certain resemblance to Tolstoy's play *The Power of Darkness*. Again one recalls the adverse comment of Nadezhda Mandelstam on the idiom of the porter and the Siberian grocer's wife in *Doctor Zhivago*.[60] Pasternak could find countless examples of peasant speech, ranging from the tales of Leskov, or from Zamyatin before the First World War, to a great many Soviet novels. His interest in all the nuances of vocabulary is attested by poems from the earliest period on. Whether he had the dramatist's ear for convincing dialogue is less certain. The scene of Pakhom's death has an authentic grimness; but the language seems a little too much of a *tour de force* using brilliantly, perhaps, the stores of popular speech in the nineteenth-century lexicon by Dahl.

The language generally in Pasternak's play is less striking than one would expect from acquaintance with his prose writings. This may be partly due to the fact that he does not primarily excel in dialogue; the originality of his prose is to be found mainly in the descriptions. A further reason may be that the entire play as we have it seems contrived and therefore external. There are few speeches in which Pasternak appears to be deeply engaged rather than illustrating an idea – however truthful – about Russian life in the nineteenth century. Only once, I think, does the ring of a genuine moral experience make itself heard, when the countess exclaims, after Rimmars has left her:

And I thank you, Lord, my great defence, my unassailable protection, that you bid me live in such difficulty and confusion; so inscrutably that you bid my heart to faint so sweetly through loss of blood... Life is a fine pain that illuminates, the quiet gift of a bright silent power, a long, a long-enduring power.[61]

This she contrasts with what Straton the police chief and his kind imagine to be power, as they 'creak in their boots, command, instruct, and impose order'. Here, and here only, do we seem to penetrate deep into the consciousness of the poet who had fallen into the hands of men like Straton after accepting the Nobel Prize.

15

The Place of Pasternak

I

It may be well at this point to go back some fifty years and try to recover the effect of Pasternak's two little volumes of verse *My Sister Life* and *Themes and Variations* upon their earliest readers. The second of these, as Grzhebin brought it out in Berlin, consisted of some 120 small pages. Even today, opening the facsimile published at Ann Arbor in 1972, one is surprised by the high tension and unexpectedness of the poems, and by how much falls within their compass. They disclose a sensibility avid for every impression that the city or the surrounding country can yield. The sun on the gloss of carriage doors, the knifegrinder, the dragonfly's wing; the questions put by a tribunal, the changing of cold coins, the sound of bells on the eve of a church holiday; the watchmaker with his tweezers, old-clothes women; dead insects at the bottom of a phial; dawn like a shot in the darkness; grand pianos, railway time-tables, the Kremlin in a snowstorm, a Dickens Christmas story, Jacobean furniture – a huge inventory could be made of the unrelated details which his verse brings into fleeting union. The effect is one of deliverance into a world where the surprising becomes the normal – and where the modern city has been at last given equal status with the natural scene. Pasternak, unlike previous urban poets, is not contrasting the ugliness and chaotic indifference of the town with the ideal harmony of field and hamlet, or of the golden age as in Poussin's landscapes. He has simply accepted that for the city dweller there need be no division between what lies in his daily environment and what stretches beyond it. The weather in the streets is also that of the steppes; and as the wind passes from a meadow to an alley littered with torn-down advertisements, so the poet's imagination must be prepared for any encounter and must give all their turn.

235

Thus for those who grew up with the poetry like Gladkov 'all the summer showers came to seem like quotations from him, all the misty daybreaks, all the gardens sprinkled with morning dew'.[1] To have enabled a generation to form and exercise its sensibility is the mark of an original poet. Not since Blok had this been done with such authority as in those two volumes by Pasternak. He was an innovator like none of the Futurists except Khlebnikov, because the inspiration of his poetry came not from a quarrel with his predecessors but from an absorption in what he found at his feet.[2] It must have been the wholeness of Pasternak's impulse that worked so strongly on his contemporaries. Of course he resembled Mayakovsky, who had been prominent some years before him. There are common features in their writing: Mayakovsky's voice too at the time he was closest to Pasternak had a strong personal timbre, it was flexible and he used audacious rhymes and a wide-ranging idiom. But his capital got sooner expended; he lacked the resources of Pasternak who wrote not of himself as hero but of an everchanging experience that waylaid him. For Mayakovsky poetry was a defensive weapon; for Pasternak an instrument of discovery.

The verse of that time and early prose fiction like *The Childhood of Luvers* has remained for some people the best of Pasternak, the writing in which he is most truly himself. As yet the pressures on him to conform were minimal. It was a period of free experimentation when the regime briefly tolerated any artist who did not oppose it, and the critics could welcome poetry which spoke for itself. And Pasternak's did exactly that. A mind of extraordinary alertness registered in these pages what it felt like to be living in the confused, exciting and, at times, dangerous world of the years immediately following the revolution. The awareness Pasternak showed was exceptional, but he heightened the general experience and made articulate for others what they had obscurely felt. In this way *My Sister Life* and its sequel *Themes and Variations* give a matchless impression of an unique period in Russian history. There was more profundity in Mandelstam's volumes of the same period, *Tristia* (1922) and *Second Book* [*Vtoraya kniga*, 1923]. But their appeal had been different from that of Pasternak's poetry. Mandelstam stood away from the time, reading it with a stern and classical eye that foresaw ruin. Pasternak immersed himself in the running flood: he was carried along by it, gasping and ecstatic.

II

In the next phase, that of *Second Birth* and *Safe Conduct*, he could still fascinate (though this had been less true of his semi-official narrative poems, *Nineteen Five* and *Lieutenant Schmidt*). He revealed a capacity to grow with the times, and yet remain essentially himself. Thus the first half of his poetic career projects a simple arc, through ecstasy to a more sober acceptance; and it is in retrospect all of a piece. Had Pasternak disappeared in the purges of 1937 his place in Russian literature would have been indisputable. Among Russian poets of the post-revolutionary era he stands very high; the only names that come into comparison are Mandelstam, Marina Tsvetaeva and Akhmatova. Of these Pasternak had been published the most frequently; in the Soviet Union he was conspicuous to a degree the others were not.

Yet, as he told Gladkov in 1942, his achievement to date did not satisfy him: 'This is my most sincere conviction: for several decades I have lived really on credit and up till now have done nothing worth-while. I am not afraid of these thoughts, they are dreadful only to spiritual bankrupts, but they only encourage me.'[3] He was then in his early fifties. One result of the Second World War was to seal off the revolutionary period in which Pasternak's most widely admired work had originated. A return to the 1920s was impossible; even to preserve continuity became difficult. The very least that can be said for his later writing both in verse and prose is that he performed the latter feat. Continuity has been kept, although *Doctor Zhivago* and the later poems disappointed some of Pasternak's adherents. Yet the novel is quite clearly an extension to *Safe Conduct*, and the very title *On Early Trains* would appear to make a bid for connection with the rail journeys of *My Sister Life*. The poetry of his last twenty years could not have been written by anybody other than himself. It resembles an evening when the light has mellowed and lost some of its force; the perspective has not changed, though objects stand out more distinctly for contemplation. The second half of his career counterbalances the first; and the achievement of *Doctor Zhivago*, a work on which he set so much store, was that it familiarised an enormously large public with the concerns and perceptions that had accompanied Pasternak through life. The emphasis was now more overtly religious, the argument at some points too explicit and even heavy-handed. None the less it would be wrong to contend that *Doctor Zhivago* represents in any way a diminution of Pasternak's powers. On the contrary in certain respects it enriched them. Particular episodes of the novel (the spring in Melyuzeevo, the long journey to the Urals, the return to Varykino) have evolved from the most successful experiments in his earlier fiction, and they provide memorable images in which the meaning of an epoch is given focus.

III

The reputation he gained throughout the world as the author of *Doctor Zhivago* made him a symbolic figure for many in his own country and abroad, in the way that Solzhenitsyn was to become. The contrast between the two is worth examining, at least cursorily. Solzhenitsyn's art belongs to an established and honourable tradition in Russian writing. He stands in the line of the Archpriest Avvakum three centuries ago, of Belinsky, Saltykov-Shchedrin and the later Tolstoy – all of them convinced opponents of an alien regime. Both his satire and his dogmatism have ample precedent in their work, and the same is true of his consistent moral emphasis. It is perhaps true that Pasternak eventually, as George Reavey has said, found himself 'in the moral situation of a Leo Tolstoy'.[4] But he arrived there by a different route from Solzhenitsyn's. That this should be his final destination need not surprise. Although he had never set his face against the Soviet regime in the way that Mandelstam and Akhmatova did (with occasional wavering), Pasternak's devotion to artistic freedom could have no other outcome. In the final balance his integrity can be matched with Solzhenitsyn's, and without being consciously heroic or seeking out martyrdom it is no less admirable, and perhaps more sympathetic. Solzhenitsyn, a whole generation younger, has been too long the prisoner of a closed society. The virtue of Pasternak's most enlightened contemporaries, which he exemplifies as well as any of them, was their civilisation. They had achieved the proper relationship with European culture, participating fully and coming to it as equals, with certain advantages from their own literary inheritance. Pasternak never saw himself as a *pravednik*, the righteous man who is pleasing to God's sight in a wicked world. Nor may Solzhenitsyn see himself like this; but sometimes he has behaved as if he did.

It is not Pasternak's civic courage, although this was considerable, that will ensure him a permanent place in Russian literature.

Courage is, of course, necessary in a great writer, but it must be of the kind Pasternak described once to Gladkov: 'The first sign of talent is courage. Courage not on the platform, or in the editor's office, but in front of a blank sheet of paper...'[5] To that particular test the writer brings all that he is, and, like Zhivago when writing poetry, he must be prepared for the moment to come in which the language takes over, and what must be said declares itself.

The moral basis of such an attitude goes deep into actual life. One may think of Hamlet in the poem by Zhivago, who lives his part in the play as a reality. In Pasternak's understanding of art, the aesthetic demand bears a moral weight: 'to be alive to the end' requires that life should have the willingness to risk all. This appears strongly in the poem 'Bacchanalia' to which reference has already been made.[6] The young actress who has taken upon herself the ordeal of the queen in Schiller's *Maria Stuart* demonstrates how for an artist it is ordained 'to play without holding back' [*igrat' bez otkaza*].[7]

Those words sum up the principle by which Pasternak lived in his difficult times. For him 'the play and the torment of an achieved triumph' in art [*Dostignutogo torzhestva/Igra i muka*[8]] were indissoluble, just as for the actress 'joy and pain' [*radost' i bol'*] go with her daring. The verb *igrat'* covers the same range of meanings as our English verb 'to play'. One is particularly emphasised in the poem. The actress's playing must follow the example of things in nature – the ravines, the river, diamonds, wine. Here the play of light seems to be indicated – its movement and brilliance. To play, then, in the sense both of acting an appointed part and rejoicing in the free movement of the imagination, defines the artist's function as Pasternak understood it. And there can be no holding back in the face of perils or sufferings. 'O, believe in my play' [*O., ver' igre moey...*] he had implored in *My Sister Life*, because even then it was serious for him.[9]

The significance of that whole-hearted play did not escape Marina Tsvetaeva, whose essay 'A Downpour of Light' is so dithyrambic in tone yet so alert in its judgment. She called his poetry 'light-writing' [*svetopis'*],[10] and she noted that 'daily life for him is nearly always in movement'.[11] 'The whole book', she said of *My Sister Life*, 'is an affirmation, for all and everything: I am!'[12] His poetic gift she considered inevitable: 'A divine "it cannot be otherwise"'.[13] The reference to Luther's saying 'Ich kann nicht anders', here concerned with an aesthetic matter, the choice of form, can be taken as prophetic for Pasternak's subsequent career. His spontaneity, unchecked throughout a life that was not free from troubles, bound him to its own law. 'To play without holding back' demanded the quality that he describes in the poem 'August' (of the *Zhivago* cycle) – 'a free persistence' [*vol'noe uporstvo*].[14]

IV

The *Essay in Autobiography* assigns to Blok a place in the chapter which also discusses Rilke and moves on to Tolstoy. This seems to be a conscious elevation of Blok into the company of two writers who meant very much to Pasternak. The interest is further shown by his 'Four Fragments on Blok' under the general title of 'The Wind' ['*Veter*'] – the only poem in *When the Weather Clears* about another poet.

Blok, as Pasternak says, had been very important for his own generation when they were growing up.[15] (Zhivago is made to reflect on the affinities between Blok's poetry and the Christmas scene around him in 1911.[16]) Now in the autobiography Pasternak attributes to him 'everything that makes up a great poet', with particular emphasis on 'his own restrained destiny, secretive, gathered into itself'. Blok appeals to Pasternak both for his example as a poet able to realise the urban scene in a deeply personal way, and for his self-commitment. In the lyrical sequence Pasternak writes of Blok's reputation which imposes itself regardless of what the pundits may prescribe. Just as Pushkin's monument in the poem of that name was 'not made with hands' [*nerukotvornyy*], so Blok is 'not fabricated by hands' [*ne izgotovlen rukami*]: his authority stands on its own.[17] Pasternak does not identify himself with Blok, but he responds fully to the sense of desolation in Blok's poetry – the wind blowing everywhere – and to the ambivalence with which Blok had regarded the inevitability of the revolutionary storm:

> Блок ждал этой бури и встряски.
> Ее огневые штрихи
> Боязнью и жаждой развязки
> Легли в его жизнь и стихи.[18]

> [Blok awaited that storm and turmoil.
> Its fiery lineaments
> With fear and thirst for the outcome
> Lay upon his life and verses.]

I have discussed elsewhere the strong sense of affinity that Pasternak came to feel with Blok.[19] The essential bond between them lay in the conception of realism informing their poetry. Because the St Petersburg of Blok was at once visionary and identifiable – 'it exists equally in life and the imagination'[20] – and because the poet, as Pasternak contends in his essay on Verlaine, expressed a whole age through his personal confessions,[21] Blok could be seen to have helped Pasternak towards discovering his own method.

Mandelstam once wrote that 'the most convenient way of measuring our poetry is by the degrees of Blok's poetry. This is live mercury.'[22] Since the days of Pushkin and Lermontov, there had not been a lyrical talent in Russian poetry to match Blok's. His tone of poignant intimacy and impersonal possession made him unique among the Russian Symbolists. Strongly present in his work as an individual, yet seeming at times a disembodied voice, he held firmly like the great romantics of a century earlier to the actual, but transformed it by his feeling. Blok was the supreme poet of his own time in Russia, and at the moment of transition into another age he offered up all that he had been in *The Twelve*, a poem that is a funeral pyre and a beacon.

Pasternak seems to have thought that one universal poet was all any age needed, and to have aspired himself to be that poet.[23] In entertaining such an idea he showed himself a true child of the romantic movement, and from such thinking came the determination to produce in *Doctor Zhivago* the central work of our time. Accordingly, when he gave this attention to Blok in the last phase of his own life, it is presumably as Blok's successor in the field that he now writes. For a while in the 1920s Pasternak had certainly dominated the minds of contemporaries as Blok had done in the first decade of the century. It might also be claimed that *Doctor Zhivago* is what he hoped it would become, the work that embraces all the main issues of the age from a poet's point of view. But this is to assume too readily that a single imagination can answer for the experience of a whole people.

Anna Akhmatova wrote a poem in 1961 which when first published bore the title 'There Are Four of Us' ['*Nas chetvero*'].[24] Those who make up the foursome with herself are Mandelstam, Pasternak and Tsvetaeva. It was more than a love of symmetry – two men, two women, one pair from each capital – that dictated this selection. They are surely the most interesting poets of high and sustained achievement after Blok. Of these four it would appear that the two indubitably major poets are Pasternak and Mandelstam. They can be contrasted in many ways. Mandelstam's

widow has done this tellingly in a chapter of *Hope Against Hope*.[25]
All through this present book the figure of Mandelstam has been
demanding entry: he must now have it.

V

In 1923 Mandelstam had ended a brief essay, 'Notes on Poetry'
['*Zametki o poezii*'], with his famous tribute to Pasternak's *My
Sister Life*. He also claimed there for poetry that, crazed and
obscurely muttering as it may seem to be, 'all the same it is the one
sober, the one fully awake thing in the whole world'.[26] The image
may have been inspired by Pasternak's well known inability in
conversation to get out what he wanted to say. At first sight the
ascription of a sober quality to the book Mandelstam was considering may appear wilful. Yet on reflection it will be found apt. The
wakefulness specified by Mandelstam means a direct and penetrating vision such as was habitual for Pasternak. Even the most
unexpected of his conceits, as we have noted, rely on sharp observation and unerring appraisal. And his moral growth as a poet
ensued from this fidelity to impressions. He wanted to attain the
'realism' which in his essay on Chopin he defines as 'the highest
level of accuracy in a writer'.[27] Pasternak said about Blok that he
manifested a soberness like the piercing eye of an eagle [*orlinaya
trezvost'*].[28] Mandelstam and Pasternak are in agreement about the
poet's basic sanity and vigilance in a somnambulant world.

It could be argued that Mandelstam who knew his adversaries
from the start was a more profoundly responsible poet than Pasternak. The authority of Mandelstam is great and growing, partly
because we are bound to admire the absoluteness of his commitment, partly because poetry that arises from an extreme situation
like his appeals irresistibly to the present age. His poems written at
Voronezh in the final years differ from the Varykino poems of Yury
Zhivago in one respect: the conditions that Pasternak imagined for
Zhivago actually were Mandelstam's. This in itself would not necessarily make the poetry superior; it could have been worse from the
writer's incapacity or unwillingness to see beyond his immediate
miseries. But in point of fact the Voronezh group of poems is distinguished by the firmness of control and the ultimate impersonality
to be expected of Mandelstam. None the less, Zhivago's poems are
impressively realised: there was enough in Pasternak's own experience, as 'Separation' shows, to give him a full sense of the possi-

bilities. These poems of Zhivago, which may be termed the quick of the novel, confront the same terror and solitude as Mandelstam's do. To quote the concluding phrase of 'The Earth' (No. 21), they too have their 'secret flow of suffering' [*taynaya struya stradan'ya*], though sometimes it may be almost or even wholly inaudible. If Mandelstam may be called Dantesque, then Pasternak is Shakespearian. These terms signify real allegiances. Pasternak's love of Shakespeare had much to do with the 'inner freedom' he exemplifies;[29] Mandelstam's love of Dante with the conviction that Dante's many-sided crystal reflects not merely his own time but ours too.[30] Eliot maintained that Dante and Shakespeare divide the modern world.[31] It is appropriate that Russian poetry at this time should have been drawn so powerfully to both poles.

Mandelstam is wonderfully concentrated, a deeply historical mind, impressive for its lucidity and control. One might too easily set up a whole battery of plausible antitheses – between the apparent fixities of Mandelstam's world and the flux of Pasternak's; between Mandelstam, if we may borrow American terms, as the poet of memory and Pasternak as the poet of hope; between Mandelstam's slowly consolidated advances, and Pasternak's rapid sorties. It may be that for our age and perhaps for others Mandelstam has more to offer; the fabric is adamantine; the poetic thinking subtle and sustained. There are inequalities in Pasternak's poetry as in his prose – the defects of an impetuous mind insatiable for the overflowing bounty of life, and for words from any quarter to express his amazement. He is naive in his poetry as Mandelstam rarely is; yet this apparent weakness constituted his real strength. Pasternak's sensibility was able to replenish itself from hidden sources of delight, and from an unassailable innocence.

The truth is that both Mandelstam and Pasternak were necessary to the development of the Russian poetic imagination in their age. Their combined presence allows it an extraordinary range and complexity.

VI

On 2 June 1960 Boris Pasternak was buried at Peredelkino. Several thousands managed to attend his funeral which, like Tolstoy's just fifty years before, turned into a manifestation. The poems read at the graveside – 'O, had I known. . .' and 'Hamlet' – dwelt on the ordeal of the artist. But the occasion was mainly one of gratitude for his creative energy no less than his courage. Pasternak had extended the bounds of Russian poetry by his innovations in language and by the originality of his perceptions. He was, in Mandelstam's words, 'the inaugurator of a new harmony, a new order in Russian verse' which could become 'the common property of all Russian poets'.[32] Simply to have shown fresh possibilities in syntax and to have transformed diction would amount to a great service. Pasternak's example will long animate the awareness of other poets; his work will remain a growing-point. But, although these things – novel perceptions inhering in a novel use of language – are inseparable, what most distinguished Pasternak was not his innovatory power so much as his unique sensibility. He kept the spring of life unchoked in himself, and his poetry is cleansing, refreshing and fortifying.

Notes

CHAPTER 1   A PORTRAIT OF THE ARTIST

1 *Soch.* I, 118.
2 *Ibid.*, p. 275.
3 Introduction by Lydia Slater to *The Last Summer* (London, 1960), p. 10.
4 *Soch.* I, 268.
5 *Soch.* III, 215.
6 Quoted by Lydia Pasternak Slater (trans.), *Fifty Poems* (London, 1963), p. 16.
7 E. Levitin, quoted in Buckman, *Leonid Pasternak: a Russian Impressionist 1862–1945* (London, 1974), p. 81.
8 *Ibid.*, pp. 24f.
9 Korney Chukovsky, '*Iz vospominaniy*', *Yunost'* XI (August 1965), 8.
10 Marina Tsvetaeva, *Neizdannye pis'ma* (Paris, 1972), p. 256.
11 Mandelstam, *Sobr. soch.* II, 2nd edn. (New York, 1971), 56.
12 *Doktor Zhivago* (Milan, 1957), IV, 12; IX, 16. The quotation is from the latter passage, p. 310.
13 Mandelstam, *Sobr. soch*, II, pp. 66–7.
14 Nadezhda Mandelstam, *Hope Against Hope: A Memoir* (London, 1971), p. 151.
15 *Zhivago*, XIV, 8.
16 Tsvetaeva, *Neizdannye pis'ma*, p. 250.
17 *Zhivago*, XVI, 5, 531.
18 *Soch.* II, 267.
19 *Paris Review* (Winter 1972).
20 Blok, *Sobr. soch.* 8 vols. (Moscow–Leningrad, 1960–3), VII, 217. His italics.
21 *Vozdushnye puti* II (1961), 84.
22 Camilla Gray, *The Russian Experiment in Art 1863–1922* (London, 1971), p. 118.
23 *Ibid.*, p. 120.
24 Blok, *Sobr. soch.* III, 296.
25 *Ibid.*, pp. 304–5.
26 *Ibid.*, p. 604.
27 *Ibid.*, p. 262.
28 *Ibid.*, p. 62.
29 *Zhivago*, XVI, 4, 530; Blok, *Sobr. soch.* III, 278.
30 *Ibid.*, p. 295.
31 *Zhivago*, II, 18, 51.
32 Mandelstam, *Sobr. soch.* II, 97.
33 *Soch.* II, 159.
34 Akhmatova, *Soch.* (2 vols., Munich–New York, 1965–8) II, 118.
35 *Posle Rossii* (Paris, 1928).
36 *Soch.* II, 281–2.
37 *Soch.* III, 220.
38 Aleksandr Gladkov, *Vstrechi s Pasternakom* (Paris, 1973), p. 11.
39 *Soch.* III, 222.
40 N. Mandelstam, *Hope Against Hope*, pp. 25–7, 299.
41 N. I. Khardzhiev, quoted in Clarence Brown, *Mandelstam* (Cambridge, 1973), p. 129. The Futurist poet Velemir Khlebnikov had become by the end of his life a vagrant and outcast from Soviet society. The Mandelstams befriended him in 1922 (*Hope Abandoned*, pp. 89–97).
42 Edmund Wilson, *The Bit Between My Teeth* (London, 1965), pp. 450–4.
43 *Zoo or Letters Not about Love*, trans. Richard Sheldon (Ithaca and London, 1971), pp. 62–3.

44 See Ehrenburg's *Portrety russkikh poetov* (Berlin, 1922), pp. 127–30.
45 Ehrenburg, *People and Life 1891–1921*, trans. Anna Bostock and Yvonne Kapp (New York, 1962), p. 281.
46 Anastasiya Tsvetaeva, *Vospominaniya* (Moscow, 1971), p. 520.
47 Note of 1960, quoted in J. van der Eng-Liedmeier and K. Verheul, *Tale without a Hero and Twenty-two Poems by Anna Axmatova* (The Hague, 1973), p. 133.

48 Letter of 30 July 1932, in *Voprosy literatury* (1 January 1966), 174.
49 A. N. Afinogenov, *Stat'i, dnevniki, pis'ma, vospominaniya* (Moscow, 1957), pp. 150–2.
50 L. Chukovskaya, 'Zapiski ob Anne Akhmatovoy', *Pamyati Anny Akhmatovoy* (Paris, 1974), pp. 179, 182.
51 *Ibid.*, p. 104.
52 Akhmatova, *Soch.* I, 2nd edn. (1967), 235.
53 *Zhivago*, IX, 1–9.
54 Gladkov, *Vstrechi s Pasternakom*, p. 112.

CHAPTER 2 MUSIC AND MARBURG

1 Letter to N. A. Tabidze, 15 April 1951, *Voprosy literatury* (January 1966), 189.
2 Letter to P. Yashvili, 30 July 1932, *ibid.*, p. 173.
3 *Soch.* II, 31.
4 A. Pasternak, 'Leto 1903 goda', *Novy Mir* XLVIII (1972), 1, 205.
5 *Soch.* II, 3–5.
6 Gladkov, *Vstrechi s Pasternakom*, p. 50.
7 *Soch.* II, 4.
8 Ezra Pound, *Literary Essays* (London, 1960), p. 437.
9 *Soch.* II, 4.
10 *Soch.* III, 171–5.
11 *Ibid.*, p. 172.
12 *Soch.* I, 345–7.
13 *Soch.* III, 175. Pasternak's italics.
14 See the essay 'Verlaine', *Soch.* III, 168–71; and on Blok, *Soch.* II, 14–17.
15 *Zhivago*, III, 17, 91.
16 *Soch.* II, 13.
17 Eliot, 'Eighteenth Century Poetry', *Selected Prose* (London, 1953), pp. 164, 168.
18 *Soch.* II, 13. My italics.
19 *Ibid.*, pp. 8–9; A. Pasternak, 'Leto 1903 goda'.
20 *Vozdushnye puti* II (1961), 213.
21 L. Danilevich, *A. N. Skryabin* (Moscow, 1953), p. 13.
22 *Soch.* III, 174–5.

23 *Ibid.*, p. 88.
24 *Ibid.*, pp. 174–5.
25 *Soch.* II, 24.
26 Letter to S. I. Chikovani, 6 October 1957, in *Voprosy literatury* (January 1966), 199.
27 *Zhivago*, XIV, 8, 447f.
28 *Soch.* II, 189.
29 *Ibid.*, p. 12.
30 A. Pasternak, 'Leto 1903 goda', p. 207; see also Pasternak, *Soch.* II, 207.
31 R. M. Plekhanova in *Aleksandr Nikolaevich Skryabin, 1915–1940* (Moscow, 1940), p. 65.
32 A. Lunacharsky, 'Taneev i Skyrabin', *Novy Mir* (1925), 6, p. 113.
33 T. S. Eliot, 'Baudelaire', *Selected Essays* (London, 1961), p. 423.
34 Nadezhda Mandelstam, *Hope Abandoned: a Memoir* (London, 1974), p. 109.
35 *Soch.* II, 10.
36 *Ibid.*, p. 11.
37 *Ibid.*, p. 11.
38 *Ibid.*, p. 12.
39 *Ibid.*, p. 13.
40 *Soch.* I, 114: *O, kuda mne bezhat'/Ot shagov moego bozhestva!*
41 *Soch.* II, 13.
42 *Ibid.*, p. 210.
43 *Soch.* I, 328.

44 Mandelstam, *'Pushkin i Skryabin'*, *Sobr. soch.* II, 2nd edn., 313f.
45 By S. Schimanski in his introduction of *The Collected Prose Works* (London, 1945), p. 13.
46 Dale L. Plank, *Pasternak's Lyric: A Study of Sound and Imagery* (The Hague, 1966), pp. 23, 63–75.
47 E.g. Pasternak's series *'Tema s variyatsiyami'*, *Soch.* I, 63–9.
48 *Soch.* II, 208f.
49 *Ibid.*, p. 208.
50 *Ibid.*, pp. 9–10.
51 *Ibid.*, p. 11.
52 Danilevich, *Skryabin*, p. 37.
53 *Soch.* II, 210.
54 Frederick Copleston, *A History of Philosophy*, VII (London, 1963), 361.
55 *Collected Works* 14 (Moscow, 1962), p. 308. See also pp. 282–3.
56 *Bol'shaya sovetskaya entsiklopediya*, 2nd edn. (Moscow, 1953), 21, p. 517.
57 *Soch.* II, 224–5.
58 *Ibid.*, p. 245.
59 *Ibid.*, p. 252.
60 *Ibid.*, p. 239. Pasternak's italics.
61 *Ibid.*, p. 239.
62 *Soch.* I, 345.
63 *Ibid.*, p. 337.
64 *Soch.* II, 238.
65 *The Prelude* (1805), IV, ll. 342–4.

66 Rainer Maria Rilke, *'Die Kathedrale'*, *Neue Gedichte* (Wiesbaden, 1955), p. 35.
67 *Soch.* II, 251.
68 *Ibid.*, p. 229.
69 See D. W. Harding's well known essay on Eliot's *Poems, 1909–35* in *Scrutiny*, V (1936), also in *Experience into Words* (London, 1970), pp. 104–11.
70 Eliot, *Selected Essays*, pp. 14–15.
71 *Soch.* I, 22–3.
72 *Ibid.*, p. 24.
73 As by Mandelstam, *Sobr. soch.* II, 2nd edn., 264.
74 Plank, *Pasternak's Lyric*, p. 52.
75 *Soch.* III, 149–50.
76 N. Mandelstam, *Hope Abandoned*, pp. 110–11.
77 *SP*, p. 54; see *Soch.* III, 149.
78 *SP*, p. 58.
79 G. Adamovich, *'Neskol'ko slov o Mandel'shtame'*, *Vozdushnye puti* II (1961), 91.
80 Victor Erlich in *The Double Image: Concepts of the Poet in Slavic Literatures* (Baltimore, 1964), p. 138, n. 20, suggests that Pasternak's view of 'objective reality' as organised by an 'intersubjective' principle may be 'a poetic extension of neo-Kantianism', and hence owing to his Marburg days.

CHAPTER 3   A COMMITMENT TO FUTURISM

1 Mandelstam, *Sobr. soch.* II, 251.
2 Charles Baudelaire, *Les Fleurs du Mal*, ed. Antoine Adam (Paris, 1959), p. 13; for dating, see p. 274.
3 James West, *Russian Symbolism: A Study of Vyacheslav Ivanov and the Russian symbolist aesthetic* (London, 1972), p. 167.
4 *Ibid.*, p. 129.
5 In a commemorative essay of 1910, *Sobr. soch.* V, 446–54.
6 K. Mochulsky, *Vladimir Solov'yov: Zhizn' i uchenie* (Paris, 1951), p. 11.

7 West, *Russian Symbolism*, pp. 86–7, 153.
8 Blok, *Sobr. soch.* VI, 161.
9 Eliot, *On Poetry and Poets* (London, 1957), p. 257.
10 Mandelstam, *Sobr. soch.* II, 262.
11 *Ibid.*, p. 255.
12 *Ibid.*, p. 324.
13 *Ibid.*, p. 253.
14 Pound, *Literary Essays*, p. 380.
15 Quoted in E. Etkind's introduction to V. Zhirmunsky, *Tvorchestvo Anny Akhmatovoy* (Leningrad, 1973), p. 8.

16 V. Markov, *Russian Futurism: A History* (London, 1969), p. 132.
17 Renato Poggioli, *The Poets of Russia 1890–1930* (Cambridge, Mass., 1960), p. 241.
18 *Ibid.*, p. 241.
19 *Sobr. soch.* VII, 232.
20 Markov, *Russian Futurism*, p. 53.
21 Mandelstam, *Sobr. soch.* II, 348.
22 Sheila Fitzpatrick, *The Commissariat of Enlightenment: Soviet organization of education and the arts under Lunacharsky* (Cambridge, 1970), p. 124.
23 The title is taken from a phrase in Tyutchev's well known poem 'Spring Thunder' ['*Vesennyaya groza*'].
24 Blok, *Sobr. soch.* VII, 232; N. Gumilyov, *Pis'ma o russkoy poezii* (Petrograd, 1923), pp. 108, 175; Mandelstam, *Sobr. soch.* III, 83.
25 Akhmatova, *Soch.* II, 192.
26 In 1922 Mandelstam recognised him as the one Moscow poet to combine invention with memory (*Sobr. soch.* II, 330).
27 Markov, *Russian Futurism*, treats the movement at length in his sixth chapter, pp. 228–75. He observes (p. 228) that it failed to show 'step-by-step development toward a simple and clear goal'; it lacked any real 'aesthetic unity or clarity'; and its ideology was less developed than that of the Ego-futurists who stemmed from Severyanin.
28 *Ibid.*, p. 229.
29 *Soch.* II, 45.
30 *Ibid.*, p. 33.
31 *Ibid.*, p. 31.
32 *Ibid.*, p. 243.
33 *Soch.* I, 364.
34 *Ibid.*, pp. 364–5.
35 *Ibid.*, p. 369.
36 *Soch.* II, 32.
37 *Ibid.*, p. 214.
38 *Soch.* I, 382.
39 *Ibid.*, p. 182.
40 *Soch.* II, 32.
41 *Soch.* I, 183.
42 *Ibid.*, p. 181.
43 Gumilyov, *Pis'ma o russkoy poezii*, p. 76.
44 *Soch.* I, 184.
45 *Ibid.*, p. 367.
46 *Soch.* II, 23.
47 Mandelstam, *Sobr. soch.* II, 2nd edn., 252.
48 Akhmatova, *Soch.* I, 2nd edn, 257.
49 Khardzhiev, 'Zametki o Mayakovskom', *Literaturnoe nasledstvo*, LXV (Moscow, 1958), p. 410.
50 *Soch.* I, 177.
51 Plank, *Pasternak's Lyric*, p. 65 n. 2. For the whole poem see Innokenty Annensky, *Stikhotvoreniya i tragedii* (Leningrad, 1959), p. 143.
52 *Soch.* I, 469.
53 See '*Zametki perevodchika*', *Soch.* III, 184.
54 *Soch.* II, 37 and on Swinburne's *Chastelard*, *ibid.*, p. 154.
55 *Ibid.*, p. 41.
56 *Soch.* I, 202.
57 F. M. Dostoevsky, *The Brothers Karamazov*, V, iii.
58 *Soch.* III, 152.
59 *Soch.* I, 222.
60 *Soch.* III, 155.
61 See *Doctor Zhivago*, II, 18, 50.
62 *Soch.* I, 190.
63 *Ibid.*, p. 200. Pasternak spent most of the First World War working for a chemical firm in this region.
64 *SP*, p. 584.
65 *Soch.* I, 186.
66 *SP*, p. 587.
67 *Ibid.*, p. 587.
68 *Soch.* I, 209.
69 *Ibid.*, p. 207.
70 *Ibid.*, pp. 188–9.
71 *SP*, p. 586.
72 *Soch.* I, 207.
73 *Ibid.*, p. 208.
74 *Ibid.*, pp. 216–17.
75 *Ibid.*, p. 221.

CHAPTER 4 *MY SISTER LIFE*: THE SUMMER OF 1917

1 *SP*, p. 631.
2 *Ibid.*, p. 631; *Zhivago*, xiv, 14, 466.
3 *SP*, p. 631; *Zhivago*, v, 8, 148
4 Shklovsky, *A Sentimental Journey* (Ithaca and London, 1970), p. 240.
5 M. Tsvetaeva, '*Svetovoy liven*'', in *Proza* (New York, 1953), p. 365.
6 Pasternak, *Poems*, trans. Eugene M. Kayden (Michigan, 1959), p. ix. Pasternak's own English.
7 Blok, *Sobr. soch*, v, 25.
8 *Literaturnoe nasledstvo*, XLIII–XLIV (Moscow, 1941), II, 554. Pasternak's father was put in charge of this edition (Buckman, *Leonid Pasternak*, p. 30).
9 Tsvetaeva, *Proza*, p. 357.
10 *Soch*. I, 3.
11 There is a possible reference in the *cherneyshiy demon* of '*Uroki angliyskogo*' ['English Lessons'] (*Soch*. I, 21). (The epigraph to '*Devochka*' (*Soch*. I, 8; see p. 445n.) is from Lermontov's '*Utyos*' ['*The Crag*'].)
12 *Soch*. II, 282.
13 Eugene Kayden, introduction, in Pasternak, *Poems*, p. ix.
14 As the epigraph from Lenau indicates, he has depicted the girl's features in the storm clouds. They become emblematic of her, and they are the inescapable weather, the cosmic conditions, of the time.
15 *Soch*. I, 18.
16 *Ibid.*, p. 5.
17 *SP*, p. 631.
18 Akhmatova, *Soch*. I, 2nd edn., 201.
19 *Zhivago*, v.
20 *Soch*. I, 18.
21 *Soch*. I, 47.
22 D. L. Plank, in *RLT* 3, 327, finds it anticipated in a novel of 1905 by Alexander Dobrolyubov.
23 *Zhivago*, III, 7, 76.
24 *Purgatorio* XI, 63. The phrase

may denote the earth as well as Eve or woman.
25 Blok, *Sobr. soch*. III, 249 ('*Na pole kulikovom*').
26 'Cantico delle creature'.
27 *Soch*. II, 241.
28 To S. I. Chikovani, 6 October 1957.
29 There were no further revisions attempted until he was preparing the edition of 1957 (*SP*, 631).
30 Yakov Chernyak, *Pechat' i revolyutsiya*, VI (1922), 303–304.
31 P. 49.
32 *Soch*. III, 107–8.
33 See Khlebnikov's '*Slovo o el*'', *Sobranie proizvedeniy Velemira Khlebnikova*, ed. Yu. Tynyanov and N. Stepanov (Moscow, 1928–33), III, 70–2.
34 *Soch*. I, 25–6; Plank, pp. 30f.
35 Yury N. Tynyanov, '*Promezhutok*', *Arkhaisty i novatory* (Leningrad, 1929), pp. 562–8; translated as 'Pasternak's "Mission"' in *Pasternak: Modern Judgements*, ed. Donald Davie and Angela Livingstone (London, 1969).
36 Eliot, *Selected Essays*, p. 326.
37 Davie–Livingstone, *Pasternak: Modern Judgements*, p. 131.
38 *Soch*. I, 33–4.
39 Cf. 'A district in the Rear', *Soch*. II, 330.
40 Angela Maria Ripellino in *Boris Pasternak: Poesie* (Turin, 1957), p. 125 understands *khrip* as *predsmertnyy khrip* and translates it *rantolo*, 'death rattle'.
41 *Soch*. I, 22.
42 *Ibid.*, p. 24.
43 *Ibid.*, p. 4.
44 *Izbrannye perevody* (Moscow, 1940).
45 *Razgulyavshiysya* also carries a sense of spreading itself, 'having free scope', and 'going on the spree'. These three lines could be

taken as a gloss on Pasternak's
final collection of verse, *When
the Weather Clears* [*Kogda
razgulyaetsya*].
46 *Soch.* II, 243.
47 As Lydia Slater does in Boris
Pasternak, *Fifty Poems*, p. 33.
48 J. M. Cohen, in Boris Pasternak,
Prose and Poems (London,
1959), ed. Stefan Schimanski,
p. 259.
49 *Pasternak: Modern Judgements*,
pp. 135–51.
50 *Soch.* I, 12.
51 *Ibid.*, p. 38.
52 Roman Jakobson, 'Marginal
Notes on the Prose of the Poet
Pasternak', in Davie–
Livingstone, *Pasternak: Modern
Judgements*, p. 142.
53 *Soch.* I, 38.

54 *Ibid.*, p. 7.
55 The first title of this poem was
'Ya sam' ['Myself'].
56 Or, as Richard Peace suggests,
the paling; *ochki* (from *ochko*)
could be the gap through which
light passes, glittering on the
lawn like spectacles.
57 *Soch.* I, 26.
58 Mandelstam, '*Zametki o poezii*'
(1923), *Sobr. soch.* II, 2nd edn.,
p. 264.
59 *Zoo*, p. 62.
60 *Soch.* I, 14.
61 Pushkin, *PSS*, II, 338–9.
62 *Soch.* I, 49–50.
63 The marriage of Yagaylo and
Jadwiga in 1386 united the
Lithuanian and Polish crowns.
64 *Soch.* I, 47.
65 *Ibid.*, p. 52.

CHAPTER 5 POETRY UNDER THE SOVIETS:
THEMES AND VARIATIONS

1 Chernyak, *Pechat' i revolyutsiya*
VI (1922), 303–4.
2 A. Menshutin and A. Sinyavsky,
*Poeziya pervykh let revolyutsii
1917–1920* (Moscow, 1964), p.
10.
3 N. Mandelstam, *Hope
Abandoned*, p. 459.
4 Mandelstam, *Sobr. soch.* II, 2nd
edn., 330.
5 *Ibid.*, p. 263.
6 *Ibid.*, pp. 264–5.
7 *Hope Abandoned*, p. 459.
8 '*Svetovoy liven''* ['A Downpour
of Light'], *Proza*, pp. 353f.
9 L. Yu. Brik, in *V. Mayakovskiy
v vospominaniyakh
sovremennikov* (Moscow, 1963),
p. 343.
10 *Soch.* II, 275.
11 Rita Wright-Kovaleva,
'Mayakovsky and Pasternak:
Fragments of Reminiscence',
OSP, XIII (1967), 129.
12 *Soch.* I, 75.
13 Letter to S. I. Chikovani, 6
October 1957.
14 *Soch.* I, 101.

15 Chernyak, *Pechat' i revolyutsiya*,
VI, 303.
16 *Soch.* I, 65–7.
17 *Pasternak's Lyric*, p. 88.
18 *Soch.* I, 67.
19 Pushkin, *PSS*, III, 265.
20 *Soch.* II, 241. The idea is also to
be found in the writings of the
Formalists.
21 'The Poetry and Prose of Boris
Pasternak', Davie–Livingstone,
Pasternak: Modern Judgements,
pp. 108ff.
22 '*Boris Pasternak i modernizm*',
Pasternak, *Soch.* I, xxxv–xliv.
23 *Ibid.*, p. 58.
24 Plank, *Pasternak's Lyric*, p. 95.
25 D. S. Mirsky, *A History of
Russian Literature*, ed. and
abridged Francis J. Whitfield
(London, 1964), pp. 501–2.
26 *Soch.* I, 78.
27 V. Mayakovsky, *PSS* (13 vols.,
Moscow, 1955–61), x, 283.
28 *Soch.* I, 79.
29 *Ibid.*, p. 80.
30 Brik. *V. Mayakovsky...*, p.
343.

31 *Soch.* I, 82.
32 *Ibid.*, p. 220.
33 *Soch.* II, 29.
34 *Soch.* I, 95.
35 *War and Peace*, II, iii, 3.
36 *Anna Karenina*, IV, xv.
37 See Plank's analysis of this poem, *Pasternak's Lyric*, pp. 82–5.
38 Blok, *Sobr. soch.* III, 37.
39 The phrase *tuskluyu, bessmyslennuyu zhizn'* ['dull, meaningless life'], appears in Chekhov's *Ward No. 6* [*Palata No. 6* (1892)].
40 Plank, *Pasternak's Lyric*, p. 84. The diminutive *zvyozdochka* can mean 'asterisk'.
41 *Soch.* I, 82.
42 M. Yu. Lermontov, *Sobr. soch.* (2 vols., Moscow, 1964–5), p. 63 (section 15 of the poem).
43 As in Blok's *Neznakomka* (1906), *Sobr. soch.* II, 184.
44 *Soch.* I, p. 67.
45 *Soch.* II, 243.
46 *Soch.* I, 104.
47 *Soch.* II, 243.
48 *Soch.* I, 101.
49 The brothel area of Moscow.

50 Prominent in the battle of Borodino, 1812.
51 See *Sbornik statey, posvyashchonnykh tvorchestvu Borisa Leonidovicha Pasternaka* (Munich, 1962), p. 248, n. 35.
52 Compare Wallace Stevens's phrase, 'the bawds of euphony' ('Thirteen Ways of Looking at a Blackbird').
53 *Soch.* I, 6.
54 'Marginal Notes on the Prose of the Poet Pasternak', p. 147.
55 *Soch.* II, 95.
56 *Ibid.*, p. 204.
57 Cf. *Zhivago*, XV, 11, 500.
58 *Soch.* II, 94–6.
59 *Soch.* I, 291.
60 *Ibid.*, p. 341.
61 *Soch.* II, 2.
62 *Zhivago*, XIV, 17, 471–2.
63 N. Mandelstam, *Hope Abandoned*, p. 343.
64 *Soch.* I, 249–51.
65 *Soch.* I, 86.
66 *Ibid.*, p. 104.
67 *Ibid.*, p. 83.
68 *Ibid.*, p. 85.
69 See the poem *O, znal by ya, chto tak byvaet* of 1931, *Soch.* I, 351.

CHAPTER 6
PASTERNAK AND THE NEW RUSSIAN PROSE

1 Evgeny Zamyatin, '*Novaya russkaya proza*' in *Litsa* (New York, 1967), pp. 193f.
2 A group of Petrograd writers formed in 1921 taking its title from Hoffmann's Serapion the Anchorite. The Soviet novelist Konstantin Fedin also belonged, and the poet Nikolay Tikhonov.
3 Zamyatin, '*Novaya russkaya proza*', p. 203.
4 *Ibid.*, p. 201.
5 Translated by George Reavey as *The Last Summer*.
6 *Soch.* II, 34.
7 *Ibid.*, pp. vii–viii.
8 *Ibid.*, p. 54.
9 'The Legend of the Poet and the Image of the Actor in the Short Stories', Davie–Livingstone,

Pasternak: Modern Judgements, pp. 220f.
10 A still earlier story, unpublished until 1974, *Istoriya odnoy kontroktavy* [*The Story of a Counteroctave*], probably of 1913, already deals with art in another aspect, its relation to human responsibilities. In this story an organist unwittingly destroys his son in the exercise of his art. This was first printed in *Izvestiya Akademii Nauk SSSR: Seriya literatury i yazyka*, 33, (1974), 2, 150–61.
11 *Soch.* II, 64.
12 *Ibid.*, p. 82.
13 *Ibid.*, p. 282.
14 *Ibid.*, p. 78. Pasternak's italics.
15 *Ibid.*, p. viii.

16 *Ibid.*, pp. 35–6.
17 *The Last Summer* (London, 1960), p. 10.
18 *Soch.* II, 86.
19 *Ibid.*, p. 2.
20 *Ibid.*, p. 90.
21 *Ibid.*, p. 84.
22 *Ibid.*, pp. 96–7.
23 *Ibid.*, p. 99.
24 *Ibid.*, p. 87.
25 *Ibid.*, p. 75.
26 *Ibid.*, p. 82.
27 *Ibid.*, p. 83.
28 *Ibid.*, p. 135.
29 *Ibid.*, p. 129. Pasternak's italics.
30 *Ibid.*, p. viii.

31 *Ibid.*, p. 105.
32 *Ibid.*, p. 89.
33 A. Tsvetaeva, *Vospominaniya*, pp. 464, 522.
34 *Literaturnoe nasledstvo*, LXX (Moscow, 1963), pp. 308–10.
35 N. Mandelstam, *Hope Abandoned*, p. 322.
36 *Soch.* II, 147.
37 *Ibid.*, p. 149.
38 *Ibid.*, p. 200.
39 Chapter 14.
40 *Soch.* II, 196.
41 The words are in English.
42 *Ibid.*, pp. 180–1.

CHAPTER 7
'FROM LYRICAL THINKING TO THE EPIC'

1 *Na literaturnom postu* (1927), IV, 74.
2 According to a note in *Na literaturnom postu* (1926), I, quoted in *SP*, p. 655, though the poem is dated in the text 'June 1925 – February 1926'.
3 *Soch.* III, 215–16.
4 See Chapter 6 above.
5 *Soch.* II, 144.
6 *V. Mayakovskiy v vospominaniyakh sovremennikov*, pp. 370–1.
7 *Soch.* I, 391.
8 V. Mayakovsky, *PSS*, X, 280–1.
9 The passage on Lenin was first published at the end of 1928, when the political climate had altered from that of five years before.
10 Foreword to Pasternak, *SP*, p. 43, quoting Blok, *Sobr. soch.* III, 297.
11 Blok, *ibid.*, VI, 83.
12 *Soch.* I, 398 (retained on p. 268).
13 *Ibid.*, p. 393. Only the first four lines of the second paragraph were retained; *Idiot* (perhaps on account of its association with Prince Myshkin) was changed to *Durak*, 'fool'.
14 *Ibid.*, p. 395; also in later version p. 267.

15 *Ibid.*, p. 395; also p. 268.
16 *SP*, p. 40.
17 Ripellino, *Pasternak: Poesie*, p. 34.
18 It may be convenient to summarise very briefly the events of this revolutionary year. War had broken out in 1904 between Russia and Japan. On 9 January 1905 (O.S.), following the fall of Port Arthur, a huge crowd of petitioners led by Father Gapon to the tsar's Winter Palace in St Petersburg was fired on with enormous casualties – perhaps 1000 dead. Strikes spread, and government broke down in many parts. The Russian army was defeated at Mukden, the fleet destroyed at Tsushima. The summer and autumn saw a new wave of action from the workers. Troops were called out at Lodz in Poland. The crew of the battleship *Potemkin* mutinied in the Black Sea. There was much arson and looting in the countryside. In September a general strike spread from St Petersburg and the whole of Russia was paralysed. In October the tsar unwillingly

granted a constitution, and a Soviet was formed in St Petersburg. The year ended with the rising of workers in Moscow, mutiny in the Black Sea Fleet at Sevastopol, and revolts in Siberia, Batum and Kharkov.

19 *Soch.* I, 109.
20 *Ibid.*, I, 47.
21 Davie–Livingstone, *Pasternak: Modern Judgements*, p. 25.
22 *Soch.* I, 275.
23 Wordsworth, *The Prelude* (1805 edn.), IV, l. 343.
24 *Soch.* I, 109. A. M. Ripellino in *Pasternak: Poesie*, p. 534 finds warrant for the image of Joan in its probable derivation from the actress Ermolova, who played the heroine in Schiller's *Jungfrau von Orleans*. He argues that she reflected in her theatrical performances the spirit of women like the terrorist Sophie Perovskaya.
25 *Soch.* I, 126.
26 The film was originally screened on 1 January 1926.
27 *Ibid.*, pp. 127–30.
28 *Ibid.*, p. 120.
29 *Ibid.*, p. 131.
30 *War and Peace*, III, ii, 21.
31 *Soch.* I, 136.
32 Sergei Eisenstein, *Film Form and Film Sense*, trans. Jay Leyda (Baltimore, 1964), p. 162
33 *SP*, p. 656, quoting *Na literaturnom postu* (1926), I.
34 *Film Form*, pp. 115–20.
35 *Soch.* I, 127–8.
36 *Ibid.*, p. 131.
37 *Ibid.*, p, 114.
38 *Ibid.*, p. 115.
39 *Ibid.*, pp. 111–12.
40 *Ibid.*, p. 118.
41 *Ibid.*, p. 110.
42 *Ibid.*, p. 110.
43 *Soch.* I, 127.
44 'Arrayed' – *oblachas'*, lit. 'robing oneself' in church vestments. There is a play here on *oblako*, 'cloud', just as Tyutchev in a poem of 1864

(*PSS* (Leningrad, 1957), p. 219) could describe Mont Blanc as shining *razoblachonnaya s utra*, 'divested [of clouds] from morning'.

45 *Soch.* I, 111. *Narodnaya Vol'ya* was the revolutionary party dominant in the 1870s and 1880s, some of whose members including Sophie Perovskaya assassinated Alexander II on 1 March 1881.
46 *SP*, p. 42.
47 *Soch.* I, 119.
48 *Soch.* III, 185, 188–90.
49 *Soch.* I, 117.
50 The latter omits some stanzas from Schmidt's final speech (III, 8; *Soch.* I, 171–3).
51 *Zhivago*, XVII, 1.
52 *Soch.* I, 78–82.
53 *Ibid.*, p. 145 (I, 6).
54 *Ibid.*, p. 172. (III, 8).
55 *Ibid.*, p. 141 (I, 3).
56 *Ibid.*, p. 153 (II, 3).
57 *SP*, p. 661.
58 Tsvetaeva, *Neizdannye pis'ma*, pp. 307–9.
59 In I, 6.
60 Tsvetaeva, *Proza*, p. 409. She means the episode 'Naval Mutiny' ['*Morskoy myatezh*'] in *Nineteen Five*. It had the title 'Potemkin' when originally published in *Novy Mir*. Her italics.
61 Henry James, *The Art of the Novel*, ed. R. P. Blackmur (London, 1937), p. 121.
62 *Neizdannye pis'ma*, p. 307.
63 *Ibid.*, p. 308.
64 Clough, *Poems*, ed. H. S. Milford (London, 1910), p. 177 (II, 1). The *Amours* was written in 1849, though not published until 1858.
65 *Soch.* I, 163.
66 *Ibid.*, p. 164.
67 *Ibid.*, p. 165 (III, 4).
68 *Resurrection*, II, xix.
69 *Soch.* I, 172 (III, 8).
70 *Ibid.*, p. 171.
71 *Ibid.*, p. 171.
72 *Ibid.*, p. 162 (III, 1).

73 Cf. Matt. xxvii. 50.
74 *Soch*, I, pp. 172–3 (III, 8).
75 *Ibid.*, p. 143.
76 *Ibid.*, p. 152 (II, 1).
77 *Na literaturnom postu* (1929), 4–5; quoted *SP*, p. 671.
78 *SP*, p. 672.
79 See below, pp. 183–4.
80 Chapter 6, p. 95.
81 As reported by D. Kalm in *Literaturnaya gazeta* (19 March 1931), quoted *SP*, p. 671.
82 *Na literaturnom postu* (1929), 4–5.
83 *Soch.* II, 159. See above p. 7.
84 '*Dvadtsat' strof s predisloviem*' ['Twenty Stanzas with a Preface'], *Soch.* I, 243–4.
85 '*Iz zapisok Spektorskogo*' ['From Spektorsky's Notes'], *SP*, pp. 603–6.
86 *Soch.* I, 139–40.

87 *Ibid.*, p. 275.
88 *Eugene Onegin*, I, xlvi–lvi.
89 *Soch.* I, 297.
90 *Ibid.*, p. 293.
91 Blok, *Sobr. soch.* III, 36.
92 *Soch.* I, 297.
93 *Ibid.*, p. 277.
94 *Ibid.*, p. 282.
95 *Ibid.*, p. 307.
96 *Ibid.*, p. 297.
97 *Ibid.*, p. 277.
98 *Ibid.*, p. 278.
99 Pushkin's miller in the unfinished verse-play *The Watersprite* [*Rusalka*, 1829–32] is crazed by the loss of his daughter.
100 *Soch.* I, 315.
101 *Ibid.*, p. 315.
102 *Ibid.*, p. 307.
103 *Ibid.*, p. 299.
104 *Ibid.*, p. 278.

CHAPTER 8
SAFE CONDUCT, RILKE AND MAYAKOVSKY

1 See Chapter 2.
2 *Soch.* II, 246.
3 *Ibid.*, p. 203.
4 *Ibid.*, p. 213.
5 *Ibid.*, p. 26.
6 *Ibid.*, p. 243.
7 *Ibid.*, p. 213.
8 Original in French, quoted by Christopher J. Barnes in 'Boris Pasternak and Rainer Maria Rilke: Some Missing Links', *Forum for Modern Language Studies*, VII, 1 (January 1972), 65.
9 N. Å. Nilsson, 'Life as Ecstasy and Sacrifice', *Scando-Slavica* 5 (1959), 195.
10 Schimanski, *The Collected Prose Works*, p. 32.
11 D. Davie, *The Poems of Doctor Zhivago* (Manchester, 1965), p. 89.
12 *Soch.* II, 20–2.
13 *Zhivago*, XVII, 19 [*Rassvet*].
14 *Ibid.*, XVII, 11 [*Svad'ba*].
15 Eudo C. Mason, *Rilke* (Edinburgh, 1963), p. 104.
16 *Ibid.*, p. 20.

17 *Soch.* II, 82.
18 Mason, *Rilke*, p. 16.
19 E. M. Butler, *Rainer Maria Rilke* (Cambridge, 1941), p. 69.
20 Eudo C. Mason, *Rilke, Europe and the English-Speaking World* (Cambridge, 1961), p. 99.
21 Mason, *Rilke*, pp. 104–5.
22 *Novy Mir*, XLV, 4 (April 1969); Tsvetaeva, *Neizdannye pis'ma*, p. 302.
23 *Soch.* II, 343–5.
24 *Ibid.*, pp. 268–9.
25 *Ibid.*, p. 270.
26 *Ibid.*, p. 273.
27 *Ibid.*, p. 282.
28 *Ibid.*, p. 281.
29 *Ibid.*, p. 38.
30 *Ibid.*, p. 282.
31 *Ibid.*, p. 243.
32 *Ibid.*, p. 241.
33 *Ibid.*, p. 262.
34 *Ibid.*, p. 273.
35 *Ibid.*, p. 281.
36 *Ibid.*, p. 40.
37 *Ibid.*, p. 271.
38 Mandelstam, *Sobr. soch.* I (2nd edn.), 85.

39 *Soch.* II, 271.
40 *Neue Gedichte* (1907).
41 *Soch.* I, 333.
42 *Ibid.*, p. 334.
43 Originally it preceded four further lines in which the 'craven men and women' are compared with bream and a pike blown by a charge out of the water (*Ibid.*, p. 485).

44 *Soch.* II, 293.
45 *Ibid.*, p. 293.
46 *Dead Souls*, I, xi.
47 *Soch.* I, 223.
48 *Ibid.*, p. 351.
49 *Soch.* II, 282.
50 *Doctor Zhivago*, XVII, 1.
51 *Novy Mir*, XLV, 8 (1969), 204. Her italics.
52 *Soch.* II, 209, 211.

CHAPTER 9 *SECOND BIRTH* AND GEORGIA

1 T. S. Eliot, *On Poetry and Poets*, pp. 253-4.
2 *Ibid.*, p. 257.
3 Mandelstam, *Sobr. soch.* III, 37.
4 For the significance to her husband of Colchis, see N. Mandelstam, *Hope Against Hope*, p. 250.
5 Titsian Tabidze, *Stikhotvoreniya i poemy* (Moscow–Leningrad, 1964), p. 47.
6 *Ibid.*, p. 21.
7 *Ibid.*, p. 22.
8 Quoted by G. Margvelashvili in *Voprosy literatury* (1 January 1966), 168.
9 *Soch.* II, 49.
10 Mandelstam, *Sobr. soch.* III, 37.
11 *Loc. cit.*
12 Letter of 30 July 1932.
13 Letter of 15 April 1951. Both these letters are given in *Voprosy literatury* (1 January 1966), 173, 189.
14 *Ibid.*, p. 168.
15 *SP*, p. 47.
16 *Soch.* I, 319.
17 *Ibid.*, p. 322.
18 *Ibid.*, p. 323.
19 *Ibid.*, p. 323. The lines belong to a couplet omitted from the poem after its 1934 edition.
20 *Ibid.*, p. 341. He is referring to *Eugene Onegin* IV, xlii for the geese and the snow.
21 *Soch.* III, 159.
22 *Soch.* I, 326.
23 *Ibid.*, p. 319.

24 *Ibid.*, p. 320.
25 *Ibid.*, p. 325.
26 *Ibid.*, p. 320.
27 'A vast shore'; 'a vast eight-versts-long beach'; 'a vast beach of bare pebbles'.
28 *Pasternak's Lyric*, p. 103.
29 *Soch.* I, 326.
30 *Ibid.*, pp. 327-8.
31 *Soch.* II, 210. See Chapter 2 above, p. 20.
32 *Soch.* I, 329-30.
33 *Ibid.*, p. 332.
34 So called in *SP*, p. 353.
35 *Soch.* I, 336.
36 Struve and Filippov however date one of them, '*Kogda ya ustayu ot pustozvonstva*' (*Soch.* I, 351-2), by the year of its appearance in *Novy Mir*, 1932.
37 *Soch.* I, 345.
38 *Ibid.*, p. 336.
39 *Ibid.*, p. 336.
40 *Ibid.*, p. 345.
41 *Zhivago*, XV, 15, 513.
42 *Soch.* I, 336
43 *Ibid.*, p. 330.
44 *Ibid.*, p. 335.
45 *Ibid.*, p. 345.
46 *Ibid.*, pp. 337-8.
47 *Ibid.*, p. 342.
48 *Ibid.*, p. 345.
49 *Ibid.*, p. 344.
50 *Zhivago*, XVII, 17 ['*Svidanie*'].
51 *Soch.* I, 352.
52 '*Stansy*' (1826), *PSS*, II, 342.
53 *Soch.* I, 360.
54 *Ibid.*, p. 341.

CHAPTER 10 PASTERNAK AS TRANSLATOR

1 Korney Chukovsky, *Vysokoe iskusstvo (Sobr. soch.* III (Moscow, 1966)), p. 341.
2 Letter to N. A. Tabidze, 5 December 1950.
3 *'Zametki perevodchika'*, *Soch*, III, 183.
4 *Ibid.*, p. 184.
5 *Soch.* II, 242–3.
6 *Soch.* III, 185.
7 *Poety Gruzii v perevodakh B. L. Pasternaka i N. S. Tikhonova*, (Tiflis, 1935).
8 Blok, *Sobr. soch.* VI, 468–9; referred to in Pasternak, *Soch.* II, 18.
9 In Tabidze, *SP*.
10 *Ibid.*, p. 41, n. 1.
11 *Ibid.*, p. 40.
12 *Ibid.*, p. 12.
13 Letter to S. I. Chikovani. 6 October 1957.
14 Tabidze, *SP*, p. 11.
15 *Ibid.*, p. 158.
16 *Soch.* II, 50.
17 See above, p. 135.
18 *Soch.* III, 17.
19 *Soch.* II, 45–52.
20 *Soch.* III, 17. *On strog, kak barel'ef,/I chist, kak samorodok.*
21 *Ibid.*, p. 194.
22 Viktor Shklovsky in *Zoo* (1923). *Zhili-byli* (Moscow, 1966), p. 217.
23 'No. Nothing at all. Simply the waves./Not a sail. The empty horizon.'
24 'I never saw the like storm in my life.'
25 As Annensky does when using blank verse in *Melanippa-filosof, Tsar' Iksion, Laodamiya* and *Famira-Kifared* (1901–6).
26 *Soch.* III, 196.
27 *Ibid.*, p. 198.
28 *Ibid.*, pp. 207, 208.
29 *Ibid.*, p. 198.
30 *Gamlet prints datskiy* (Moscow, 1940).
31 *Soch.* III, 197.
32 *Ibid.*, pp. 190–1 (*'Ot perevodchika'* ['From the Translator']).
33 *Ibid.*, p. 191.
34 *Ibid.*, p. 191.
35 *Ibid.*, p. 195.
36 *Zhivago*, p. 532.
37 *Soch.* III, 207.
38 Eliot, *Selected Essays*, p. 145.
39 Lawrence, *Twilight in Italy* (London, 1926), p. 93.
40 *Soch.* III, 197.
41 'I too have heard, and also in part believe,/But here the morning in rosy mantle/ Tramples the dew of the hillocks to the east.'
42 'How fascinating a mind has perished!/The union of knowledge, eloquence/And valour, ours to celebrate, flower of hopes,/Arbiter of tastes and proprieties/, Their looking-glass. . .all in pieces. All, all. . . /And I, who am I, most wretched of women,/With the recent honey of his vows in my soul, /Now that this mighty reason/Like a cracked bell, jangles/And the matchless youthful countenance/Is furrowed with madness. Heavens!/Where has it all vanished? What is before me?'
43 'Still here, Laertes? Be off, be off! You should be ashamed, truly!/Already the wind has curved the shoulders of your sails, /And where are you? Kneel for my blessing/And take good note of this. . .']
44 *Hamlet*, V, ii, 336.
45 *Hamlet*, V, ii, 350. 'But who would bear the sham grandeur/ Of rulers, the ignorance of magnates,/The general pretence, the impossibility/Of saying all one feels, unhappy love/And the unreality of merit in the eyes of nonentities.'
46 *Grani*, 45 (1960), quoted by L. Rzhevsky in *Sbornik statey*, p. 179.

47 *Soch.* III, 204.
48 The essays are on Verlaine (1944) and Chopin (1945); see *ibid.*, pp. 168f.
49 *Ibid.*, p. 202.
50 Pushkin, *PSS*, VII, 625.
51 *Soch.* III, 202.
52 'I call down no arrows upon your brow, /Send no complaints up to Jupiter. /Mend as you can. I shall wait.'
53 'Howl, whirlwind, to the utmost! Scorch, lightning! Flood, downpour!/Whirlwind, thunder and downpour, you are not my daughters, /I do not reproach you with heartlessness.'
54 'A king, and to the finger-tips – a king!/I stare at him straight, and the subject trembles.'
55 'Do not laugh at me. I am an old simpleton/Of eighty years and more. I fear/I am not altogether in my right mind. To be frank, /I begin to understand something/And it seems I know who both of you are,/You and he, but I am not sure/For the reason that I do not know where I am, /My own dress I do not recognise, /Where I spent last night I do not remember, /Pray do not laugh at me.'
56 'My/Poor wretch they have strangled. No, she does not

breathe. /A horse, a dog, a rat may live, /But not you. You are gone for ever, /Ever, ever, ever, ever, ever!/I suffer. Unfasten this button. /I thank you. Look sir!/Do you see? Look at her!'
57 Renate Schweitzer, *Freundschaft mit Boris Pasternak* (Munich, 1963), p. 25; for dates of translation, p. 24.
58 *Ibid.*, p. 123.
59 *Soch.* III, 94–6; *Mariya Styuart: Tragediya v pyati deystviyakh* (Moscow, 1958), p. 188.
60 *Soch.* III, 96.
61 *Schiller's 'Mary Stuart'* freely translated and adapted by Stephen Spender (London, 1959).
62 *Ibid.*, p. 7.
63 *Ibid.*, pp. 12–13.
64 *Mariya Styuart*, p. 127. (III, vi, 2540: Unsinniger, zurück. . .').
65 V, vi, 3480f.
66 V, ix, 1f.
67 I.e. the sheriff.
68 *Soch.* III, 95.
69 II, viii, 1932–7.
70 *Schiller's 'Mary Stuart'*, pp. 51–2.
71 *Vstrechi s Pasternakom*, p. 63.
72 *Ibid.*, p. 41.
73 *Ibid.*, p. 19.
74 *Ibid.*, p. 90.

CHAPTER 11
A FRESH START IN POETRY: *ON EARLY TRAINS*

1 *'O skromnosti i smelosti'*, *Soch.* III, 218f.
2 *Ibid.*, p. 222.
3 *Ibid.*, p. 138.
4 *SP*, p. 682.
5 Pushkin, *PSS*, III, 174.
6 *Soch.* III, 3.
7 Blok, *Sobr. soch.* VI, 160f.
8 Oddly Pasternak uses the Russian word for *artiste*, though in the nineteenth century this could stand for 'artist'. Cf. *Soch.* III, 32.
9 *Ibid.*, p. 6.
10 *Zhivago*, XIV, 8.

11 See his introduction to *Soch.* III, and the earlier essay of 1928 in Davie–Livingstone, *Pasternak: Modern Judgments*, pp. 108f.
12 *Soch.* II, 45.
13 *Soch.* III, x.
14 Unpublished note, *SP*, p. 618.
15 *Soch.* II, 13.
16 *Soch.* III, 219.
17 *Ibid.*, p. 217.
18 *Ibid.*, p. x.
19 *Letters to Georgian Friends*, trans. David Magarshack (London, 1971), pp. 61–2.
20 *Soch.* II, 13.

21 *Ibid.*, p. 38.
22 *SP*, p. 59.
23 *Ibid.*, pp. 59–60.
24 Mandelstam, *Sobr. soch.* II (2nd edn.), 263.
25 *Zhivago*, II, 10, 44.
26 Erich Auerbach, *Literary Language and its public in late Latin antiquity and in the Middle Ages* (London, 1965).
27 *SP*, p. 59.
28 *Zhivago*, XIV, 7, 448.
29 *Soch.* III, 22–3; *SP*, p. 399.
30 See *Soch.* III, 235–6; *SP*, p. 686.
31 *Soch.* III, X.
32 *Soch.* II, 29 v pervonachal'noy svezhesti, po-novomu, i kak by vpervye.
33 *Soch.* III, 24.
34 *Ibid.*, p. 27.
35 *Ibid.*, p. 19.
36 *Ibid.*, pp. 28–9.
37 *SP*, p. 686.
38 *Soch.* III, 162–6.
39 N. Mandelstam, *Hope Against Hope*, p. 150.
40 Gladkov, *Vstrechi s Pasternakom*, p. 20.
41 *Soch.* III, 162.
42 *Zhivago*, XVI, 2, 519.
43 *Soch.* II, 30.
44 *Soch.* III, 33.

45 *Ibid.*, pp. 57–8.
46 Akhmatova, *Soch.* I (2nd edn.), 262.
47 *Soch.* III, 39–40.
48 *SP*, pp. 703–4.
49 *Soch.* II, 46–7.
50 *Soch.* III, 39.
51 Tsvetaeva, *Neizdannye pis'ma*, p. 256.
52 See above p. 3.
53 Tsvetaeva, *Neizdannye pis'ma*, pp. 249–50.
54 An unpublished dedication quoted in Tsvetaeva, *Izbrannye proizvedeniya* (Moscow–Leningrad, 1965), p. 753.
55 *Ibid.*, pp. 259–60.
56 Translated in Davie–Livingstone, *Pasternak: Modern Judgements*, pp. 42–6.
57 *Neizdannye pis'ma*, p. 277.
58 *Soch.* II, 47.
59 *Ibid.*, p. 45.
60 *Ibid.*, p. 46.
61 See her *Stikhi o Moskve* [*Poems on Moscow*] of 1916, especially the one in which she presents her 'city not made with hands' to the young Mandelstam (*Izbrannye proizvedeniya*, p. 79).
62 *Neizdannye pis'ma*, p. 278.
63 *Ibid.*. p. 252.

CHAPTER 12 *DOCTOR ZHIVAGO*

1 *Hawthorne* (London, 1879), p. 110.
2 *Soch.* II, 359.
3 *Ibid.*, p. 300.
4 *Zhivago*, II, 9, 40.
5 *Ibid.*, III, 1.
6 *The Last Summer*, pp. 127f.
7 *Zhivago*, IV, 6.
8 *Soch.* II, 337.
9 *Ibid.*, p. 329.
10 Afinogenov, *Stat'i, dnevniki. . .*, pp. 152–4; *Hope Abandoned*, pp. 343f.
11 *Soch.* II, 301.
12 Akhmatova, *Soch.* I (2nd edn.), 234. Cf. Tsvetaeva, *Proza*, p. 354: 'something in his face at once of the Arab and of his horse'.

13 Gladkov, *Vstrechi s Pasternakom*, p. 114.
14 *Zhivago*, III, 2, 65–6.
15 *Poems*, p. vii. Pasternak wrote in English.
16 *Davie–Livingstone, Pasternak: Modern Judgements*, p. 232.
17 *Hope Abandoned*, p. 26.
18 VI, 1, 169.
19 *Znamya* no. 4 (1954). *SP*, p. 690. On Pasternak's chronology in *Zhivago* see V. Frank, 'Realizm chetyryokh izmereniy', *Mosty* II (1959), 192f.
20 Zamyatin, *Litsa*, p. 202.
21 Gladkov, *Vstrechi s Pasternakom*, p. 139.
22 *Hope Abandoned*, 31; also see above, Chapter 7.

23 D. H. Lawrence, *Phoenix* (London 1967), pp. 537–8.
24 Letter to N. N. Strakhov, 23 April 1876.
25 IV, 10, 121.
26 XIV, 14, 465.
27 V, 8, 148.
28 XV, 15, 513.
29 See John Bayley's note on p. 134 of his *Pushkin* (Cambridge, 1971), where he makes this point.
30 See Mary F. Rowland and Paul Rowland, *Pasternak's 'Doctor Zhivago'* (Carbondale and Edwardsville, 1968), pp. 58–9.
31 IX, 1–9.
32 *Encounter* X (May 1958). 43.
33 E.g. IX, 1, 287.
34 *Doctor Faustus*, Chapter 46. This point is made by Davie in *The Poems of Doctor Zhivago*, p. 6.
35 V, 3.
36 *No. 19: Ya imi vsemi pobezhdyon,/I tol'ko v tom moya pobeda.*
37 XV, 14, 512.
38 VI, 1, 169.
39 VII, 2, 214.
40 XV, 2, 479.
41 VII, 27; VIII, 4.
42 XIII, 1.
43 XV, 5, 484–5. NEP=New Economic Policy.
44 IV, 12, 122–3.
45 XIV, 14, 466.
46 *Encounter*, XV (August 1960), p. 5.
47 *Encounter*, XI (November 1958); see *Encounter*, XV (August 1960), 3–6.
48 *Soch.* III, 194.
49 I, 5, 10.
50 VI, 4, 181.
51 XV, 14, 512.
52 XV, 12, 503.
53 I, 7, 13.
54 VII, 30, 257.
55 XV, 7, 495.
56 II, 15, 48.
57 VII, 26, 247.
58 III, 10, 81.
59 VII, 16, 236.
60 VII, 21, 239–40.
61 VIII. 7, 274.
62 XI, 5, 347–8.
63 XII, 6, 372.
64 XII, 7, 377.
65 XII, 9, 385. *Ya uvizhu tebya, krasota moya pisanaya, knyaginya moya ryabinushka, rodnaya krovinushka.*
66 *Soch.* II, 16.
67 XVI, 5, 530–1.
68 XI, 7, 353.
69 I, 5, 10.
70 XV, 17, 515.
71 No. 21, *'Zemlya'* ['The Earth'].
72 *Soch.* II, 6.
73 XIII, 17.
74 V, 8, 148.
75 XIII, 11–14.
76 XIV, 16–17.
77 X, 1, 316.
78 *Ibid.*, p. 318.
79 Gladkov would point to this as a weakness. For him such elements in the book are derived from literature (*Vstrechi s Pasternakom*, p. 140). To me as a foreign reader this whole episode seems alive and cherished by Pasternak.
80 Blok, *Sobr. soch.* III, 274 (*'Greshit' besstydno, neprobudno...'*).
81 XI, 4, 343.
82 XI, 4, 346.
83 IX, 14, 307–8.
84 XIII, 14, 414–15.
85 *Ibid.*, pp. 414–15.
86 *Hope Against Hope*, p. 333.
87 IX, 7, 294.
88 XIV, 9, 452.
89 XV, 5, 486.
90 XV, 16, 513.
91 IX, 7, 294.
92 IV, 5, 106–7.
93 XII, 8, 403.
94 *Soch.* III, 198.
95 III, 2, 64.
96 III, 3, 68.
97 VII, 30, 257.
98 V, 8, 148.
99 XIV, 1, 431.

100 VII, 4, 267.
101 XV, 7, 493.
102 XI, 5, 348.
103 VII, 30, 256.
104 VII, 29, 254.
105 XIV, 17, 474.
106 XII, 14, 415.
107 *Sobr. soch.* III, 305. See above, p. 6.
108 XIV, 16, 469.
109 XII, 14, 413.
110 XIII, 18, 428.
111 XIV, 3, 437.
112 VI, 5, 187.
113 XIV, 6, 443–4.
114 XIV, 9, 451–2. The poem is No. 13, 'Fable' ['*Skazka*'].
115 'Legend and Symbol in "Doctor Zhivago" ', *The Bit Between My Teeth*, p. 447.
116 *Pasternak's 'Doctor Zhivago'*, p. ix.
117 Pasternak, *Poems*, trans. Kayden, p. viii.
118 *Soch.* II, 243–4.
119 *Zhivago*, I, 5, 10.
120 III, 10, 81–2; the poem is 'Winter Night' ['*Zimnyaya noch"*], No. 15.
121 XIV, 18, 476.
122 IV, 2, 96.

123 XIII, 4, 392.
124 Olga Andreyev Carlisle. *Voices in the Snow: Encounters with Russian Writers* (New York, 1962), p. 192.
125 See G. Ivask, 'A Note on the Real Zhivago', *The Russian Review*, XXV (October 1966), 405–8.
126 Luke xxiv, 5.
127 *Soch.* I, 238.
128 VI, 15, 211.
129 III, 17, 91.
130 VIII. 4, 266.
131 As for instance in Pushkin's *Skazka o zolotom petushke* [*Tale of the Golden Cockerel*], l. 1.
132 XIII, 11, 408–9.
133 VIII, 5, 269.
134 Rowland, *Pasternak's 'Doctor Zhivago'*, p. 122.
135 *Ibid.*, pp. 109–10.
136 *Encounter*, XV (August 1960), 4–5.
137 IX, 9, 297.
138 XIII, 14, 414.
139 *Hope Abandoned*, p. 322.
140 III, 14, 85.
141 See N. Mandelstam's comments in *Hope Abandoned*, p. 79.

CHAPTER 13 THE POEMS OF YURY ZHIVAGO

1 Coleridge, *Biographia Literaria* (Oxford, 1907), II, Chapter 14, p. 12.
2 *Soch.* II, 189f.
3 Coleridge, *Biographia Literaria*, II, Chapter 14, p. 12.
4 *PSS*, III, 264–5.
5 *Soch.* I (2nd edn.), 251.
6 *Zhivago*, XIV, 4, 448.
7 See above, Chapter 12, p. 191.
8 *Zhivago*, XIV, 9, 452. Cf. *Soch.* II, 13.
9 *Zhivago*, XV, 11, 500.
10 *Soch.* II, 42.
11 *Soch.* III, 168.
12 *Ibid.*, p. 171. See also the pages on Blok, pp. 15–17.
13 *Zhivago*, XV, 11, 501.
14 *Ibid.*, p. 501.
15 *Soch.* III, 93–100.

16 *Zhivago*, IX, 6, 293.
17 *Ibid.*, p. 536.
18 *Ibid.*, p. 540.
19 V, 6, 142.
20 *Ibid.*, p. 560.
21 *Soch.* II, 6.
22 *Moskva i moskvichi: ocherki staromodskogo byta* (Moscow, 1959).
23 B. Pasternak, *In the Interlude: Poems 1945–1960*, trans. Henry Kamen, notes by George Katkov (London, 1962), p. 123.
24 Thus *spodobit'* is often used jocularly, and *smertel' no* can mean 'terribly' in the slang sense.
25 XIV, 14, 464.
26 Davie, *The Poems of Doctor Zhivago*, pp. 56–7.

27 *Ibid.*, p. 58.
28 xiv, 13.
29 Katkov, *In the Interlude*, p. 128.
30 *Soch.* iii, 169.
31 *Ibid.*, p. 172.
32 xiv, 14, 466.
33 xiv, 14, 465.
34 'The Poems of Doctor Zhivago',
   SEER xl (1961), 123–35.
35 *In the Interlude*, pp. 117–34.
36 Obolensky, 'Poems of Zhivago',
   p. 133.
37 iii, 10, 81.
38 Katkov, *In the Interlude*, p. 129.
39 i, 7, 13.
40 Obolensky, 'Poems of Zhivago',
   p. 133.
41 xvii, 25, 564.
42 *Soch.* iii, 197.
43 Blok, *Sobr. soch.* iii, 81–2.
44 Katkov, *In the Interlude*, p. 121.
   Nightingale the Robber was
   overcome by the epic hero Ilya
   of Murom. Zhivago's poem
   makes reference to a ballad
   (*bylina*) narrating the encounter.
45 *Zhivago*, xvii, 11, 543.
46 *Ibid.*, pp. 550–1.
47 iii, 10, 81.
48 xv, 14, 511.
49 *Ibid.*, p. 545.
50 xiv, 9, 452.

51 ix, 8, 296.
52 *Poems of Zhivago*, p. 101.
53 *Zhivago*, xvii, 1, 532.
54 *Stikhi*, ed. Z. and E. Pasternak
   (Moscow, 1966).
55 xiv, 13, 464; also v, 9, 152, and
   ix, 16, 314 (Katkov).
56 xiv, 13, 463.
57 xvii, 17, 553.
58 xv, 11, 500.
59 *Poems of Zhivago*, p. 126.
60 Blok, *Sobr. soch.* iii, 538–9.
61 Eliot, *The Use of Poetry and the
   Use of Criticism* (London, 1964),
   p. 148.
62 ix, 6, 292.
63 Pasternak wrote of himself to
   Jacqueline de Proyart: 'Je vivais
   le plus de ma vie dans la pensée
   chrétienne dans les années 1910–
   1912' (*Soch.* i, xi).
64 *Zhivago*, xvii, 19, 558.
65 Matthew xxi, 17–22; Mark xi,
   12–14.
66 Obolensky, 'Poems of Zhivago',
   p. 133.
67 i, 5, 10.
68 Matthew xxvi, 36–55.
69 Bulgakov's *The Master and
   Margarita* had to await
   publication until after this
   time.

CHAPTER 14   THE FINAL STAGE:
AN ESSAY IN AUTOBIOGRAPHY;
WHEN THE WEATHER CLEARS; *THE BLIND BEAUTY*

1 Schweitzer, *Freundschaft mit
   Boris Pasternak*, p. 41.
2 Letter to S. I. and M. N.
   Chikovani, 14 June 1952.
3 Gladkov, *Vstrechi s
   Pasternakom*, p. 109.
4 *Ibid.*, p. 127.
5 Herbert E. Bowman, 'Postscript
   on Pasternak', in E. J. Brown
   (ed.), *Major Soviet Writers*
   (London, 1973), p. 139.
6 *Soch.* iii, 62.
7 *Ibid.*, p. 227.
8 *Ibid.*, pp. 107–8.
9 Gladkov, *Vstrechi s
   Pasternakom*, pp. 135–6.

10 Akhmatova, *Soch.* i (2nd edn.),
   322.
11 He dated it 'May–June 1956' and
   gave it the title 'In Lieu of a
   Preface', ['*Vmesto predisloviya*']
   (*Soch.* ii, 351).
12 *Soch.* ii, 1.
13 *Ibid.*, p. 39.
14 *The Brothers Karamazov*, i, i, 6;
   ii, vi, 1.
15 *Soch.* iii, 168.
16 *Soch.* ii, 38.
17 *Ibid.*, p. 44.
18 *Ibid.*, p. 52.
19 *SP*, p. 446.
20 *Soch.* ii, 34.

21 *Soch*, III, 63–4.
22 *Doctor Zhivago*, XV, 13, 505.
23 *Ibid.*, XIV, 14, 464–5.
24 *Soch.* III, 62.
25 *Ibid.*, pp. 62–3.
26 *Soch.* I, 22.
27 *Hope Abandoned*, p. 331.
28 *Soch.* III, 67.
29 *Ibid.*, p. 82.
30 See Chapter 8 above, p. 123.
31 *Soch.* III, 106.
32 *Ibid.*, pp. 109–10.
33 *'Pakhota'* ['Ploughing'], *Soch.* III, 102.
34 *Ibid.*, p. 102, *'Vsyo sbylos''* ['It Has All Happened'].
35 *Ibid.*, p. 75.
36 *Ibid.*, p. 70.
37 *Ibid.*, p. 67.
38 *Ibid.*, p. 77.
39 *Ibid.*, p. 87.
40 *Ibid.*, pp. 85–7.
41 Pasternak's italics.
42 *Hope Abandoned*, p. 233.
43 *Ibid.*, p. 230.
44 *Zhivago*, XVII, 18: *'Rozhdestvenskaya zvezda'*.
45 Foreshadowed by his statement in *The Last Summer* about 'colloquial speech that is formed from the union of rapture with everyday things' (*Soch.* II, 189).
46 *Soch.* III, 65–6.

47 *Ibid.*, p. 88.
48 Carlisle, *Voices in the Snow*, p. 208.
49 This is the view of Pasternak's translators, who point out that 'to his other correspondents he spoke in terms of a single play' (*The Blind Beauty*, trans. Max Hayward and Manya Harari (London, 1969), p. 6, n. 4).
50 Yeats, *Autobiographies* (London, 1961), p. 417.
51 He had tried a play in blank verse, fragments of which were published in 1918 (*SP*, pp. 528–538). It seems to have been very much on the lines of Pushkin's 'little tragedies'.
52 I, ii, dated 1860; Dumas made his visit, to be precise, in 1858.
53 *Slepaya krasavitsa* (London, 1969), *kartina chetvyortaya*, p. 62.
54 *Ibid.*, p. 75.
55 *Ibid.*, p. 50.
56 *Voices in the Snow*, p. 208. For Shchukin, see Gray, *The Russian Experiment in Art*, pp. 67–9.
57 *Slepaya krasavitsa*, p. 70.
58 *Blind Beauty*, p. 7, n. 2.
59 *Ibid.*, p. 8.
60 *Hope Abandoned*, p. 79.
61 *Slepaya krasavitsa*, p. 51.

CHAPTER 15 THE PLACE OF PASTERNAK

1 *Vstrechi s Pasternakom*, p. 13.
2 See his *'Slovo o poezii'* (1935), quoted in *Sbornik statey . . .*, p. 9 where he speaks of poetry as something that 'lies in the grass at one's feet', waiting to be picked up.
3 *Vstrechi s Pasternakom*, p. 51.
4 *The Last Summer*, p. xxiii.
5 Gladkov, *Vstrechi s Pasternakom*, p. 35.
6 See above, Chapter 10, pp. 158–9.
7 *Soch.* III, 96.
8 *Ibid.*, p. 62.
9 *Soch.* I, 25.
10 Tsvetaeva, *Proza*, p. 358. 'Photography' would be an exact

but misleading translation of this invented term.
11 *Ibid.*, p. 362.
12 *Ibid.*, p. 369.
13 *Ibid.*, p. 355.
14 *Zhivago*, XVII, 14.
15 *Soch.* II, 15.
16 *Zhivago*, III, 10, 81.
17 Pushkin, *PSS*, III, 373; Pasternak, *Soch.* III, 82.
18 *Ibid.*, p. 84.
19 'Pasternak and the "Realism" of Blok', *OSP* XIII (1967), 96–106.
20 *Soch.* II, 16.
21 *Soch.* III, 169.
22 *Sobr. soch.* III, 33.
23 See for example Gladkov,

Vstrechi s Pasternakom, p. 34;
N. Mandelstam, *Hope
Abandoned*, p. 230.
24 *Vozdushnye puti*, III (1963), p. 9,
with epigraphs from
Mandelstam, Pasternak and
Tsvetaeva, all in the form of
addresses to her. These and the
title are missing from
Akhmatova, *Soch.* I (2nd edn.),
328.

25 Chapter 33 'The Antipodes', pp.
149–55.
26 Mandelstam, *Sobr. soch.* II (2nd
edn., 1971), p. 265.
27 *Soch.* III, 172.
28 *Ibid.*, p. 171.
29 Gladkov, *Vstrechi s
Pasternakom*, p. 90.
30 Mandelstam, *Sobr. soch.* II, 388–9
31 Eliot, *Selected Essays*, p. 265.
32 Mandelstam, *Sobr. soch.* II, 351.

Chronological Table

Life of Pasternak	Publication of works by him	Other events
1889		Anna Akhmatova born
1890	Boris Leonidovich Pasternak born in Moscow, 29 January (O.S.).	
1891		Osip Mandelstam born.
1892		Marina Tsvetaeva born.
1893		Vladimir Mayakovsky born.
1895		Sergey Esenin born.
1900	First meets Rilke.	
1901	Enters Moscow Fifth *Gymnasium*.	
1903	First meets Scriabin. Begins study of music in earnest.	
1904		Outbreak of Russo-Japanese war.
1905		First Russian revolution. Moscow insurrection December.
1906	Pasternak family visits Berlin.	

1907	Joints artistic and literary circle 'Serdarda'.		
1908	Leaves school. Takes post as tutor.		
1909	Enters Law Faculty of Moscow University. Scriabin gives him an audition. Transfers to philosophy.		Death of Innokenty Annensky.
1910	Gives talk on 'Symbolism and immortality'. Accompanies father to Tolstoy's deathbed.		Annensky's *Cypress Chest.*
1911	Joins Futurist group 'Centrifuge'.		Gumilyov founds 'Poets' Guild' initiating Acmeism.
1912	Studies at Marburg for semester. Visits Italy.		Akhmatova's *Evening.* December: Futurist manifesto *A Slap in the Face of Public Taste.*
1913	Graduates from Moscow University. Private tutor in house of German merchant living in Moscow.		Mandelstam's *Stone.*
1914	Meets Mayakovsky. Tutor at country estate of poet Baltrushaitis. Exempt from military service (former leg injury).	*A Twin in the Clouds*	Russia enters First World War. Akhmatova's *Rosary.*

Life of Pasternak	Publication of works by him	Other events
1915 Travels; works in management of Urals chemical factories.		Death of Scriabin. Mayakovsky's *A Cloud in Trousers*.
1917 Returns to Moscow.	*Above the Barriers*	February Revolution in Russia. Akhmatova's *White Flock*. October Revolution.
1918 Works as librarian in Soviet Ministry of Education.		Blok's *The Twelve*. Treaty of Brest-Litovsk. Outbreak of civil war.
1921 Leonid and Rosa Pasternak emigrate to Germany.		Civil war ends. Kronstadt naval mutiny. New Economic Policy announced. Death of Blok. Execution of Gumilyov. Akhmatova's *Plantain* and *Anno Domini*. Mayakovsky's *150,000,000*. Tsvetaeva's *Versts*.

1922	Journeys to Berlin and Marburg. Marries Evgeniya Lourié.	*My Sister Life* *The Childhood of Luvers*	Death of Khlebnikov. Tsvetaeva emigrates to Prague. Mandelstam's *Tristia*.
1923	Birth of son Evgeny.	*Themes and Variations* (published in Berlin)	Mayakovsky founds LEF.
1924		*The High Malady*	Death of Lenin.
1925		*Tales (Childhood of Luvers; The Line of Apelles; Letters from Tula; Aerial Ways)*	Suicide of Esenin.
1926			Death of Rilke.
1927		*Nineteen Five*	Trotsky expelled from Bolshevik Party.
1928			End of NEP; inauguration of first Five Year Plan. Mandelstam's *Poems* and essays *On Poetry*. Tsvetaeva's *After Russia*.
1930			Suicide of Mayakovsky.
1931	First trip to Georgia. Separation from wife.	*Spektorsky* *Safe Conduct*	

CHRONOLOGICAL TABLE—*contd*

Life of Pasternak	Publication of works by him	Other events
1932	*Second Birth*	
1933 Second trip to Georgia.		
1934 Marries Zinaida Neuhaus. Begins regular work as verse translator. Offers to intercede for Mandelstam (**under arrest**).	*The Last Summer*	First Congress of Soviet Writers. Doctrine of Socialist realism promulgated.
1935 Attends Anti-Fascist Congress in Paris. Meets Tsvetaeva	*Georgian Lyrics*	
1936 Settles in Peredelkino. Speech at Minsk conference of Soviet Writers.		New Stalin Constitution. Yezhov head of secret police.
1937		Year of Terror: Execution of Tabidze. Suicide of Yashvili.
1938 Son Leonid born.		The purge. Bukharin and others sentenced. Final arrest of Mandelstam.

1939			Soviet–German Pact. Tsvetaeva returns to U.S.S.R.
1940			Akhmatova's *From the Six Books.*
1941	October: Evacuated to Chistopol.	*Selected Translations* *Hamlet*	June: German invasion of U.S.S.R. August: Suicide of Tsvetaeva.
1942	After return to Moscow rejoins family in Chistopol.		
1943	Visit to Orel front with other writers.	*On Early Trains* *Romeo and Juliet*	Battle of Stalingrad.
1944		*Antony and Cleopatra*	
1945		*Earth's Vastness* *Othello*	Soviet troops enter Berlin.
1946	Awarded medal 'For Valiant Labour'. Criticised by Fadeev, secretary of Writers' Union.		Zhdanov denounces Akhmatova and Zoshchenko.
1948		*Henry IV*	First arrest of Olga Ivinskaya.
1949		*King Lear*	
1953	January: Serious heart attack.	Goethe's *Faust*	March: **Death of Stalin.** Execution of Beria.

CHRONOLOGICAL TABLE—*contd*

Life of Pasternak	Publication of works by him	Other events
1954		Ehrenburg's *The Thaw*
	Ten poems from *Zhivago* published in *Znamya*	
1956		Khrushchev's 'secret speech' at Twentieth Party Congress. Suicide of Fadeev. Uprisings in Poland and Hungary.
Novy Mir refuses *Doctor Zhivago*		
1957	November: *Zhivago* published in Italy.	
Edition of Pasternak's poetry in the press.		
1958	Schiller's *Maria Stuart*	
October: Awarded Nobel Prize, which he is compelled to renounce. Appeal to Khrushchev.		
1959		
March: Last visit to Georgia.		
1960		
30 May: Boris Pasternak dies at Peredelkino.		

Select Bibliography

RUSSIAN TEXTS OF WORKS BY PASTERNAK

Sochineniya, ed. G. P. Struve and B. A. Filippov, 3 vols., Michigan, 1961. (*Soch.*)
Stikhotvoreniya i poemy, ed. L. A. Ozerov, introductory essay by A. D. Sinyavsky, Moscow–Leningrad, 1965. (*SP*).
Stikhi, ed. Z. Pasternak and E. Pasternak, with introduction by Korney Chukovsky, Moscow, 1966. (Dates some poems undated in *Soch.* III, also sixteen poems from the *Zhivago* cycle. Certain poems are dated differently from ascriptions in *Soch.* III.)
Doktor Zhivago, Milan, 1957. (Pagination is the same in the Michigan vol. 4.)
Slepaya krasavitsa, London, 1969.
Istoriya odnoy kontroktavy, ed. with introduction Evg. B. Pasternak, *Izvestiya Akademii Nauk SSSR: Seriya literatury i yazyka* 33 (1974), 2, 150–61.
A number of Pasternak's letters to Georgian writers are to be found in *Voprosy literatury* (1 January 1966), 166–201, ed. G. Margvelashvili.
Izbrannye perevody, Moscow 1940.
Mariya Styuyart: Tragediya v pyati deystviyakh, trans. B. Pasternak, Moscow, 1958. (Schiller's *Maria Stuart*.)
Vil'yam Shekspir, *Izbrannye proizvedeniya*, Moscow, 1953. (Includes Pasternak's versions of *Romeo and Juliet, 1 and 2 Henry IV, Hamlet, Othello, Lear, Macbeth, Antony and Cleopatra*.)

TRANSLATIONS CITED OF SEPARATE WORKS

The Blind Beauty, trans. Max Hayward and Manya Harari, foreword by Max Hayward, London, 1969.
The Collected Prose Works, ed. S. Schimanski, London, 1945.
Doctor Zhivago, trans. Max Hayward and Manya Harari, London, 1958.
An Essay in Autobiography, trans. Manya Harari, introduction by Edward Crankshaw, London 1959.
Fifty Poems, trans. Lydia Pasternak Slater, London, 1963.
In the Interlude: Poems 1945–1960, trans. Henry Kamen, foreword by Sir Maurice Bowra, notes by George Katkov, London, 1962.
The Last Summer, trans. George Reavey, New York, 1959 (with 'A District Behind the Front'); revised, with introduction by Lydia Slater, London, 1960.
Letters to Georgian Friends, trans. David Magarshack, London, 1971.
Poems, trans. Eugene M. Kayden, Michigan, 1959.

271

BIBLIOGRAPHY

The Poems of Doctor Zhivago, trans. with commentary Donald Davie, Manchester, 1965.

The Poetry of Boris Pasternak, trans. George Reavey, New York, 1959.

Prose and Poems, ed. Stefan Schimanski, introduction by J. M. Cohen, London, 1959.

MEMOIRS AND BIOGRAPHICAL

Afinogenov, A. N., *Stat'i, dnevniki, pis'ma, vospominaniya*, Moscow, 1957.

Carlisle, Olga Andreyev, *Voices in the Snow: Encounters with Russian Writers*, New York, 1962.

Chukovskaya, L., '*Zapiski ob Anne Akhmatovoy*', *Pamyati Anny Akhmatovoy*, Paris, 1974.

Ehrenburg, Ilya, *People and Life 1891–1921*, trans. Anna Bostock and Yvonne Kapp, New York, 1962.

Gladkov, Aleksandr, *Vstrechi s Pasternakom*, Paris, 1973.

Mandelstam, Nadezhda, *Hope Against Hope: A Memoir*, London, 1971.

Hope Abandoned: A Memoir, London 1974.

V. Mayakovskiy v vospominaniyakh sovremennikov, Moscow, 1963.

Pasternak, A., '*Leto 1903 goda*', *Novy Mir XLVIII* (1972), 1, 203–11.

Pasternak, Josephine, 'Patior', *The London Magazine* (September 1964), 42–57.

Porman, R. M., '*Pasternak v Chistopole*', *Russkaya literatura* (1966), 3, 193–5.

Schweitzer, Renate, *Freundschaft mit Boris Pasternak*, Munich, 1963.

Shklovsky, Viktor, *Zoo or Letters Not about Love*, trans. Richard Sheldon, Ithaca and London, 1971.

Taubman, Jane Andelman, 'Marina Tsvetaeva and Boris Pasternak: Toward the History of a Friendship', *RLT*, 3 (May 1972), 303–21.

Tsvetaeva, Anastasiya, *Vospominaniya*, Moscow, 1971.

Wright-Kovaleva, Rita, 'Mayakovsky and Pasternak: Fragments of reminisence [*Vse luchshie vospominan'ya. . .*] *OSP* XIII (1967), 108–32.

CRITICISM

Aucouturier, Michel, 'The Legend of the Poet and the Image of the Actor in the Short Stories' (1966), trans. in Davie and Livingstone, *Pasternak: Modern Judgements* (see below).

Barnes, Christopher J., 'Boris Pasternak and Rainer Maria Rilke: Some Missing Links', *Forum for Modern Language Studies* VII, 1 (January 1972), 61–78.

'Boris Pasternak's Revolutionary Year,' *Studies in Twentieth Century Russian Literature*, Edinburgh and London, 1976.

Bowman, Herbert E., 'Postscript on Pasternak', in E. J. Brown (ed.), *Major Soviet Writers*, London, 1973.

Bowra, Maurice, *The Creative Experiment*, London, 1949.

Chernyak, Yakov, review of *Sestra moya zhizn'* in *Pechat' i revolyutsiya* VI (1922), 303–4.

Chiaromonte, Nicola, 'Pasternak's Message' (1958) trans. in Davie and Livingstone, *Pasternak: Modern Judgements*.

Chukovsky, Korney, *Vysokoe iskusstvo, Sobranie Sochineniy*, III Moscow, 1966

Davie, Donald and Livingstone, Angela (eds.), *Pasternak: Modern Judgements*, London, 1969.

BIBLIOGRAPHY

Ehrenburg, Ilya, *Portrety russkikh poetov*, Berlin, 1922.

Erlich, Victor, *The Double Image: Concepts of the Poet in Slavic Literatures*, Baltimore, 1964.

Frank, V., '*Realizm chetyryokh izmereniy*', *Mosty* II (1959), 189–209.

'*Vodyanoy znak*', *Sbornik statey*. . .Munich, 1962 (*see below*), pp. 240–52.

Gifford, Henry, 'Pasternak and the "Realism" of Blok', *OSP* XIII (1967), 96–106.

Hughes, Olga R., *The Poetic World of Boris Pasternak*, Princeton, 1974.

Jackson, Robert L., '*Doktor Živago* and the Living Tradition', *The Slavic and East European Journal*, N.S. IV (XVIII) (1960), 103–18.

Jakobson, Roman, 'Marginal Notes on the Prose of the Poet Pasternak' (1935), trans. Davie and Livingstone, *Pasternak: Modern Judgements*.

Mandelstam, Osip, *Sobranie sochineniy*, 3 vols., Washington, 1964–9. Vol. II revised, New York, 1971. Criticism on Pasternak (1923), trans. Davie and Livingstone, *Pasternak: Modern Judgements* ('Notes on Poetry').

Menshutin, A., and Sinyavsky, A., *Poeziya pervykh let revolyutsii 1917–1920*, Moscow, 1964.

Mirsky, D. S., *A History of Russian Literature*, ed. and abridged Francis J. Whitfield, London, 1964.

Mossman, Elliott, 'Pasternak's Short Fiction', *RLT* 3 (May 1972), 279–302.

Muchnic, Helen, *From Gorky to Pasternak*, London, 1963.

Nilsson, N. Å., 'Life as Ecstasy and Sacrifice', *Scando-Slavica* 5 (1959), 180–198.

Obolensky, Dimitri, 'The Poems of Doctor Zhivago', *SEER* XL (1961), 123–135.

Ripellino, Angelo Maria (ed.), *Boris Pasternak: Poesie. Introduzione e note di Angelo Maria Ripellino*, Turin, 1957.

Plank, Dale L., *Pasternak's Lyric: A Study of Sound and Imagery*, The Hague, 1966.

'Readings of *My Sister Life*', *RLT* 3 (May 1972), 323–37.

Poggioli, Renato, *The Poets of Russia 1890–1930*, Cambridge, Mass., 1960.

Pomorska, Krystyna, *Themes and Variations in Pasternak's Poetics*, Lisse, 1975.

de Proyart, Jacqueline, *Pasternak*, Paris, 1964.

Rowland, Mary F., and Rowland, Paul, *Pasternak's 'Doctor Zhivago'*, Carbondale and Edwardsville, 1968.

Sbornik statey, posvyashchonnykh tvorchestvu Borisa Leonidovicha Pasternaka, Munich, 1962.

Sinyavsky, Andrey, 'Boris Pasternak' (1965), trans. Davie and Livingstone, *Pasternak: Modern Judgements*. (His introduction to *SP*.)

Tsvetaeva, Marina, *Neizdannye pis'ma*, Paris, 1972.

'*Svetovoy liven'*' (1923), in *Proza*, New York, 1953, trans. Davie and Livingstone, *Pasternak: Modern Judgements* ('A Downpour of Light').

Tynyanov, Yury N., *Arkhaisty i novatory*, Leningrad, 1929; reprinted Munich, 1967. Criticism on Pasternak (1924), trans. Davie and Livingstone, *Pasternak: Modern Judgements* ('Pasternak's "Mission"').

Wain, John, 'The Meaning of *Dr. Zhivago*', *Critical Quarterly* 10 (1968), 1 & 2, 113–37.

Weidlé, Wladimir, 'The Poetry and Prose of Boris Pasternak' (1928), trans. Davie and Livingstone, *Pasternak: Modern Judgements*.

BIBLIOGRAPHY

Wilson, Edmund, 'Doctor Life and his Guardian Angel', *The Bit Between My Teeth*, London, 1965.

'Legend and Symbol in *Doctor Zhivago*', *ibid.*

Wrenn, C. L., 'Boris Pasternak', *OSP* II (1951), 82–96.

Zamyatin, Evgeny, '*Novaya russkaya proza*' (1923), *Litsa*, New York, 1967.

GENERAL

Akhmatova, Anna, *Sochineniya*, 2 vols., Munich–New York, 1965–8. Vol. I revised, 1967.

Annensky, Innokenty, *Stikhotvoreniya i tragedii*, Leningrad, 1959.

Blok, Aleksandr, *Sobranie sochineniy*, 8 vols., Moscow–Leningrad, 1960–3. *Zapisnye knigi 1901–20*, Moscow, 1965.

Brodsky, N. L., *et al.* (eds.), *Literaturnye manifesty ot simvolizma k oktyabryu: Sbornik materialov*, The Hague, 1969.

Brown, Clarence, *Mandelstam*, Cambridge, 1973.

Buckman, David, *Leonid Pasternak: A Russian Impressionist 1862–1945*, London, 1974.

Butler, E. M., *Rainer Maria Rilke*, Cambridge. 1941.

Danilevich, L., *A. N. Skryabin*, Moscow, 1953.

Eisenstein, Sergei, *Film Form and Film Sense*, trans. Jay Leyda, Baltimore, 1964.

Eliot, T. S., *On Poetry and Poets*, London, 1957. *Selected Essays*, London, 1961. *The Use of Poetry and the Use of Criticism* (1933), London, 1964.

Fitzpatrick, Sheila, *The Commissariat of Enlightenment: Soviet organization of education and the arts under Lunacharsky*, Cambridge, 1970.

Gray, Camilla, *The Russian Experiment in Art 1863–1922*, London, 1971.

Gumilyov, N., *Pis'ma o russkoy poezii*, Petrograd, 1923.

Karlinsky, Simon, *Marina Cvetaeva: Her Life and Art*, Berkeley and Los Angeles, 1966.

Lermontov, M. Yu., *Sobranie sochineniy*, 2 vols., Moscow, 1964–5.

Markov, V., *Russian Futurism: A History*, London, 1969.

Mason, Eudo C., *Rilke*, Edinburgh, 1963.

Mayakovsky, V., *Polnoe sobranie sochineniy*, 13 vols., Moscow, 1955–61.

Pushkin, A. S., *Polnoe sobranie sochineniy*, 10 vols., Moscow, 1956–8.

Schiller's 'Mary Stuart', freely translated and adapted by Stephen Spender, London, 1959.

Tabidze, Titsian, *Stikhotvoreniya i poemy*, Moscow–Leningrad, 1964.

Tsvetaeva, Marina, *Izbrannye proizvedeniya*, Moscow–Leningrad, 1965.

Tyutchev, F. I., *Polnoe sobranie sochineniy*, Leningrad, 1957.

West, James, *Russian Symbolism: A study of Vyacheslav Ivanov and the Russian symbolist aesthetic*, London 1972.

Zamyatin, Evgeny, *Litsa*, New York, 1967.

Index

Titles of works are listed under the names of the authors